"In our postmodern world, it is so critical to become grounded in the historic doctrines of our Christian faith—this is why I commend Kenneth Erisman for this excellent discipleship guide, *Grounded in the Faith*. Both new and mature believers in Christ can benefit from these timeless and faith-strengthening insights."

**Joni Eareckson Tada**, Joni and Friends International

"*Grounded in the Faith* is an outstanding tool to use in helping believers understand and embrace the basic doctrines of Scripture. It is simple enough to use with new believers and comprehensive enough to use with those who have been believers for some time but have never been taught basic theology. *I know of no other discipleship tool like it available today.*"

**Jerry Bridges**, author of *The Pursuit of Holiness*

"Some books are like steak without sizzle, and others have sizzle and no steak. This guide to becoming grounded in historic, sound, biblical theology is steak that sizzles. Profound theology is presented in such an engaging manner that it is a meal to be savored and shared. Changing the metaphor, under Coach Erisman's tutelage, the Christian learns the heavenly game plan and how to execute it well, and the church team will come to its destined maturity in Christ Jesus."

**Bruce K. Waltke**, professor of Old Testament
at Knox Theological Seminary

"To be a Christian of depth and substance we must first understand what we believe. Here is an exciting discipleship tool that delivers sound, biblical theology in a way that is compelling and fresh! *Grounded in the Faith* offers a great corrective to our message-lite and method-driven culture. I know it will benefit not only the young Christian but the mature believer as well."

**Rebecca Pippert**, author of *Out of the Salt Shaker*

"Discipleship guides are a dime a dozen these days, and rarely worth the price. They typically lack the theological depth and practical wisdom so essential for successful Christian living in a postmodern world. That's why I'm so excited about Ken Erisman's new work. This is discipleship as it was meant to be: God-centered, Christ-exalting, and solidly grounded in the authority of Holy Scripture. There's nothing superficial in the spirituality Erisman promotes. It is biblically rigorous, culturally relevant, and focused on producing grace-empowered and spiritually discerning followers of Christ. I highly and heartily recommend it."

**Sam Storms**, Enjoying God Ministries,
author of *Pleasures Evermore*

# GROUNDED
## *in the*
# FAITH

*An Essential Guide to Knowing
What You Believe and Why*

## KENNETH ERISMAN

With a Foreword by J. I. PACKER

BakerBooks

*a division of Baker Publishing Group*
Grand Rapids, Michigan

Published by Baker Books
a division of Baker Publishing Group
P.O. Box 6287, Grand Rapids, MI 49516-6287
www.bakerbooks.com

Printed in the United States of America

Library of Congress Cataloging-in-Publication Data
Erisman, Kenneth, 1949–
Grounded in the faith : an essential guide to knowing what you believe and why / Kenneth Erisman.
    pages cm
   Includes bibliographical references.
   ISBN 978-0-8010-1513-7 (pbk.)
    1. Theology, Doctrinal—Popular works. 2. Apologetics. I. Title.
BT77.E64  2013
230—dc23
                                           2013004327

13  14  15  16  17  18  19       7  6  5  4  3  2  1

# Contents

# Foreword

Every church member a disciple? A sweet dream, but how may it be made reality? A step in the right direction is the provision of this interactive, user-friendly teaching tool for disciple and friend to work through together. Its theology is mainstream evangelical at its crisp, clear best; its choice of ground to cover reveals good judgment; and its interactions are thoughtfully calculated. All in all, it is a very useful adult catechetical resource. I commend it most warmly.

J. I. Packer
Board of Governors' Professor of Theology, Regent College

# How This Guide Works

**The Aim:** J. I. Packer, after an extraordinary lifetime of scholarship, concludes that the greatest challenge for the twenty-first-century church is catechesis. By "catechesis" Packer means the process whereby believers in Christ are grounded in the essentials of the faith. He concludes, "Where wise catechesis has flourished, the church has flourished. Where it has been neglected, the church has floundered."[1] The aim of this book is to see the church flourish for the glory of God. We are convinced that by designing this guide to be user-friendly but at the same time keeping Reformation depth, followers of Christ will have a transferable tool to become grounded in the faith.

## EVERYONE NEEDS A COACH

Even world-class athletes need coaches. And you are in a real sense a spiritual athlete because the Christian life is described in the New Testament as a race—"Let us run with endurance the race that is set before us looking unto Jesus, the author and finisher of our faith" (Heb. 12:1–2). In order to run well we need the encouragement and wisdom that comes from God's Word. There is no better training than to get grounded in the faith. These sessions will give you the opportunity to become established in those timeless essentials of the Christian faith. What you will gain from this guide is classic, historic, sound biblical theology that is a reflection of the best biblical scholarship through the centuries. This training guide will give you important, in-depth knowledge to understand God and his plan for your life. This process of coaching and training is what is called "discipleship." We have designed a training method that has three simple steps—Listen, Absorb, and Interact. This creates an easy-flow format that allows the discipleship process to virtually run on its own.

The first step is *Listen.* It should be no surprise that this guide is deliberately formatted "to teach"—to impart to you valuable information. If you entered medical school and were introduced to a class on the makeup of the brain, you would not be expected to immediately come up with your own answers about brain surgery, but you would want to learn and build upon the history of medical knowledge that has been passed down through the years. This is what we are seeking to do with this guide—help disciples learn by passing on historic, sound, biblical theology so that individuals can build their faith upon that foundation. We believe that followers of Christ can grasp deep biblical truths if they are presented in manageable-sized bites. After the material is presented there is then a much better platform from which to interact and engage in meaningful discussion.

The second step is *Absorb*. It often takes a moment of time to think about and process new concepts, so we designed a moment to pause and allow our minds to concentrate on the most essential elements presented in the *Listen* step. It's a way to pull everything together and focus on what matters most as well as reinforce what was presented in step one.

The third step is *Interact*. The questions under the *Interact* step are intentionally crafted to enhance your understanding of the truths being presented. Interaction is valuable because it is during this time that we come to grips with how well we are comprehending the truth being conveyed. Also, in the process of interaction, more questions naturally surface that give a greater breadth of comprehension. Quite often the questions help us think about how we can apply the material to real life. It is also noteworthy that friendships and relationships are deepened as we interact with one another. We desperately need fellowship with one another, especially in the context of seeking to grow in our faith. If discussion and interaction take up more time than you had anticipated, then next time simply pick up where you had left off. It is often better to be "relationship driven" rather than "cover-the-content driven."

You will notice that at the end of each session there are two brief sections, *Reflect* and *Cultivating Spiritual Habits*. The *Reflect* segment is primarily a challenge to take what you have learned in the session and think about how to live it out in real life. Discipleship is not just about growing in knowledge of the Christian faith, but it is equally about letting biblical knowledge shape how we actually trust God and treat people. *Cultivating Spiritual Habits* is designed to get us into the habit of reading the Bible, journaling, and memorizing key verses. Journaling has been a helpful spiritual discipline for many, assisting them in meditating upon the truth of the Scriptures. Also, memorizing key verses in the Bible can be invaluable. It is noteworthy that Jesus, the Son of God, memorized much of the Old Testament. If the Son of God found it important to memorize Scripture, then we know it is indispensable for us. One way to begin the process is to jot down the verse on a note card and tape it on your mirror, or use it as a bookmark, or carry it with you during the week. Reviewing the verse just a few times a day will embed it in your memory, and you will discover that if you keep reviewing, the verses will stay in your mind for a lifetime.

When you are finished with these twenty-four sessions, you will have discovered that this methodology is highly transferable. Somewhere in the future you will no doubt feel the confidence to help coach someone else to become *grounded in the faith*.

# LEVEL ONE

# Declared Not Guilty

## Understanding Justification (Part 1)

**Purpose of Session One:** In this session, you will learn that all humans are lawbreakers—we all have broken at least one of God's laws. You will also learn that God declares the Christian righteous—morally perfect—not by the Christian's good acts but by faith in Jesus Christ. This amazing truth is called "justification," and understanding it will give you an astonishing appreciation of God's love and mercy and a deep sense of relief from guilt. Justification—being declared righteous before God—is one of the most significant and encouraging truths of the Christian faith.

## LISTEN: Are You Good Enough?

As we start this initial session, it would be interesting to discover how you view our society. How do you think most people in our culture would answer this question: *How does a person get into heaven?*

The most common responses given go something like this:

- "By trying to be a good person—or doing enough good."
- "By not hurting people and not being selfish."
- "By being the best I can be—doing what is right."
- "By trying to live a moral life—letting the good you do outweigh the bad."

- "There are lots of different ways and different religions but by being sincere in whichever one you choose."
- "By keeping the laws of God (or trying not to break the commandments)."
- "By trying to be religious in some way."

The New Testament describes these types of attempts to get right with God as "works."[1] In other words, people try to "work" for God's approval by trying to keep the laws of God and trying to do enough good. The New Testament also describes this attempt to gain God's approval as "observing the law," "deeds of the law" (or "works of the law"), and "law" (as a system of salvation).

Whenever you see phrases such as "observing the law," "deeds of the law," and "works of the law" in the New Testament, you will know what they normally mean: a strategy where you try to *work for* your salvation so that you will become righteous enough in God's assessment of you. It means you are trying to do enough good or to be moral enough to gain eternal life. It describes what people do when they turn the commandments into a virtual job description for how to earn salvation. In other words, it means using the law as a *system of salvation*. Understanding the meaning of these phrases is an important key to understanding many parts of the New Testament.

"To be justified" means that you are "declared (or pronounced) righteous before God." In Romans 3:20, we learn that no person will ever be declared righteous before God by keeping the law: "Therefore by the deeds of the law no flesh [no one] will be justified in His sight, for by the law is the knowledge of sin."

## ABSORB

**According to the New Testament, our moral record could never be good enough to be accepted by God.**

## INTERACT

○ Why do you think no person will be declared "righteous" before God by trying to keep the laws of God or by trying to be a good person?

○ Rephrase in your own words what Romans 3:20 means to you.

## LISTEN: The Law Itself Tells Me I'm a Sinner

Again, Romans 3:20 reads, "Therefore by the deeds of the law no flesh will be justified in His sight, *for by the law is the knowledge of sin.*" This verse says that you cannot be justified (declared righteous) by trying to keep the law of God, and it says that one of the primary purposes of the law is *to make you aware that you actually do sin.* When you look carefully at the Ten Commandments (often called "the Law") and comprehend the spirit of the law as Jesus explained them, it is eye-opening to see how miserably we fail. We are clearly found to be sinners.

While this might be a little uncomfortable, we're going to look at each of the Ten Commandments and evaluate how we measure up. Be thinking about how you measure up. Remember: "By the law is the knowledge of sin." One of the main purposes of the law is to help us see that truly we are sinners. Although this can be very hard, it is not until we admit we are sinners that we will ever look to God for his mercy and grace. And by looking at the Ten Commandments we can better appreciate what God has done for us so that we can be justified (declared righteous).

### ABSORB

One of the primary purposes of the law is to make us aware that we do in fact sin against God. The law is designed to show us that we have, without a doubt, violated God's moral code. If we are humble enough to admit that we are sinners, then the law can lead us to see how much we need God's grace.

### INTERACT

Below are a series of questions concerning how well we have kept the Ten Commandments. How we answer these questions can tell us a great deal about our spiritual need.

1. "You shall have no other gods before Me" (Exod. 20:3).

   *This means nothing should have first place in our lives other than God. Oftentimes people put jobs, relationships, possessions, and money before him. God should have center stage in our affections, priorities, goals, and so on.*

   ○ What do you think it means to put God first in your life? Have you always kept God first?

2. "You shall not make for yourself a carved image—any likeness of anything that is in heaven above, or that is in the earth beneath, or that is in the water under the earth" (Exod. 20:4).

   *Although most people in Western societies do not carve or shape physical idols, many people do shape a mental image of God from their own ideas. They say, "To me God is like . . . ," even though their ideas about God contradict the Scriptures. When they do this they are mentally shaping an image of God to fit what they want God to look like.*

○ What was your concept or mental image of God as you were growing up? (The nature of discipleship is to help us align our concepts of God to his Word.)

3. "You shall not take the name of the LORD your God in vain, for the LORD will not hold him guiltless who takes His name in vain" (Exod. 20:7).

   *The phrase "in vain" means "with no good purpose."[2] Most people have spoken the name of God in vain by using it in a profane way or by the habit of saying, "Oh my God!" That is using his name "with no good purpose"!*

○ How does our culture go against this commandment?

4. "Remember the Sabbath day, to keep it holy" (Exod. 20:8).

   *Because Jesus was resurrected on Sunday, first-century Christians set aside time to worship together on that day—the Lord's Day. Throughout church history Christians have gathered together on Sunday to corporately worship Christ. The spirit of this command is carried out when Christians gather together each week to worship the Lord.*

○ How much importance is put on this commandment in our society?

## The Human Heart Is an "Idol Factory"

"When most people think of 'idols' they have in mind literal statues—or the next pop star anointed by Simon Cowell. Yet while traditional idol worship still occurs in many places of the world, internal idol worship, within the heart, is universal. In Ezekiel 14:3, God says about elders of Israel, 'These men have set up their idols in their hearts.' Like us, the elders must have responded to this charge, 'Idols? What idols? I don't see any idols.' God was saying that the human heart takes good things like a successful career, love, material possessions, even family, and turns them into ultimate things. Our hearts deify them as the center of our lives, because, we think, they can give us significance and security, safety and fulfillment, if we attain them. . . . Most people know you can make a god out of money. Most know you can make a god out of sex. However, anything in life can serve as an idol, a God-alternative, a counterfeit. . . . But counterfeit gods always disappoint, and often destructively so."

**Timothy Keller**[a]

[a]*Counterfeit Gods* (New York: Dutton, 2009), xiv–xvi.

5. "Honor your father and your mother" (Exod. 20:12).

> *When you are young, this means to obey them. As a grown adult, this means to respect them and treat them as valuable. The respect and honor we show our (imperfect) parents is closely related to the respect and honor we show God.*

○ Why might God command us to obey, honor, and value our parents, who cannot parent perfectly?

6. "You shall not murder" (Exod. 20:13).

> *Jesus recognized that murder stems from resentment, anger, and hate in our hearts. Jesus, in the Sermon on the Mount, said that sin is not only related to our external actions but has to do with what goes on inside our hearts. So if someone has unrighteous anger, according to Christ, the spirit of this command is broken.*

○ Have you ever had anger that got out of hand or had bitterness in your heart toward someone?

7. "You shall not commit adultery" (Exod. 20:14).

*Again, Jesus makes it plain that sin is not just an external act; it also involves our inward thoughts. He explains that if we lust, we have broken the spirit of this command. Jesus said that "whoever looks at a woman to lust for her has already committed adultery with her in his heart" (Matt. 5:28).*

○ Do you think our culture takes Jesus's words seriously? What are some indicators that show this?

8. "You shall not steal" (Exod. 20:15).

*When a person steals, he or she takes possession of something that does not belong to him or her. You normally do not feel the depth of the wrongness of stealing until you have something of value stolen from you!*

○ Have you ever had something stolen from you? If so, how did you feel at the time? Have you ever stolen something?

9. "You shall not bear false witness against your neighbor" (Exod. 20:16).

*This commandment includes lying. It is interesting that Jesus connects the origin of lying with the devil. The Lord said of the devil in John 8:44 that "there is no truth in him. When he speaks a lie, he speaks from his own resources, for he is a liar and the father of it." C. S. Lewis recognized the subtlety of lying; in his novel, The Last Battle, at a critical moment he has one of the main characters realize a terrible truth: "And then she understood the devilish cunning of the enemies' plan. By mixing a little truth with it they had made their lie far stronger."*[3]

○ Why does mixing a little truth with a lie make the lie stronger?

10. "You shall not covet your neighbor's house; you shall not covet your neighbor's wife, nor his male servant, nor his female servant, nor his ox, nor his donkey, nor anything that is your neighbor's" (Exod. 20:17).

> *Coveting is to intensely desire something that God doesn't want you to have. It is an inordinate desire. At the core of coveting is being discontent with God. Often we ignore God's will by trying to acquire something he has chosen not to give us. Although we can be blessed with affluence, it is easy to become discontented.*

○ In our society, what types of things are most often coveted?

○ After looking closely at how you've kept the Ten Commandments, ask yourself: If God were to judge me purely on the basis of keeping the Ten Commandments perfectly, how would I measure up? Why do you think there are people who, although they have clearly broken some of the Ten Commandments, still consider themselves fairly good people?

The law never came to save men. It never was its intention at all. It came on purpose to make the evidence complete that salvation by works is impossible.

**—Charles Spurgeon, "Law and Grace"**

## LISTEN: God's Definition of "Good"

To be *good*, by God's definition, means to have *absolute moral perfection*. Humans settle for a less strict definition of what it means to be a good person. However, God's evaluation is what counts! Listen to what the apostle Paul says about God's evaluation of you and me and all humanity from Romans 3:20: "Therefore by the deeds of the law [by trying to keep the Ten Commandments] *no flesh* will be justified." The Scriptures also categorically state: "There is none righteous, no, not one" (Rom. 3:10). Humans don't like to think of themselves as not being good enough to go to heaven. It is hard for us to admit that we are that desperate. In our pride we do not want to admit that we are not good enough to be accepted by God.

### ABSORB

**Only God is absolutely morally perfect. God says no one is justified by "works" or "deeds of the law."**

---

INTERACT

○ Why do you think it is so common that people try to be justified by the good things they do?

○ Do you think most people have done a self-evaluation by going through the Ten Commandments and being honest about how well they have kept God's moral law? Why not?

## LISTEN: What It Means to Be Justified

Listen carefully to this amazing verse: "Knowing that a man is *not justified by the works of the law* but by *faith in Jesus Christ*, even we have believed in Christ Jesus, that we might be justified by faith in Christ and not by the works of the law; for by the works of the law no flesh shall be justified" (Gal. 2:16).

"Justification" is a technical, legal, courtroom term; it is a legal pronouncement and a legal rescue. God is pictured as the majestic, righteous, perfect judge over all the universe. In his heavenly courtroom you and I will either be acquitted or condemned and sentenced. "To be justified" means that God declares that you are acquitted—free from condemnation and free from the sentence of hell. It implies the removal of our guilt and of God's wrath against us. "To be justified" means to be *pronounced righteous* (or *declared righteous*) in the sight of God.[4]

Theologian John Stott explains what justification is in legal terms and what it is not.

"Justification" is a legal term, borrowed from the law courts. It is the exact opposite of "condemnation." "To condemn" is to declare somebody guilty; "to justify" is to declare him . . . righteous. In the Bible it refers to God's act of unmerited favor by which He puts a sinner right with Himself, not only pardoning or acquitting him, but accepting him and treating him as righteous.[5]

Justification is not a synonym for amnesty, which strictly is pardon without principle, a forgiveness which overlooks—even forgets—wrongdoing and declines to bring it to justice. No, justification is an act of justice, of gracious justice. . . . When God justifies sinners, he is not declaring bad people to be good, or saying that they are not sinners after all. He is pronouncing them legally righteous, free from any liability to the broken law, because he himself in his Son has borne the penalty of their law-breaking.[6]

As we think more deeply about what Galatians 2:16 means, we realize that we are justified only by faith in Jesus Christ and not at all by works of the law (that is, not by trying to keep the Ten Commandments). This means that when you believe in Christ Jesus—when you believe that Christ died in your place and took your punishment—it is only then that you are justified, only then that you are acquitted and are free from condemnation.

## ABSORB

### According to God's Word, the only way you can be justified is by faith in Jesus Christ.

## INTERACT

○ How does it make you feel to know that even though you have broken the laws of God, you can still be declared righteous before God by faith alone in Christ?

○ Write out the meaning of the phrase "to be justified" so that the definition can be firmly fixed in your mind.

○ If God has shown so much mercy to us, how should we, then, treat people who don't deserve our mercy?

**Reflect:** One of the most important traits of being a follower of Christ is to "follow Christ." This means the more we integrate the truth we learn about God with real-life experiences, the more real our spiritual lives feel. After understanding even a little bit about justification, be thinking this week how that knowledge could make a difference in the way you think about God and treat people.

## Our Desperate Predicament

"Picture the scene: An accused criminal stands before an impartial judge to receive his just sentence. The legal proceedings begin with a court official reciting the laws of the kingdom. As he listens, the criminal starts to realize that he is doomed to be condemned, for it turns out that he has violated every single law in the book. Whatever the charge, he is certain to be found guilty. When the judge finally turns to the defendant and asks how he pleads, the man is speechless. He stands before the judge in mute terror, unable to utter anything in his defense. This is the desperate legal predicament described in the opening chapters of Romans. . . . The problem of humanity is sin, plain and simple. We are guilty sinners who deserve nothing except God's wrath. Nor is there anything we can do to save ourselves. God's righteous requirements cannot save us; they can only condemn us because we cannot keep them. Therefore, when we stand before God for judgment, there is not the slightest chance that we can be accepted on the basis of anything that we have done. This is not a trial in which we are innocent until proven guilty; instead, it is a trial in which we have already been proven guilty and must remain guilty until we are declared righteous. It is only when we recognize how desperate our situation is from the legal standpoint that we can begin to understand the biblical doctrine of justification. It is only when we see the stark and ugly reality of our sin that we are truly ready to turn to God for help—specifically, for the forgiveness and the righteousness of Jesus Christ."

**Philip Graham Ryken[a]**

[a]"*Justification*," in *The Gospel as Center*, ed. D. A. Carson and Timothy Keller (Wheaton: Crossway, 2012), 151–53.

Are there any questions that this session has raised in your mind? Is there anything I can be praying about for you until we meet for the next session? Where do you feel the most pressure in your life at this point in time?

## CULTIVATING SPIRITUAL HABITS

**Read:** Matthew 27:1–50 and Romans 3:9–31

**Journal:** Write down any verse or thought from your reading that stands out to you or encourages you. Also, jot down any questions you might have concerning your reading or the Christian faith. We're here to learn together, and one of the best ways we can grow is to search the Scriptures and find answers for our questions.

## Memorize

*Knowing that a man is not justified by the works of the law\**
*but by faith in Jesus Christ, even we have believed in Christ*
*Jesus, that we might be justified by faith in Christ and not by*
*the works of the law; for by the works of the law no flesh*
*shall be justified.*

GALATIANS 2:16

---

\* Remember the phrase "works of the law"? It describes when someone is trying to *work* *for* God's acceptance by keeping the law or trying to do enough good in order to have a right standing before God—in order to be saved. Also, remember that "to be justified" means "to be declared righteous" by God.

# God Pays the Price

## Understanding Justification (Part 2)

**Purpose of Session Two:** In the last session you learned how you are justified (declared righteous before God)—it is by faith in Christ. In this session, you will learn how God can be just when he justifies you. You will also be introduced to three important biblical concepts that will help explain what it cost God to justify you.

## LISTEN: Our Inborn Sense of Justice

C. S. Lewis, well-known author of The Chronicles of Narnia, was a brilliant writer and had unusual insight into human nature. In one of his books, *Mere Christianity*, he describes how all humans have a built-in sense of what is right and wrong.

> Everyone has heard people quarrelling. Sometimes it sounds funny and sometimes it sounds merely unpleasant; but however it sounds, I believe we can learn something very important from listening to the kind of things they say. They say things like this: "How'd you like it if anyone did the same to you?"—"That's my seat, I was there first"—"Leave him alone, he isn't doing you any harm"—"Why should you shove in first?"—"Give me a bit of your orange, I gave you a bit of mine"—"Come on, you promised." People say things like that every day, educated people as well as uneducated, and children as well as grown-ups. Now what interests me about all these remarks is that the man who makes them is not merely saying that the other man's behavior does not happen to please him. He

is appealing to some kind of standard of behavior which he expects the other man to know about.[1]

Lewis is saying that every person has a built-in sense of what is just and what is unjust. We are simply hardwired to want justice—because we are made in the image of God.

--- **ABSORB** ---

### Because humans are made in the image of God we value justice and fair play.

--- **INTERACT** ---

○ Choose one of the following three questions to answer:

1. What are justice and injustice?
2. Have you ever experienced something in your life that you felt was an injustice?
3. What do you think of when you hear the phrase "an eye for an eye, a tooth for a tooth"?

## LISTEN: A Judge's Dilemma

When we learn about how God justifies us there appears at first to be a dilemma: "How can God justify (pronounce righteous) people who are absolutely guilty? How can God justify guilty people and still be a just judge? How can God justify the ungodly?"

For example, try to imagine the worst injustice someone could ever carry out against you. Maybe it would be kidnapping or injuring someone you deeply love. Maybe it would be taking something that is irreplaceable—your health, your most treasured keepsakes, or the life of a loved one. We all would agree that the perpetrator of such a crime should be severely punished. But suppose the judge decided to show the criminal mercy by ruling: "Because I am a merciful judge and feel compassion for this criminal, I will therefore let him go free."

--- **ABSORB** ---

**Because God is a just judge he must have a way to satisfy his own sense of justice when he lets offenders (sinners like you and me) go free.**

--- **INTERACT** ---

○ If the judge mentioned above were to simply show mercy, would you have a problem with that? Why?

## LISTEN: Your Release Was Paid For (Redemption)

Justice matters to you and me, but it matters infinitely more to God! Justice is part of the glory of God. That is why when God justifies sinners, when he pronounces the sinner acquitted—no longer condemned—he does it in such a way that he demonstrates that he is just. God is both the justifier and just. Our inborn desire to see justice carried out is completely satisfied in Christianity! There are three biblical concepts that you need to understand concerning how God can be just when he justifies you. They are redemption, propitiation, and imputation.

Redemption means "deliverance at a cost" or "release by payment" of a price.[2] The Bible says that God has redeemed you at an immeasurably great cost to himself. It cost him the sacrifice of his own Son. God redeemed you out of your slavery to sin. You and I were in bondage to sin; that is, we were in the bondage of guilt and condemnation because of our sin. The sentence of death and hell was held over our heads. We were on *death row*, spiritually speaking. We were enslaved to the enemy, the devil, because we had given in to his temptations to sin. But thank God we were released by the payment of a price—God purchased our redemption. Christ paid the ransom price to free you from your slavery to sin. Every genuine follower of Christ has been redeemed!

The classic nineteenth-century hymn written by the poet Fanny Crosby captures how we love to praise God because he has purchased our redemption:

> Redeemed, how I love to proclaim it!
> Redeemed by the blood of the Lamb;
> Redeemed through His infinite mercy,
> His child and forever I am.

When you consider the idea of redemption, remember that there is always a price paid to set the slave free. This price is called the "ransom" or "ransom price."[3] The ransom price that God paid was the *blood of Christ*. The unique feature of your redemption is that the price was paid to God *by God himself*. This surprising idea will be explained later in this session. Christ came from heaven to be crucified for our sins. Jesus said that he came "to give His life a ransom for many" (Mark 10:45). Listen to what the apostle Peter writes: "knowing that you were not *redeemed* with corruptible things, like silver or gold, from your aimless conduct received by tradition from your fathers, but with the *precious blood of Christ*, as of a lamb without blemish and without spot" (1 Pet. 1:18–19). God purchased our redemption with the blood of his Son! Any parent understands that there could be nothing more valuable to you than your own child and nothing more difficult to give away.

## — ABSORB —

### God is just when he justifies us because God himself redeemed us with the blood of Christ.

## — INTERACT —

○ Can you imagine giving your child as a sacrifice—giving up your child to die so that others could be set free? Why do you think it would be such an outrageous insult to God to try to be justified on the basis of your own works rather than through the blood of Christ?

○ If you had been living as a slave back in the days of slavery in the United States, what would you have disliked most?

## LISTEN: God's Wrath Is Satisfied . . . by God (Propitiation)

The second reason why God is just when he justifies us is that Christ's death on the cross was a sacrifice that satisfied God's wrath against injustice. "Propitiation" means "to satisfy God's wrath by an offering." Propitiation is the

## Jesus Came to Give His Life a Ransom for Many

"Jesus Christ came not to be served but to die, to give his life. That sets him apart from the founder of every other major religion. Their purpose was to live and be an example; Jesus's purpose was to die and be a sacrifice. . . .

"Jesus came to pay that kind of ransom. But since the slavery he is dealing with is of a cosmic kind—that is, cosmic evil—it required a cosmic payment. Jesus is saying, 'I will pay the ransom that you couldn't possibly pay, and it will procure your freedom.' The payment is Jesus's death on the cross. . . .

"This will be hard for you if you're among those who struggle with the Christian teaching about the cross. It's natural to assume that the Bible is giving us one more example of those ancient, primitive, bloodthirsty gods worshiped by those ancient, primitive, bloodthirsty societies. In *The Iliad* by Homer, for example, Agamemnon didn't get fair winds to Troy until he sacrificed his daughter. That appeased the wrath of the gods, and then they let him go to Troy. What Jesus says in Mark [10:45] may seem to be just another variation on that theme. . . .

"But that's not what's going on here at all. And why not, you may say? If God is really a loving God, why doesn't he just forgive everybody? Why did Jesus have to go through suffering into death? Why did he have to be a ransom?

"Here's the beginning of an answer: Jesus didn't have to die despite God's love, he had to die *because* of God's love. And it had to be this way because *all life-changing love is substitutionary sacrifice*."

**Timothy Keller[a]**

[a]*The King's Cross* (New York: Dutton, 2011), 141–42.

removal of God's wrath by providing a substitute offering.[4] According to the Scriptures, the substitute offering given to remove God's wrath is Christ himself, shedding his blood on the cross. Romans 3:24–25 describes how God set forth Jesus as a propitiation: "being justified freely by His grace through the redemption that is in Christ Jesus, whom God set forth as a propitiation by His blood, through faith."

Many tribal religions employ the concept of people satisfying the wrath of "the gods." But Christianity is totally different—propitiation is a work that God himself does. God's nature is such that his justice must be satisfied. So God (not humans) provides the offering, which turns out to be God's own Son, and the ransom price (the blood of Christ) is paid by God himself, to himself. The death of the Son of God satisfied the wrath of God against the injustice of our sin.

John Stott points out that propitiation "does not make God gracious. . . . God does not love us because Christ died for us, Christ died for us because God loves us."[5] The fourth-century theologian Augustine also observes, "Our being reconciled by the death of Christ must not be understood as if the

Son reconciled us, in order that the Father, then hating, might begin to love us."[6] In other words, it was God's love that prompted him to give Christ as the substitute offering to remove his wrath: "In this is love, not that we loved God, but that He loved us and sent His Son to be the propitiation for our sins" (1 John 4:10).

---

### ABSORB

**God is just when he justifies us because God gave his own Son as the propitiation (offering) for our sins.**

---

### INTERACT

○ Explain this saying, "God's grace is free, but it is not cheap."

According to the Christian revelation, God's own great love propitiated his own holy wrath through the gift of his own dear Son, who took our place, bore our sin and died our death. *Thus God himself gave himself to save us from himself.*

**—John R. W. Stott,**
***The Message of Romans***

## LISTEN: The Unfair Trade (Imputation)

The third reason why God is just when he justifies us is that our sin is *imputed* (credited) to Christ, and Christ's righteousness is imputed to us.

Imputation means that God did something amazing, which could be described as "The Great Exchange."[7] God exchanged Christ's perfect life of obedience for our disobedience. Our sins were placed on Christ as he suffered for us. Therefore, although Christ was just, he was judicially credited with our sins, and the Father executed judgment on him. As a result we are clothed in Christ's righteousness, and therefore we are judicially counted as righteous in God's sight. God thinks of Christ's righteousness as belonging to us. This is imputation! Our sin was imputed to Christ and Christ bore the punishment for our sin. Christ's righteousness is imputed to the sinner through faith in Christ. One of the clearest passages in the Bible that teaches this is 2 Corinthians 5:21: "For He made Him who knew no sin to be sin for us, that we might become the righteousness of God in Him." This does not mean that Christ personally committed any acts of sin, nor does it mean he was morally a sinner. What it does mean is that our sin was judicially credited to Christ so that his sufferings satisfied the justice of God.[8]

## ABSORB

**God is just when he justifies us because Christ's perfect life of obedience is imputed (credited) to us and our sins are imputed to Christ. God executed perfect justice on his Son.**

## INTERACT

○ Analogies often break down at certain points, but discuss one of the following analogies:

Analogy 1: Suppose you had a diseased heart, and it was certain that you would die. Someone with a perfect heart offered to do a double heart transplant—his good heart would be transplanted into you and your bad heart would be transplanted into him. How would you feel about this person? Now relate that to what God has done for you.

---

### Martin Luther's Famous Latin Formula— *Simul Justus et Peccator*

"*Simul* is the word from which we get the English *simultaneous*; it means 'at the same time.' *Justus* is the Latin word for 'just' or 'righteous.' *Et* simply means 'and.' *Peccator* means 'sinner.' So, with this formula—'at the same time just and sinner'— Luther was saying that in our justification, we are at the same time righteous and sinful. Now, if he had said we are just *and* sinful at the same time and in the same relationship, that would have been a contradiction in terms. But that is not what he was saying. He was saying that, in one sense, we are just. In another sense, we are sinners. In and of ourselves, under God's scrutiny, we still have sin. But by God's imputation of the righteousness of Jesus Christ to our accounts, we are considered just. This is the very heart of the gospel. In order to get into heaven, will I be judged by my righteousness or by the righteousness of Christ? If I have to trust in my righteousness to get into heaven, I must completely and utterly despair of any possibility of ever being redeemed. But when we see that the righteousness that is ours by faith is the perfect righteousness of Christ, we see how glorious is the good news of the gospel."

R. C. Sproul[a]

[a]*Are We Together?* (Sanford, FL: Reformation Trust, 2012), 43–44.

Analogy 2: Suppose you incurred an enormous financial debt that you could never repay. Someone, at a great cost to himself or herself, stepped forward and credited to your bank account the money to pay off your debt. How would you feel about this person? Now relate that to what God has done for you.

## LISTEN: God Pays, You Receive

God can justify the ungodly because when a sinner trusts in Christ, God imputes (credits) the righteousness of Christ to the sinner. Because the sinner (the ungodly one) is now clothed in the righteousness of Christ, God then makes the legal declaration, "you are righteous." In this way God is just when he justifies us because he has executed judgment on his own Son, and the obedience of Christ has been credited to us who are sinners. If you enjoy language of the 1640s, then you will appreciate this description of justification given in the Westminster Shorter Catechism (a teaching tool to educate lay people in theology): "Justification is an act of God's free grace, wherein He pardoneth all our sins, and accepteth us as righteous in His sight, only for the righteousness of Christ, imputed to us, and received by faith alone" (a. 33).

A major difference between Christianity and all other religions is that in some form or some way, other religions try to appease the displeasure of the deity by offering something that *people* do—whether it be self-denial, or kind deeds, or moral improvement. But in Christianity, *God himself* satisfies his displeasure of our injustice and sin. Can you see the vast difference between these two approaches?

--- **ABSORB** ---

### God is both just and the justifier of those who have faith in Christ.

--- **INTERACT** ---

○ Justification is not about you and me becoming good enough for God to declare us righteous, but it is about God stepping in and doing for us what we could never do for ourselves. Why does "justification" give all the glory to God, not humans? Are you glad that this is the way God justifies you?

**Reflect:** It is amazing that God would go to such lengths to justify us. That reality creates gratefulness in our hearts. Think about how having a grateful spirit could affect our attitudes and outlook at work, home, school, or wherever. This good news about justification has the potential of changing everything about how we respond to life!

Look back at the main "Absorb" points for a few moments, and then rephrase in your own words what redemption, propitiation, and imputation mean. Is there anything I can be praying about for you until we meet for the next session?

## CULTIVATING SPIRITUAL HABITS

**Read:** 1 Corinthians 1:18–31; John 6:28–65; Romans 8:14–39

**Journal:** Review the first and second sessions, jot down the main points of each session, think about them, and meditate on them.

### Memorize

*For even the Son of Man\* did not come to be served, but to serve, and to give His life a ransom for many.*

MARK 10:45

---

\* The term "Son of Man" was a favorite title and description Jesus used to refer to himself. The term alludes to the reality that although Jesus is divine (the Son of God), he is also *fully human* (the Son of Man). It is also a messianic title. Daniel 7:13–14 uses it in this description of a messianic scene: "I was watching in the night visions, / And behold, One like the *Son of Man*, / Coming with the clouds of heaven! / . . . to Him was given dominion and glory and a kingdom, / That all peoples, nations, and languages should serve Him. His dominion is an everlasting dominion."

# Incredible Spiritual Benefits

Calling, Regeneration, Conversion, Salvation, Adoption

**Purpose of Session Three:** When you were justified (declared righteous by God), God was at work to give you other incredible benefits. In this session you will come to understand that you were also *called*, *regenerated*, *converted*, *saved*, and *adopted* by God. Understanding each one of these will help you appreciate to a greater degree the mercy and grace of God in your life.

## LISTEN: "Come!"—God's General Calling

The New Testament describes Christians as those who are called by almighty God himself. This means that we were spiritually lost, and God called us to himself through the gospel. It is incredible to think that God would call us! As you read through the Scriptures, you discover that God uses a *general calling* and a *special calling*.[1] *General calling* is a call to know God and is offered to all persons of all times. This general call is seen in Isaiah 45:22, where the Lord invites all on the earth to be saved: "Look to Me, and be saved, / All you ends of the earth! / For I am God, and there is no other." Also, Jesus graciously gives an open, general call for anyone to come to him for spiritual rest and salvation: "Come to Me, all you who labor and are heavy laden, and I will give you rest" (Matt. 11:28). The Spirit of God also gives an open invitation to all people to take of salvation that is freely offered: "And the Spirit and the bride say, 'Come!'. . . And let him who thirsts come. Whoever desires, let him take the water of life freely" (Rev. 22:17). God's gracious offer extends to all peoples throughout the earth. At the judgment day, *no one* will be able to say that he or she had no opportunity to know God.

## How Does Everybody Receive Knowledge of God?

The apostle Paul makes a compelling case in Romans 1:20–23 that God has revealed enough about himself in order for everyone to receive true, authentic knowledge of God. Paul concludes that if anyone does not come to know this true God, then they are "without excuse." The apostle's point is that because humans have a bias toward sin, they choose not to pursue the true knowledge of God, which is available. Their pursuit of knowing God is diverted and distorted by sin.

Also the apostle Paul states in Romans 2:14–15 that the gentiles (those who have not formally received the written Word of God) still have an internal, moral law imprinted on their hearts. This means that every rational person knows the difference between right and wrong—no matter where they live on the face of the earth. And every person who knows this moral law also knows that he or she has not perfectly lived up to it. So these people (just like you and me) must cry out by faith for God's mercy.

There is an underlying assumption in the New Testament that if anyone looks to God's mercy and grace for salvation, then God sends to them a fuller revelation of himself through the message of the gospel of Christ (for example, Cornelius in Acts 10, and the vision of the man from Macedonia calling out for help in Acts 16:9–10). Also, Jesus himself taught, "To you who hear, more will be given. For whoever has, to him more will be given" (Mark 4:24–25). The Great Commission in Matthew 28:19–20 is directed at all of us to take seriously the mandate to take this message of the gospel to the very ends of the earth. We must never forget the enormous responsibility and privilege that we have of taking the gospel to the ends of the earth.

---

### ABSORB

**God is gracious to extend a general call to all to come to him. No one will ever be able to say that there wasn't enough knowledge available to know God.**

---

### INTERACT

○ When God calls people to come to Christ, some people ignore or refuse the offer. What are some of the most common reasons for refusing the call?

## LISTEN: "I Choose You"—God's Special Calling

Although Jesus graciously gives an open, general call for *anyone* to know him, that call is often rejected. Believers have come to realize that God does not leave us to ourselves. He extends to us even further grace! Jesus said, "No one can come to Me unless the Father who sent Me draws him; and I will raise him up at the last day" (John 6:44). Christ also said, "Therefore I have said to you that no one can come to Me unless it has been granted to him by My Father" (John 6:65). This means that if we were left to ourselves, we would not choose to come to Christ. And God would be totally just in letting us remain in our choice to ignore him and suffer the consequences. But God, in an amazing extension of his grace, actually draws us to Christ. This is what theologians refer to as our *special calling* (sometimes called an *effectual* or *inward calling*). This special calling is (in a real sense) a gracious and powerful divine summons.

When I was a kid, my best friend, Orville, would often ignore his mother's call for him to come home for supper. She would call out, "Orville, come home." I noticed he wouldn't respond. But then after a while, she would give a formal summons: "Orville George Knebel Jr., you come home!" And Orville would go home. This call evoked a response of obedience; it was effective!

In a sense, this is what God does with us—he gives us a divine summons that is *effective* (effectual). He calls us in such a way that we are drawn to his Son. His "special calling" enables our hearts to respond to Christ.

Christians are referred to in the New Testament as "the called" (Rom. 1:6; 8:28). It is true that we must respond personally and willingly to the gospel message with faith, but when the Bible describes Christians as "the called," it underscores the truth that it is *God* who does the special work of opening our hearts so that we want to respond to the gospel. Acts 16:14 says that it was *the Lord* who opened Lydia's heart to the gospel. Notice how the Bible labels only believers as being called in this special sense: "For you see your calling, brethren, that not many wise according to the flesh, not many mighty, not many noble, *are called*. But God has chosen the foolish things . . . that no flesh should glory in His presence" (1 Cor. 1:26–27, 29). God calls us in such a way that the glory goes to him. Also, it is important to observe that when God extends this special calling to someone, that calling begins a chain of events that does not stop until we are in heaven. Romans 8:30 describes that chain of events (notice that what God begins, he always finishes): "these He also called; whom He called, these He also justified; and whom He justified, these He also glorified." It is also noteworthy that Jesus himself said, "For many are called but few *are* chosen" (Matt. 22:14), which indicates that there is a general call of God extended to all people, but few are chosen to receive this special extension of grace. This grace is purely undeserved and magnifies God's overflowing mercy, compassion, and loving-kindness. Our only reasonable response is to be eternally grateful to God for our special calling.

## ABSORB

God graciously gives to everyone the call to know him. This is God's *general calling.* Believers, however, are described as *the called of God—* this is God's *special calling,* whereby he draws us to his Son.

## INTERACT

○ Jesus said, "No one can come to Me unless the Father who sent Me draws him" (John 6:44). How does it make you feel to know that the Father has actually drawn you to come to Christ? Are you thankful for his special calling in your life?

## LISTEN: New Birth—Regeneration

"Regeneration" is a work of God, not humans, in which he imparts new spiritual life to us. It marks the beginning of a new life, a new beginning, a new birth (often called being "born again"). To be regenerated means that you were spiritually dead and now have been made alive in Christ. This is more than "turning over a new leaf." The Scriptures state that we are actually a new creation in Christ: "Therefore, if anyone is in Christ, he is a new creation; old things have passed away; behold, all things have become new" (2 Cor. 5:17). This means that we are absolutely not what we were. The New Testament speaks of us in terms of the old man (old self) and new man. Romans 6:6 says, "knowing this, that our old man was crucified with Him . . . that we should no longer be slaves of sin." We were slaves of sin, but when we are born again (regenerated), we are set free from the dominating power sin had over us. God regenerates through his Word, not without it. The apostle Peter records that we have been born again through the Word of God: "having been born again, not of corruptible seed but incorruptible, through the Word of God which lives and abides forever" (1 Pet. 1:23).

When the Holy Spirit regenerates us, a profound change occurs in our identity. Our new identity is first and foremost that of a new person. In the deepest sense of personhood I am no longer "a sinner" but "a saint," which means "holy one." ("Saint" is a common identifying label that the New Testament uses for all Christians.) I am now *righteous* not *unrighteous*. The "old me" (the unregenerate me) was constantly dominated by sin and the flesh. The flesh was constantly pulling me down and causing me to live in ways that were in opposition to the will of God. But now the old person is dead—crucified! If I have been regenerated then I can say, "I am not who I was." A regenerated person still struggles with sin, but the bent and inclination and desire of our new nature is toward righteousness. We are a new person with a new nature.[2] The "flesh" has lost its controlling power, but it still clings and tempts us, although it doesn't have the dominion over us that it had before we were saved. The key is that we are learning to become in practice who God keeps insisting that we already are. The issue of identity is letting what God says about us shape what we believe about ourselves.

## — ABSORB —

**Regeneration is a work of God in which the Holy Spirit brings about in us a new (spiritual) birth and creates in us a new heart and a new nature so that our deepest desire and disposition now is to believe and trust God.**

## — INTERACT —

○ When you feel like you are trapped in a particular sin, how can knowing that you are fundamentally a new person with a new nature help you overcome that sin or habit?

## LISTEN: Turn, Turn, Turn—Conversion

Jesus said: "Assuredly, I say to you, unless you are converted and become as little children, you will by no means enter the kingdom of heaven" (Matt. 18:3). The word "converted" in its basic sense means "to turn." Therefore, "conversion" is turning from sin and unbelief and turning to Christ.

This turning includes repentance and faith. Repentance and faith are two sides of a single coin; therefore, sometimes in the Bible the terms *faith* and *repentance* appear to be interchangeable. But each term does have a specific emphasis. "Repentance" is a radical change of mind where there is authentic (godly) sorrow for your sin together with a resolution to turn from it. "Faith" is turning to Christ (God) by trusting in Christ to save you and forgive you for your sins.

Repentance means "to undergo a change of one's mind." Theologian Louis Berkhof rightly observes that repentance is a totally inward act and should not be confused with the change of life that proceeds from it. But he points out that where there is true repentance there will follow the "fruits" of repentance.[3] In other words, your deeds (how you live) will demonstrate whether or not your repentance and faith are real. The apostle Paul makes this clear when he stands before King Agrippa and describes how he was converted and given a message from Christ to give to the world. That message was that people would be turned from darkness to light and receive the forgiveness of sins through faith in Christ (Acts 26:18) and *"that they should repent*, turn to God, *and do works befitting repentance* [performing deeds appropriate to repentance]" (Acts 26:20). In other words, if you genuinely repent, then the way you live must show that you have turned away from your sins.

There is a pattern in all these incredible benefits of God—God reaches out to us in such a way that he deserves the glory. God should be given the glory because even our repentance is a gift that he grants: "They glorified God, saying, 'Then God has also granted to the Gentiles repentance to life'" (Acts 11:18).

--- **ABSORB** ---

**"Conversion is our willing response to the gospel call in which we sincerely repent of sins and trust in Christ for salvation."[4]**

--- **INTERACT** ---

○ Do you think that there might be people in our culture who call themselves Christians but have never been converted? Why would it be important to talk about the component of repentance (turning from our sins) when helping someone to understand the gospel of Christ?

## LISTEN: Rescued by Grace—Salvation

The New Testament says, "For by grace you have been saved through faith, and that not of yourselves; it is the gift of God" (Eph. 2:8). To be "saved" means to be delivered or rescued. God in his grace delivers us from many things, including the *dominion* of sin, the flesh, the devil, and the power of death. He also delivers us from a life of fear and selfish futility. But the ultimate calamity from which he rescues us is the coming judgment and wrath of God (Rom. 5:9). Jesus himself stated in the clearest terms that there will be a coming day, which he called "that day" (Matt. 7:22) and the "day of judgment" (Matt. 12:36), when God pours out his wrath in judgment against all the unrepentant—all those who remain unconverted. To be saved is to be rescued from the condemnation of hell: "There is therefore now no condemnation to those who are in Christ Jesus" (Rom. 8:1). Notice again that it is by God's free grace that you have been saved; Ephesians 2:8–9 says: "For by grace you have been saved through faith, and that not of yourselves; it is the gift of God, not of works, lest anyone should boast." The means of receiving salvation is through faith—faith is the hand that opens up to receive the gift. Acts 4:12 clearly states that salvation is found only in Christ: "Nor is there salvation in any other, for there is no other name under heaven given among men by which we must be saved." J. I. Packer makes the observation that God not only saves us *from* certain things but also *for* something extremely important:

> Believers are saved from sin and death, but what are they saved for? To live for time and eternity in love to God—Father, Son, and Spirit—and to their neighbors. The source of love for God is knowledge of God's redeeming love for us, and the evidence of love for God is neighbor-love. (1 John 4:19–21)[5]

## ― ABSORB ―

**Salvation is rescue from the ultimate calamity, which is the coming judgment and wrath of God.[6] Christ saves us to live in love to God and to our neighbors for time and eternity.[7]**

## ― INTERACT ―

○ How does it make you feel to know that because of God's grace you will never experience the condemnation of hell? If a friend asked you to explain how to become saved, what would be some key ideas that you would include?

## LISTEN: Becoming a Child of God—Adoption

Romans 8:15–17 explains that every Christian has received adoption by our Father in heaven, and therefore we are heirs of God and even joint heirs with Christ. J. I. Packer's statements on the subject of becoming children of God are classic:

> What is a Christian? The question can be answered in many ways, but the richest answer I know is that a Christian is one who has God for his Father. But cannot this be said of every man, Christian or not? Emphatically no! The idea that all

---

*Sidebar:*

Much more then, having now been justified by His blood, we shall be saved from wrath through Him.
**—Romans 5:9**

The Gospel is not just the ABCs but the A to Z of the Christian life. It is inaccurate to think the gospel is what saves non-Christians, and then Christians mature by trying hard to live according to biblical principles. It is more accurate to say that we are saved by believing the gospel, and then we are transformed in every part of our minds, hearts, and lives by believing the gospel more and more deeply as life goes on (see Rom. 12:1–2; Phil. 1:6; 3:13–14).
**—Timothy Keller, Center Church**

For you did not receive the spirit of bondage again to fear, but you received the Spirit of adoption by whom we cry out, "Abba, Father." The Spirit Himself bears witness with our spirit that we are children of God, and if children, then heirs—heirs of God and joint heirs with Christ.

**—Romans 8:15–17**

men are children of God is not found in the Bible anywhere. The Old Testament shows God as the Father, not of all men, but of His own people, the seed of Abraham, "*Israel is my son, even my firstborn: and I say unto thee, Let my son go. . .*' (Exod. 4:22 f.). The New Testament has a world vision, but it too shows God as the Father, not of all men, but of those who, knowing themselves to be sinners, put their trust in the Lord Jesus Christ as their divine sin-bearer and master. . . . "*You are all sons of God, through faith, in Christ Jesus.*" . . . Sonship to God is not, therefore, a universal status upon which everyone enters by natural birth, but a supernatural gift which one receives through receiving Jesus. . . . If you want to judge how well a person understands Christianity, find out how much he makes of the thought of being God's child, and having God as his Father. If this is not the thought that prompts and controls his worship and prayers and his whole outlook on life, it means that he does not understand Christianity very well at all. For everything that Christ taught, everything that makes the New Testament new, and better than the Old, everything that is distinctively Christian as opposed to merely Jewish, is summed up in the knowledge of the Fatherhood of God. "Father" is the Christian name for God.[8]

John 1:12 says that we become children of God through faith in his Son: "But as many as received Him, to them He gave the right to become children of God, to those who believe in His name." Also 1 John 3:1 says: "Behold what manner of love the Father has bestowed on us, that we should be called children of God!" Only those who trust Christ receive the status of being called children of God—only believers are members of his family. After we were

---

## Becoming a Father

"My relationship with God took a major turn when I became a father myself. After my oldest daughter was born, I began to see how wrong I was in my thinking about God. For the first time I got a taste of what I believe God feels toward us. I thought about my daughter often. I prayed for her while she slept at night. I showed her picture to anyone who would look. I wanted to give her the world.

"Sometimes when I come home from work, my little girl greets me by running out to the driveway and jumping into my arms before I can even get out of the car. As you can imagine, arriving home has become one of my favorite moments of the day.

"My own love and desire for my kids' love is so strong that it opened my eyes to how much God desires and loves us. . . .

"Through this experience, I came to understand that my desire for my children is only a faint echo of God's great love for me. . . . I am just an earthly, sinful father, and I love my kids so much it hurts. How could I not trust a heavenly, perfect Father who loves me infinitely more than I will ever love my kids?"

**Francis Chan**[a]

[a]*Crazy Love* (Colorado Springs: David C. Cook, 2008), 54.

## God Is the Gospel

"Today—as in every generation—it is stunning to watch the shift away from God as the all-satisfying gift of God's love. It is stunning how seldom God Himself is proclaimed as the greatest gift of the gospel. . . . The best and final gift of the gospel is that we gain Christ. . . . My point in this book is that all the saving events and all the saving blessings of the gospel are means of getting obstacles out of the way so that we might know and enjoy God most fully. *Propitiation, redemption, forgiveness, imputation, sanctification, liberation, healing, heaven*—none of these is good news except for one reason: they bring us to God for our everlasting enjoyment of Him. . . . The gospel is not a way to get people to heaven; it is a way to get people to God. It's a way of overcoming every obstacle to everlasting joy in God."

**John Piper[a]**

[a]*God Is the Gospel* (Wheaton: Crossway, 2005), 11, 47.

justified, God then gave to us the new status of being "sons and daughters of God." We are heirs of God, and we have been given the status of "sonship," which means we have all the rights and privileges that come with being children of God. Romans 8:16 says: "The Spirit Himself bears witness with our spirit that we are children of God."

— ABSORB —

*"Adoption is an act of God whereby He makes us members of His family"*[9] *and grants to us all the liberties, privileges, and promises of having God as our Father.*

— INTERACT —

○ How could it make a difference in our attitude in life if we lived every day with the full realization that we are children of God? God is our Father!

**Reflect:** The spiritual reality of being called, regenerated, converted, saved, and adopted into God's family has the potential of revolutionizing our self-image. If we really have been shown this kind of favor from God, think about how that knowledge could free us up to help and serve others instead of being consumed with feeding and pampering our own egos.

What stands out most in your mind from your understanding of this session? Is there anything I can be praying about for you until we meet for the next session?

## CULTIVATING SPIRITUAL HABITS

**Read:** Galatians 5:16–26 and Romans 7:7–8:17

**Journal:** Jot down in your journal each of the five benefits: *calling, regeneration, conversion, salvation,* and *adoption.* Write out what it is about each one that you appreciate most.

### Memorize

*For by grace you have been saved through faith, and that not of yourselves; it is the gift of God, not of works, lest anyone should boast.*

EPHESIANS 2:8–9

# Temptations of the Flesh

## Overcoming Temptation (Part 1)

**Purpose of Session Four:** Every Christian faces temptation, and as you understand the sources of temptation and how to overcome temptation you will be equipped to face the struggles of life. This session focuses on "the flesh," which is one of the three sources of temptation—the flesh, the devil, and the world. The next session will focus on the devil and the world.

## LISTEN: The Deception of Temptation

In the Disney classic *A Bug's Life*, there is a scene where a bug named Harry is mesmerized by an electrical light zapper. He starts flying toward the light, even though his friend strongly warns: "No, Harry, no! Don't look at the light." But Harry responds, "I can't help it, it's so beautiful." The light is so alluring that he voluntarily flies right into the light and then *zap!* The bug is destroyed by what he thought would bring him great pleasure and happiness. Harry was deceived.

The potential power of temptation is in its deceit. Temptation promises to give us more pleasure, more happiness, and more satisfaction and fulfillment than can be found by following God's will for our lives. But such promises are deceiving because the greatest benefits, advantages, and blessings come from making choices that God says are the best. Temptations appear promising, but they conceal the eventual negative and destructive consequences of sin. God has infinite knowledge, and he knows what will ultimately harm us and what will bring us the greatest happiness.

There are three enemies of our soul that use temptation to draw the Christian away from God—the *flesh*, the *devil*, and the *world*. We will take time now to understand "the flesh." If you understand the nature and makeup of the flesh, you will realize where many of our temptations come from.

## ABSORB

**The power of temptation is in its deceit. Temptations conceal the destructive consequences of sin.**

## INTERACT

○ Have you ever used some allurement or enticement to catch or trap an insect or animal? Describe the process of how you did that. Why did the insect or animal fall into your trap?

## LISTEN: The Enemy Within—The Flesh

The flesh is one of our enemies that tempts us into disobedience. To get a good grasp of what the Bible teaches about the flesh, we'll look closely at some Scriptures that describe our nature.

The flesh is that element within humans that generates desires that are hostile to God and oppose his will for our lives. The flesh is the ego that feels an emptiness inside and tries to satisfy that emptiness with anything but God.[1] Some versions of the Bible translate the word for "flesh" as the "sinful nature," but this can be confusing when we talk about becoming a "new creation." However, a simple but good definition of the flesh is: *The flesh is the selfish, God-resisting impulse, bent, or inclination within us that opposes God and his will.*

Where did we all get this bent that is so obvious in humans? A common saying is "nobody's perfect," but the question is, "Why not? Why isn't there even one perfect person?" The New Testament affirms our universal sinfulness: "There is none righteous, no, not one" (Rom. 3:10). Scriptures tell us that this selfish, God-resisting bent within us is derived from Adam. When Adam sinned against God, in some mysterious way, this affected the whole human race. Romans 5:12, 19 says, "Therefore, just as through one man sin entered the world, and death through sin, and thus death spread to all men, because all sinned . . . For as by one man's disobedience many were made sinners." Adam fell into temptation, and now we are descendants of Adam's fallen race; we too are affected by Adam's disobedience. The Bible teaches that we are sinful by nature. In our union with Adam we are counted as sinners.

## Sin = Social Disintegration

"According to Genesis 3 [the account of Adam and Eve sinning], when our relationship with God unraveled, all our other relationships disintegrated as well. Self-centeredness creates psychological alienation. Nothing makes us more miserable than self-absorption, the endless, unsmiling concentration on our needs, wants, treatment, ego, and record. In addition, self-centeredness leads to social disintegration. It is at the root of the breakdown in relationships between nations, races and classes, and individuals. Finally, in some mysterious way, humanity's refusal to serve God has led to our alienation from the natural world as well."

**Timothy Keller[a]**

[a]*The Reason for God* (New York: Dutton, 2008), 220.

This is what is referred to as "original sin," and it affects us all. "Ephesians 2:3 also establishes this, saying that we are all '*by nature* children of wrath.' If we are all 'by nature children of wrath,' it can only be because we are all by nature sinners—for God does not direct His wrath towards those who are not guilty. God did not create the human race sinful, but upright. But we fell into sin and became sinful due to the sin of Adam."[2]

If there was ever any debate about this truth, just look around—we all demonstrate that we are sinful by our acts of disobedience to God. Any parent can attest to the reality that you do not have to teach a child selfish and disobedient behavior—it comes naturally. The philosopher G. K. Chesterton once wrote with a touch of satire: "The only Christian doctrine for which there is empirical evidence is that of original sin." In other words, he was saying, just look at human behavior through the centuries—the hurt, pain, and suffering that humans have inflicted on each other and the way we have dishonored and ignored God—and it is obvious that something is sadly broken within all of human nature.

John Owen, who wrote the classic, seventeenth-century work *Sin and Temptation*, gives further elaboration on what the flesh does (while this quote is a bit archaic in its English, it is profound in its explanation): "It adheres as a depraved principle, unto our minds in darkness and vanity, unto our affections in sensuality, unto our wills in a loathing of and aversation from that which is good; and by some, more, or all of these, is continually putting itself upon us, in inclinations, motives, or suggestions to evil."[3]

—— ABSORB ——

**The flesh is the selfish, God-resisting impulse, bent, or inclination within us that opposes God and his will.**

---

### INTERACT

○ Since you have become a Christian, have you struggled with any of the desires of the flesh listed below in Galatians 5:19–20?

> Now the works of the flesh are evident, which are: adultery, sexual immorality, impure thoughts and activities, sensuality, putting other things as first place before God in your life, delving into occult practices, hatred, strife, jealousy, outbursts of anger, selfish ambition, dissensions, divisions, envy, getting intoxicated, wild parties, and other kinds of sin that you know are against God's will. [*Author's paraphrase, designed to clarify all the biblical terms.*]

## LISTEN: New Life Within—The Holy Spirit

The New Testament informs us that before we became followers of Christ the flesh dominated our lives. Our spiritual condition is described as being "in the flesh" (Rom. 8:8–9), which means that we were mastered and controlled by the flesh. The New Testament describes our unregenerated state as being the "old man" (the "old self"). The "old man" was dominated by the flesh. We were slaves of sin (Rom. 6:6, 17), and sin was our master. But when we are born again, we are set free from the dominating power that the flesh had over us. Now the Spirit of God indwells us, and we have a new power and a new nature that can overcome the flesh. Listen to a very important verse: "But you are not in the flesh but in the Spirit. . . . Now if anyone does not have the Spirit of Christ, he is not His" (Rom. 8:9). This means that when you believe in Christ you are no longer "in the flesh." The flesh no longer has the controlling power that it had. You now have the Spirit of God. The flesh no longer has the power to be the master of your life and your decisions. When you put your faith in Christ, who was crucified in your place, in a very real sense your flesh is crucified as well. This is brought out in Galatians 5:24: "And those who are Christ's have crucified the flesh with its passions and desires." But the question then arises, does that mean you and I will never experience any inner desires or cravings that are against the will of God?

Here is a description of what happens when you become a believer. When you are regenerated (born again) you are given a new nature. As Ephesians 2:3 explains, we "*were* by nature children of wrath." The "old man" (the old unregenerated you) *was* in slavery to the flesh. The old you was dominated by the flesh, but now you have been regenerated and given a new nature. We are new beings with all new affections and longings and desires—an incredible transformation has occurred. You are a "new man," with a distinct identity as a new creation in Christ. The tyrannical power of the flesh is broken. It has been dethroned. Now the Spirit of God is the dominant factor, and you have a new identity, a new heart, and a new nature. Although the flesh is still present within you, there is a life-changing difference: the flesh was master over you, but now the flesh has lost its controlling power and is simply an opposing force that seeks to tempt you.[4] (Note: The word "simply" does not imply that there will be no battles and that life will become simple but that the flesh has truly been dethroned.)

John Piper gives a graphic analogy of how the flesh no longer has the power it had over our old unregenerated self. His analogy gives insight into what happens to us when we are regenerated.

> When the Bible speaks of our flesh having been crucified it is like saying that the enemy has been conquered—the decisive battle against the flesh has been fought and won by Christ. The enemy has lost. The Spirit has captured the capital and broken the back of the resistance movement. The flesh is as good as dead. Its doom is sure. But there are outlying pockets of resistance. The guerrillas [or terrorists] of the flesh will not lay down their arms and must be fought back daily. A Christian is not a person who experiences no bad desires. A Christian is a person who is at war with those desires by the power of the Spirit. Conflict in your soul is not all bad. Even though we long for the day when our flesh will be utterly defunct and only pure and loving desires will fill our hearts, yet there is something worse than the war within between flesh and Spirit—namely, no war within because the flesh controls the citadel and all the outposts. Praise God for the war within! Serenity in sin is death. The Spirit has landed to do battle with the flesh. So take heart if your soul feels like a battlefield at times. The sign of whether you are indwelt by the Spirit is not that you have no bad desires, but that you are at war with them![5]

## ABSORB

**The flesh was the controlling master over you before you came to faith, but now you are indwelt by the Holy Spirit, and the flesh is an opposing force that has lost its controlling power. You are now *new*!**

## INTERACT

○ What do you think it means that the flesh was master over you but now the flesh has lost its controlling power and is simply an opposing force that seeks to tempt you?

○ How do we feel as Christians when we give in to any of these desires of the flesh?

○ How can knowing that the flesh has been dethroned give you hope as you are tempted by bad desires?

## LISTEN: Our Ongoing Struggle

The Bible says that as we walk in the Spirit, we will not carry out the desires of the flesh. Galatians 5:16–17 gives the Christian insight into the inner struggles we face: "Walk in the Spirit, and you shall not fulfill the lust of the flesh. For the flesh lusts against the Spirit [the flesh sets its desire against the Spirit], and the Spirit against the flesh; and these are contrary to one another, so that you do not do the things that you wish."

This means that there is great hope that we can face these desires of the flesh and overcome them by walking in the Spirit. To walk in the Spirit (or "by the Spirit") means to live out your life by allowing the Holy Spirit to control you. When you act on the counsel and guidance and empowerment of the Holy Spirit, you are able to resist the desires of the flesh. It is not wrong to be tempted by the desires of the flesh, but it does become sin when you give in to these desires.

When you seek to walk in the Spirit, you can have real victory over these desires. But it is the common experience of Christians to struggle with the flesh at certain points and to end up not doing the right thing but rather doing the very thing they don't want to do.[6] Even the apostle Paul admits that he finds himself struggling with the flesh and winds up not doing what he really wants to and should do.

> For what I will to do [*for what I want to do that is right*], that I do not practice; but what I hate, that I do [*the wrong that I hate to do, that I do*]. If, then, I do what I will not to do [*if, then, I do the wrong that I don't want to do*], I agree with the law that it is good. But now, it is no longer I who do it, but sin that dwells in me. For I know that in me (that is, in my flesh) nothing good dwells; for to will [*for to want to do what is right*] is present with me, but how to perform what is good I do not find. For the good that I will to do [*for the good that I want to do*], I do not do; but the evil I will not to do, that I practice. Now if I do what I will not to do [*now if I do what I don't want to do*], it is no longer I who do it, but sin that dwells* in me. (Rom. 7:15–20)

---

\* "Indwelling sin" is another way of describing "the flesh."

Paul describes the true-life process that Christians go through in our journey in this world. This is not a picture of ongoing defeat but a description of the realistic struggle with sin that every Christian goes through and that is a part of our sanctification (the process of becoming more like Christ). This passage rescues us from the devastating hopelessness of perfectionism—thinking that if you are not perfect in your walk with Christ you will be rejected by God. This also keeps us from becoming filled with pride and helps us live in humility. It makes us realize all the more that the "just shall live *by faith*." We realize that, concerning our salvation, all the glory goes to Jesus Christ our Lord!

"Is Romans 7 a description of the *normal* Christian life?" The answer to this question is "No" if by *normal* one means constant, with no hope of improvement or victory. On the other hand, it *is* normal if by that one means *universal*. Undoubtedly all Christians have at one time or another, some more and some less, experienced a struggle with sin analogous to what is described in Romans 7.

—**Sam Storms,** **"Romans 7"**

## ABSORB

**Although we are in a struggle with the flesh, if we walk in the Spirit, we will not carry out the desires of the flesh.**

## INTERACT

○ Do you ever experience what Paul describes: you really want to do what is right, but you don't do it; instead, you do the very thing you know is wrong? How does that make you feel?

○ Our culture considers certain sins to be "acceptable." How does society's approval of certain sins make them even more tempting?

○ Do you think some Christians might use this passage (Rom. 7) as an excuse to develop a pessimistic, defeatist attitude toward the Christian life?

## LISTEN: Walking in the Spirit

Galatians 5:16 states, "Walk in the Spirit, and you shall not fulfill [*carry out*] the lust [*desire*] of the flesh." But the underlying question is, *how do we actually walk in the Spirit?*

First, we must acknowledge that we are helpless to overcome the desires of the flesh apart from the enablement of the Holy Spirit.

Second, we must understand why our new identity is so important. Identity precedes and affects behavior (also attitudes, emotions, values, and so on)! If you perceive yourself as no longer enslaved to the flesh, then that will affect how you face the struggles of temptation from the flesh. One pastor explains how our identity radically affects our decisions, behaviors, and choices:

> While visiting downtown Manaus (Brazil) one evening, I noticed a pack of young boys picking pockets, stealing from shops, etc. When I asked a native about these boys, he replied, "Oh, those are the 'throw-away' kids." These children were abandoned downtown by their parents, and left to survive on their own. They (correctly) viewed themselves as throw-away children, so they stole to survive. Suppose I adopted one of those children and took him home with me. If I took him with me to the grocery store the next day, I wouldn't be surprised if he stole food and stuffed it under his shirt. *Until* he really understood and believed that his identity had changed (from a throw-away kid to my son), he would probably continue to act as if he didn't have two parents to care for him; once he understood his new identity as a child of loving, caring parents, he would look to us for his provision and his action of stealing would cease.[7]

The key is that we are learning to become *in practice* who God keeps insisting that we already are *in actuality*. The issue of identity is letting what God says about us shape what we believe about ourselves.

Third, we must be active and not passive in taking hold of the means of grace that God has given us to grow spiritually. Paul wrote: "Fight the good

All the great temptations appear first in the region of the mind and can be fought and conquered there. We have been given the power to close the door of the mind. We can lose this power through disuse or increase it by use, by the daily discipline of the inner man in things which seem small and by reliance upon the Word of the Spirit of truth. It is God that worketh in you, both to will and to do of His good pleasure. It is as though He said, "Learn to live in your will, not in your feelings."

**—Amy Carmichael (1867–1951), Protestant missionary to India**

---

## Mortify Sin

There is an old theological phrase that describes how to overcome the flesh when it tempts us: "mortify sin." It comes from verses like Romans 8:13, which instruct us: "For if you live according to the flesh you will die; but if by the Spirit you *put to death* [mortify] the deeds of the body, you will live."

Thomas Watson, an English Puritan preacher, spells out what this means. He gives the common strategy that Christians for centuries have used when faced with fleshly temptations. Watson says, "How do I mortify the flesh? 1. Withdraw the fuel that may make lust burn. . . . Take heed of that which doth nourish sin. . . . 2. Fight against fleshly lusts with spiritual weapons; faith and prayer. The best way to combat with sin, is, upon our knees."[a]

First Peter 2:11 gives further light as to what "putting to death" sin means: "Beloved, I beg you as sojourners and pilgrims, abstain from fleshly lusts which war against the soul." Simply put: *stay away from it and stop doing it!*

[a]Thomas Watson, *The Christian Soldier; or Heaven Taken by Storm: Shewing the Holy Violence a Christian Is to Put Forth in the Pursuit after Glory* (New York: Robert Moore, 1810), 19.

fight of faith" (1 Tim. 6:12). The four things listed below are God's primary means of grace that for centuries Christians have understood are essential for walking in the Spirit and conforming more and more to the image of Christ.

- **Word.** Read the Word of God, and think and meditate on it. The Holy Spirit will use the Word to strengthen your faith.
- **Prayer.** Earnestly seek God, and pray especially that God would grant new desires to overcome the desires of the flesh.
- **Church.** Gather for worship, for hearing the communication of the Word, for fellowship, and for communion.
- **Live out your faith (serve).** Be real, believe God's promises, and authentically serve Christ. (This includes seeking first the kingdom of God and seeking to make disciples by reaching people with the gospel.)

This is not a mechanical formula. Your heart before God is what matters most. But if you, with an honest heart, act upon the means of grace that God offers, then you can experience walking in the Spirit.

### — ABSORB —

**We overcome the temptations of the flesh by mortifying sin and walking in the Spirit.**

### — INTERACT —

○ How would you counsel someone who is struggling spiritually but does not feel like taking advantage of the means of grace?

**Reflect:** We know that the Word, prayer, church, and service are all vital to walking in the Spirit. It would be a good and healthy thing to often evaluate our personal lives by asking: "Am I actually taking hold of God's means of grace?"

What stands out most in your mind from your understanding of this session? Is there anything I can be praying about for you until we meet for the next session?

---

If we do not abide in prayer, we will abide in temptation. Let this be one aspect of our daily intercession: "God, preserve my soul, and keep my heart and all its ways so that I will not be entangled." When this is true in our lives, a passing temptation will not overcome us. We will remain free while others lie in bondage.

**—John Owen (1616–83), Puritan theologian**

## *CULTIVATING SPIRITUAL HABITS*

**Read:** Matthew 4:1–11 and John 15:18–25

**Journal:** Write out in your journal the following paragraph and then rethink how we are to combat fleshly temptations.

> "The flesh is a bosom-traitor; it is like the Trojan horse within the walls, which doth all the mischief. The flesh is a sly enemy; . . . it kills by embracing. The embraces of the flesh are like the ivy embracing the oak; which sucks out the strength of it for its own leaves and berries: So the flesh by its soft embraces, sucks out of the heart all good. . . . The flesh chokes and stifles holy motions. . . . The flesh inclines us more to believe a temptation than a promise."
>
> Thomas Watson, *The Christian Soldier*[8]

### Memorize

*I say then: Walk in the Spirit, and you shall not fulfill the lust of the flesh.*

GALATIANS 5:16

# Temptations of the Devil and the World

## Overcoming Temptation (Part 2)

**Purpose of Session Five:** There are three enemies of our soul that use temptation to try to draw us away from God—the flesh, the devil, and the world. The last session focused on temptations of the flesh. This session focuses on temptations that come from the devil and the world. You will learn how to identify the schemes of the devil and be prepared to face temptations when they seek to pull you away from God's will for your life.

## LISTEN: Christ Was Tempted

It is not wrong to be tempted—even Jesus the Son of God was tempted by the devil. Temptation only becomes sin when you give in to the temptation. The sixteenth-century reformer Martin Luther gave some practical advice about temptations: "You can't stop the birds from flying over your head. But only let them fly. Don't let them nest in your hair."[1]

When we talk about temptation we should not feel awkward or embarrassed to admit that we are tempted because Christ himself was tempted in all categories of temptation. Hebrews 4:15 clearly states, "For we do not have a High Priest who cannot sympathize with our weaknesses, but [Christ] was in *all* points *tempted* as we are, *yet without sin.*"

Notice that Christ was tempted but did not fall to the temptations. He can authentically sympathize with you and me because he actually endured the full weight of these temptations.

―――― ABSORB ――――

Christ himself was tempted, yet without sin. Temptation
becomes sin only when we give in to it.

―――― INTERACT ――――

○ What do you think Luther meant by his statement: "You can't stop
the birds from flying over your head. But only let them fly. Don't
let them nest in your hair"?

○ Think for a moment about the kinds of temptations that we face
and identify two or three that you have faced in the last month.
Remember, it is not wrong to be tempted.

Temptation to . . .

lose your temper

be bitter toward another person

talk negatively about someone

exaggerate or shade the truth

have malice (hateful thoughts)

be impatient, not wait for God's
   timing

take revenge into your own
   hands

lust in your mind

be slothful

overeat (gluttony)

stir up strife

use corrupt language

take what doesn't belong to you

be envious/jealous or proud

revile (cut someone down with
   words)

be drawn into an immoral
   relationship

be selfish and unloving

put money, things, or people
   before God

use the Lord's name in vain

abuse substances

reject clear teaching from God's
   Word

self-pity

not say "I am sorry"

## LISTEN: The Nature of Temptation

"To tempt" means to attempt to entice or allure someone to do something
sinful.[2] It is important to note that God never tempts us to do wrong. James

1:13 says, "Let no one say when he is tempted, 'I am tempted by God'; for God cannot be tempted by evil, nor does He Himself tempt anyone."

God does not *tempt*, but he does *test* us. God brings testings (trials) into the lives of his children. God tested Abraham; Genesis 22:1 says, "Now it came to pass after these things that God *tested* Abraham." God put Abraham under a severe test (trial): would Abraham be willing to sacrifice his son for God? A test (trial) can be painful. Usually our plans are jolted, and we feel that our "cage is being rattled." But tests are designed by God to in some way move us closer to him. God's motives are for our good. We understand this as parents. For example, our daughter Emily was exceptionally good at putting puzzles together when she was a toddler. By the time she was two years old, she was no longer challenged by just a single puzzle. So one day my wife mixed together four different puzzles for Emily to put together. Why did my wife do this? To cause Emily to be frustrated or discouraged? No. It was to help her stretch and grow intellectually. The same is true with God. Sometimes he tests us—he mixes up the puzzles of our lives to help us grow spiritually.

Temptations come from three sources—the flesh, the devil, and the world. And all three often work in concert with each other. Sometimes a testing from God and a temptation from the devil will overlap. The devil will often use one of God's testings as an opportunity to tempt us to distrust God and become bitter against him. And sometimes God will allow the devil to tempt us, but he will use that as an occasion to stretch us and make us stronger.

### ABSORB

**Temptation is a tool of the devil to lure us into sin and destruction.**
**Testing (or trial) is a tool of God to lead us into spiritual maturity.**

### INTERACT

○ Why do you think that God would never tempt or entice you to do evil?

○ In the Old Testament book of Job, the devil destroys Job's family and health with the motive of tempting Job to curse God. When God permitted the devil to bring great suffering upon Job, God was at the same time introducing a severe trial (testing) into Job's life. What was God's motive for "testing" Job?

Satan will seldom come to a Christian with a gross temptation. A green log and a candle may be safely left together, but a few shavings, some small sticks and then larger, and you may bring the green log to ashes.

**—John Newton, author of "Amazing Grace"**

## LISTEN: Jesus and His Enemy—The Devil

Jesus, the Son of God, faced very real temptations from the devil. You and I can learn a great deal about how to overcome temptation by observing how Jesus faced temptation. First, we will take a closer look at his (and our) enemy, then we will look at three specific temptations used by the devil.

Here is the first act in the drama between Jesus and the devil:

> Then Jesus was led up by the Spirit* into the wilderness to be tempted by the devil. And when He had fasted forty days and forty nights, afterward He was hungry. Now when the tempter came to Him, he said, "If You are the Son of God, command that these stones become bread."
> But He answered and said, "It is written, 'Man shall not live by bread alone, but by every word that proceeds from the mouth of God.'" (Matt. 4:1–4)

According to the Bible, the devil is one of the magnificent, intelligent, powerful, angelic creatures that God created before the world began. This exalted spirit being (Heb. 1:7 says that angels are "spirits"—spirit beings) became filled with pride and led a rebellion against almighty God, taking along with him a portion of the other angels in heaven. The title "devil" (the Greek word is *diabolos* from which we get our English word "diabolical") means "slanderer"; the devil slanders and distorts the truth about God. He is also called "Satan," which means "adversary"—he is the opponent, the one who opposes the cause of God and the people of God. In John 8:44 Jesus describes how from long ago the devil is the father of lies: "You [those who were defaming Christ] are of your father the devil. . . . When he speaks a lie, he speaks from his own resources, for he is a liar and the father of it." Jesus reveals that hell itself was originally created for the devil and his angels who rebelled with him: "Then He will also say to those on the left hand, 'Depart from Me, you cursed, into the everlasting fire prepared for the devil and his angels'" (Matt. 25:41). The devil is the author of sin. You could correctly say that God is the author of the divine plan that included the creation of the devil who became the author of sin.[3] The Westminster Confession states that the Scriptures teach that God is the primary cause of all things, but it explains that God is not the author of sin, and sin and evil are not morally chargeable to him: "God from all eternity did, by the most wise and holy counsel of His own will, freely and unchangeably ordain whatsoever comes to pass; yet so, as thereby *neither is God the author of sin*, nor is violence offered to the will of the creatures."[4]

---

* Notice that the Spirit of God actually led Jesus into the desert to be tempted by the devil. Again, God does not tempt with evil, but he will use and allow the devil to tempt his children. The devil's aim is to destroy; God's aim is to make us stronger and realize that we must depend on God for victory over temptation.

God in his divine plan has given the devil the freedom to influence the world during this time of human history. God will put an end to the devil's influence at the final judgment at the end of the age (Rev. 20:10). C. S. Lewis wrote in his classic work *The Screwtape Letters*, "There are two equal and opposite errors into which our race can fall about the devils [the Bible also calls these unclean spirits, or demons]. One is to disbelieve in their existence. The other is to believe, and to feel an excessive and unhealthy interest in them."[5]

The reality is that Jesus, the Son of God, faced a real enemy, and we too are tempted by the same enemy. The devil is not omnipresent (having the ability to be everywhere at once), but his "angels" (called "demons" and "unclean spirits") are committed to helping the devil tempt humans.

In Matthew 4 the devil is called "the tempter" because his fundamental weapon is temptation. Sin gains its power through promising a false future. The tempter is always promising, "The future with God is restricted and limited and will in no way give you the pleasant and satisfying future that I offer." The power of sin is in the power of this lie. Satan's main strategy is to present us with a thousand deceptive allurements to make this lie look appealing and look like the better choice. And he does so in subtle ways.

Satan gives Adam an apple [a fruit], and takes away Paradise. Therefore in all temptations let us consider not what he offers, but what we shall lose.

**—Richard Sibbes (1577–1635), English Puritan theologian**

---

### ABSORB

**Jesus faced a real enemy (the devil); this helps us understand that we too face a real enemy in the spiritual conflicts of life.**

---

### INTERACT

○ What do some people normally envision when they think of "the devil"?

○ Have you ever bought something when everything looked great on the surface, only to later discover that you had been deceived and you wished you had never paid the price? In what way does the devil do something similar to us when he tempts us?

## LISTEN: Turning Stones into Bread

The first temptation recorded in Matthew 4 is the devil tempting Jesus with food: Satan tries to get Jesus to turn stones into bread. Jesus always perfectly followed the will of his Father; Jesus was committed to following only his Father's will and directions. In this situation, Jesus had a legitimate need: he was extremely hungry! An illegitimate way to meet his need would be to use his powers to turn stones into bread. Jesus only used his powers when led by the Father; this was not one of those times. Jesus said: "I can of Myself do nothing. . . . I do not seek My own will but the will of the Father who sent Me" (John 5:30). It was not the Father's will for Jesus to turn the stones into bread. Satan was trying to get Jesus to meet a legitimate need in an illegitimate way.

Jesus responded to the devil's temptation by quoting Scripture; he says, "It is written, 'Man shall not live by bread alone, but by every word that proceeds from the mouth of God'" (Matt. 4:4). Jesus is saying that there is something more than physical food that sustains us. Food sustains us by providing temporary relief from hunger. The Word of God nurtures us in a way that benefits us eternally.

### — ABSORB —

**Christ overcame the temptation to meet a legitimate need in an illegitimate way.**

### — INTERACT —

○ Can you give another example in everyday life of a temptation to meet a legitimate need in an illegitimate way?

## LISTEN: Jumping Off the Temple Roof

The second temptation that the devil offers is very subtle and deceptive.

> Then the devil took Him up into the holy city, set Him on the pinnacle of the temple, and said to Him, "If You are the Son of God, throw Yourself down. For it is written: 'He shall give His angels charge over you,' and, 'In their hands they shall bear you up, / Lest you dash your foot against a stone.'"
>
> Jesus said to him, "It is written again, 'You shall not tempt [put to the test] the Lord your God.'" (Matt. 4:5–7)

It is important to remember that the devil quotes Scripture to Jesus; the devil is quoting Psalm 91:11–12. The apostle Paul writes concerning the devil that he is the master of counterfeiting and distorting truth: "For such are false apostles, deceitful workers, transforming themselves into apostles of Christ. And no wonder! For Satan himself transforms himself into an angel of light. Therefore it is no great thing if his ministers also transform themselves into ministers of righteousness, whose end will be according to their works" (2 Cor. 11:13–15). Notice carefully that in Matthew 4:6 the devil is using the Scriptures but is taking this promise out of context. He actually uses the Bible to try to entice Jesus to "put God to the test." If Jesus were to jump off the pinnacle of the temple, he would be *challenging* God's faithfulness instead of *trusting* God's faithfulness. This is a subtle temptation, and Jesus understood the real intention of Psalm 91, which is that God will send his angels to protect those who make him their refuge in the normal course of life, not in some bizarre challenge to test the limits of his protecting faithfulness. This is a good lesson for us—to see that the Bible can easily be distorted from its original intent. That is why the apostle Paul warns us concerning rightly understanding and interpreting the Word of God: "Be diligent to present yourself approved to God, a worker who does not need to be ashamed, rightly dividing the word of truth" (2 Tim. 2:15).

John Piper in his book *Future Grace* gives an excellent analysis of what lies at the core of temptation and how temptation is countered by believing the superior promises of the Word of God.

> Sin is what you do when your heart is not satisfied with God. No one sins out of duty. We sin because it holds out some promise of happiness. That promise enslaves us until we believe that God is more to be desired than life itself (Ps. 63:3). Which means that the power of sin's promise [temptation] is broken by the power of God's. All that God promises to be for us in Jesus stands over against what sin promises to be for us without Him. . . . Satan's only hope of success is to hide the truth and beauty of Christ from the mind of man. It is the glory of Christ that compels the heart to embrace Him in the promises of future grace. . . . Our chief enemy is the lie that says sin will make our future happier. Our chief weapon is the Truth that says God will make our future happier.[6]

## — ABSORB —

**Christ overcame the temptation to put God to the test. Our chief weapon against temptation is the truth of God's Word that promises us a better future if we listen to him.**

## INTERACT

○ Why is it important and beneficial to know and understand God's Word *before* you face temptations?

## LISTEN: Worshiping the Devil

Jesus's third temptation is recorded in Matthew 4:8–10:

> Again, the devil took Him up on an exceedingly high mountain, and showed Him all the kingdoms of the world and their glory. And he said to Him, "All these things I will give You if You will fall down and worship me."
> Then Jesus said to him, "Away with you, Satan! For it is written, 'You shall worship the LORD your God, and Him only you shall serve.'"

The devil was trying to get Jesus to sell out for the temporary instead of waiting for the eternal. Satan wanted Jesus to choose the crown without the cross. He was trying to get Jesus to exchange the future eternal glory designed by the Father for the temporary glory now. The devil wanted Jesus to doubt the Father's goodness! He was tempting Jesus to try to satisfy his heart with something other than God himself. He wanted Jesus to transgress the first of the Ten Commandments, which states that God alone is to be worshiped ("you shall have no other gods before Me" [Exod. 20:3]). Satan is also tempting Jesus to ignore the greatest commandment of all—"And you shall love the LORD your God with all your heart, with all your soul, with all your mind, and with all your strength" (Mark 12:30).

## ABSORB

**Christ overcame the temptation to sell out for temporary glory instead of waiting for the promised glory.**

## INTERACT

○ Can you think of ways where we are tempted to sell out for temporary glory instead of waiting for the promised glory of God?

## LISTEN: The World Tempts Us

Remember that there are three enemies of our soul that try to tempt us away from God—the flesh, the devil, and the world. We will now discuss "the world" as our enemy. The term "world" is used in more than one way in the Bible. First, there is the *physical world* that God created. Second, there is the *world of people*; John 3:16 says: "For God so loved the world that He gave His only begotten Son. . . ." God loved the *world of people* so much that he sent Christ to die for sinners. We are to love people of the world, even our enemies. But there is a third sense in which the term "world" is used, and we are instructed *not* to love the world in this sense: "And do not be conformed to this *world*, but be transformed by the renewing of your mind" (Rom. 12:2). The Scriptures also tell us that "friendship with the *world* is enmity with God" (James 4:4). Because Jesus was a "friend of sinners," this verse obviously does not mean that you cannot befriend people (even sinners). But it does mean you are not to embrace the world's viewpoints and values that are at odds with God. In this sense, the world is an enemy of Christ and his people. Jesus said, "They [his disciples] are not of the world, just as I am not of the world. . . . If you [Christ's disciples] were of the world, the world would love its own. Yet because you are not of the world, but I chose you out of the world, therefore the world hates you" (John 17:16; 15:19).

Here is a working definition of "the world" in the sense that it is our enemy and a source of temptation: the world is that system that has sold out to the values, ideas, and mind-set of the devil and the flesh, that system of living that opposes the will of God. When we adopt philosophies, ideas, advice, values, practices, attitudes, and beliefs that are against the will of God but are accepted by this world, then we are falling to the temptations of the world. The world tempts us (and people of the world tempt us) by holding out choices that claim to be better options than God's will for our lives. The world system (including people who have sold out to the world) does not want to give God the glory that he rightly deserves.

Worldliness is whatever makes sin look normal and righteousness look strange.

**—Kevin DeYoung,** *The Hole in Our Holiness*

— ABSORB —

The *world* is that system that has sold out to the values, ideas, and mind-set of the devil and the flesh. The world is a powerful enemy presenting alluring temptations. Yet as we resist the temptations of the world, we are to love people who are held captive by the world.

## How to Love the World Without Falling for It

"God so loved the world that he gave his Son to save it. Yet the Bible warns us not to love the world. What do we make of these seemingly conflicting messages?

"Most of us respond in one of four ways. We retreat into holy cocoons from the surrounding culture; or we love the world so well that it's hard to tell us apart from it; or we develop a complacency that robs our effectiveness for the Gospel; or we become combative religionists who show little of Christ's love.

"There is a better way: the one Jesus took. In him, holiness met sinners in their own world and surprised them with hope, mercy, and redemption.

"God's methods haven't changed. He wants to do the same thing today—through us."

**Dick Staub**[a]

[a]*Too Christian, Too Pagan* (Grand Rapids: Zondervan, 2000), 1.

### INTERACT

○ Can you describe some attitudes, ideas, values, or advice that the world gives that are at odds with the will of God?

○ When Jesus was praying for his followers, he said, "They are not of the world, just as I am not of the world" (John 17:16). How can we as Christians be *in* the world but not *of* the world? How can we be like Jesus—"a friend of sinners"—but not give in to the temptations of the world that entice us to make the sinful choices?

**Reflect:** Perhaps a good way to reflect on how to apply this session to our own lives is to read the prayer of Peter Marshall (1902–49):

I need Thee, O Lord, for a curb on my tongue; when I am tempted to make carping criticisms and cruel judgments, keep me from speaking barbed words that hurt, and in which I find perverted satisfaction. Keep me from unkind words and from unkind silences. Restrain my judgments. Make my criticisms kind, generous, and constructive. Make me sweet inside, that I may be gentle with other people, gentle in the things I say, kind in what I do. Create in me that warmth of mercy that shall enable others to find Thy strength for their weakness, Thy peace for their strife, Thy joy for their sorrow, Thy love for their hatred, Thy compassion for their weakness. In Thine own strong name, I pray. Amen.[7]

Is there anything I can be praying about for you until we meet for the next session?

## CULTIVATING SPIRITUAL HABITS

**Read:** Philippians 3:9–21; 1 John 1:1–2:3; Romans 8:28–39

**Journal:** Go back through the above list of the kinds of temptations that you personally face most and jot them down and ask God for wisdom in how to resist these temptations. Think and meditate on how Jesus combated temptation.

### Memorize

*No temptation has overtaken you except such as is common to man; but God is faithful, who will not allow you to be tempted beyond what you are able, but with the temptation will also make the way of escape, that you may be able to bear it.*

1 CORINTHIANS 10:13

# Becoming More and More Like Christ

## Sanctification

**Purpose of Session Six:** When you were justified, you were declared righteous by God. Now that you are justified, there is a process of growth and transformation in which you are enabled more and more to grasp the reality that you are dead to your old sinful life and that you actually become more and more like Christ. In this session you will learn what sanctification is and how we are transformed into the likeness of Christ. There are three aspects to our sanctification: definitive sanctification, progressive sanctification, and ultimate sanctification.

## LISTEN: Our Status as Saints—Definitive Sanctification

Like many words in the New Testament, the term "sanctification" carries with it more than one shade of meaning. The phrase "to sanctify" in its basic form means "separation" or "to set apart."[1] The idea is that you are *set apart for God*, meaning you are holy. Therefore when a person is *set apart for God*, he or she is considered holy.

When you were saved, you were at the same time permanently *sanctified* in the sense that you were set apart for God (1 Cor. 6:11). This *definite* "setting apart for God" flows from the cross, where God through Christ purchased and claimed us for himself. [2] (Therefore it is called *definitive sanctification*.) God set you apart for himself, so now you belong to God—*all* Christians in the New Testament are actually called "saints" (which means "holy ones"). This describes the status that has been conferred on you, which is why some theologians refer to this as "positional sanctification" (also sometimes referred to as "relational sanctification"). You have probably noticed that many of the letters in the New Testament begin with an introduction addressing the Christians and referring to them all as "saints." For example, Philippians 1:1 begins with the greeting, "Paul and Timothy, bondservants of Jesus Christ, / To all the *saints* in Christ Jesus who are in Philippi." When God saved you, he also set you apart for himself, and in that sense you are already holy. But now that you are one of the "holy ones" (saints), you are to live out that holiness, which means you are to become more and more like Christ.

## — ABSORB —

*Definitive sanctification* is the state of being permanently set apart for God. If you are a believer, then you are a saint (a "holy one").

## — INTERACT —

○ Normally people in our culture use the term "saint" to refer to a "super-spiritual" person. Yet in the New Testament the term "saint" means "holy one," and it refers to every true Christian. How does it make you feel to be called a "saint"?

○ How would seeing yourself as "set apart for God" make a difference in how you view the purpose of your life?

## LISTEN: Dying to Sin—Progressive Sanctification

When pastors and teachers speak about sanctification, they normally are talking about the *progressive* aspect of our sanctification (sometimes called "experiential" or "practical" sanctification). The Westminster Shorter Catechism question 35 asks:

> *What is sanctification?*—Sanctification is the work of God's free grace, whereby we are renewed in the whole man after the image of God, and are *enabled more and more to die unto sin, and live unto righteousness.*[3]

This *progressive* aspect of sanctification describes the ongoing transformation (a process) where we become more and more like Christ. J. I. Packer

Be killing sin or sin will be killing you.

**—John Owen, English theologian**

## Holiness Is the Sum of a Million Little Things

"The avoidance of little evils and little foibles, the setting aside of little bits of worldliness and little acts of compromise, the putting to death of little inconsistencies and little indiscretions, the attention to little duties and little dealings, the hard work of little self-denials and little self-restraints, the cultivation of little benevolences and little forbearances. Are you trustworthy? Are you kind? Are you patient? Are you joyful? Do you love? These qualities, worked out in all the little things of life, determine whether you are blight or blessing to everyone around you, whether you are an ugly spiritual eyesore or growing up into a good-looking Christian."

**Kevin DeYoung[a]**

[a]*The Hole in Our Holiness* (Wheaton: Crossway, 2012), 145.

describes this as God working in us to produce "character change freeing us from sinful habits and forming in us Christ-like affections, dispositions, and virtues."[4] We grow in *holiness*, which means we become more conformed to the likeness of Christ.

There is an interesting verse in Hebrews that tells us that in one sense we have been made holy ("perfected") in God's eyes but in another sense we are still being made holy ("being sanctified") by Christ: "For by one offering He has perfected forever those who are being sanctified" (Heb. 10:14). In this verse we can see both the relational aspect of sanctification and the experiential, present aspect. In other words when we as believers were called into union with Christ, we died to sin when Christ died, and we rose to newness of life when Christ arose. Theologian John Murray describes it like this: "The breach with sin and the newness of life are as definitive as were the death and resurrection of Christ."[5] In a real sense Christ secured our holiness! But as Hebrews 10:14 says, we are presently and experientially living out who and what we are in Christ—we are in the *process* of being sanctified.

Below is a definition of sanctification. Because sanctification is usually thought of in the progressive sense, the following definition will simply leave off the word "progressive."

### ABSORB

**The main definition of *sanctification* is the lifelong process (after we are saved) of growing more and more like Christ.**

## INTERACT

○ Can you think of some areas of life where you are presently being sanctified (for example, becoming more truthful, patient, joyful, kind, disciplined, contented; becoming less judgmental, negative, lustful, prideful, angry)?

○ Does your sanctification sometimes feel slow?

## LISTEN: A Lifelong Transformational Process—Progressive Sanctification (Continued)

When does sanctification begin? Titus 3:5 gives us a hint that it begins when we are born again—at regeneration: "He saved us, through the washing of regeneration and renewing of the Holy Spirit." Something happens to us at the moment we are regenerated. The Holy Spirit gives to us new life and new power so that renewal begins at the same time. There is an initial step in sanctification where the Holy Spirit begins immediately the renewal work of breaking the ruling power of sin that once held us as slaves of sin.

J. I. Packer explains what happens from here:

> Regeneration is birth; sanctification is growth. In regeneration, God implants desires that were not there before: desire for God, for holiness, and for the hallowing and glorifying of God's name in this world; desire to pray, worship, love, serve, honor, and please God; desire to show love and bring benefit to others. In sanctification, the Holy Spirit "works in you to will and to act" according to God's purpose; what he does is prompt you to "work out your salvation" (i.e., express it in action) by fulfilling these new desires (Phil. 2:12–13). Christians become increasingly Christ-like as the moral profile of Jesus (the "fruit of the Spirit") is progressively formed in them (2 Cor. 3:18; 4:19; 5:22–25).[6]

Our sanctification is a lifelong moral renovation and transformation brought about by the indwelling of the Holy Spirit. In a real sense we are *already* new creations in Christ (2 Cor. 5:17), and through the Holy Spirit we are infused with a new power. The Holy Spirit sets in motion the process of continual character change and freedom from sinful habits. At the same time, we are being transformed to become more like Christ in our emotions, dispositions, attitudes, and actions. R. C. Sproul summarizes well how, in our sanctification, God himself gives us the desire and power to live righteously, but we must also actively *work* to do God's will.

## Cooperating with the Holy Spirit

"The New Testament calls upon us to take action; it does not tell us that the work of sanctification is going to be done for us.... We are in the 'good fight of faith,' and we have to do the fighting. But, thank God, we are enabled to do it; for the moment we believe, and are justified by faith, and are born again of the Spirit of God, we have the ability. So the New Testament method of sanctification is to remind us of that; and having reminded us of it, it says, 'Now then, go and do it.'"

**D. Martyn Lloyd-Jones[a]**

[a]*Romans: Exposition of Chapter 6: The New Man* (Edinburgh: Banner of Truth, 1972), 178.

Our sanctification is a cooperative venture. We must work with the Holy Spirit to grow in sanctification. The apostle Paul expressed this idea in his letter to the church at Philippi: "Therefore, my beloved, as you have always obeyed not as in my presence only, but now much more in my absence, work out your own salvation with fear and trembling; *for it is God who works in you both to will and to do for His good pleasure*" (Philippians 2:12–13). The call to cooperation is one that involves work. We are to work in earnest. To work with fear and trembling does not suggest a spirit of terror but of reverence coupled with effort. We are consoled by the knowledge that we are not left to do this work alone or by our own efforts. God is working within us to accomplish our sanctification.[7]

— ABSORB —

### Sanctification is a lifelong transformational process in which we must work with the Holy Spirit to grow.

— INTERACT —

○ What is wrong with the mind-set of a Christian who says, "Well, I have a problem with my bad temper (or substitute any vice, such as lust, greed, gossip, and so on), and I guess there is nothing I can do about it. If God doesn't change me then people will just have to put up with me the way I am!"?

○ Kevin DeYoung in his book *The Hole in Our Holiness* says that "holiness is plain hard work, and we're often lazy. We like our sins, and dying to them is painful. Almost everything is easier than growing in godliness." Talk about why it is plain hard work and why we feel lazy.

## LISTEN: Being Glorified—Ultimate Sanctification

A third and last sense in which we are sanctified is the final step in our journey and is often called "glorification." Our sanctification will not be complete and perfect until we see Christ (either at death or the return of Christ). Hebrews 12:23 speaks of the believers in heaven who have been made perfect. The apostle Paul, who lived a very holy life, was still in the process of sanctification when he wrote: "Not that I have already attained, or am already perfected; but I press on, that I may lay hold of that for which Christ Jesus has also laid hold of me" (Phil. 3:12). This final sense of sanctification will be realized when we are *glorified*—when we receive new spiritual bodies and will no longer sin. The process of sanctification will have reached its goal; 1 John 3:2 says: "But we know that when He [Jesus] is revealed, *we shall be like Him*, for we shall see Him as He is." This future aspect of sanctification is *glorification*—when these bodies of ours are fully redeemed and we will be able to sin no more. The apostle Paul in Philippians 3:20–21 says: "We also eagerly wait for the Savior, the Lord Jesus Christ, who will transform our lowly body that it may be conformed to His *glorious* body, according to the working by which He is able even to subdue all things to Himself."

— ABSORB —

**In heaven we will experience ultimate sanctification, *glorification*. Then we will be like Jesus, and we will no longer sin.**

— INTERACT —

○ How do you picture what life will be like in heaven, where you will no longer be tempted to sin nor will you be able to sin?

## LISTEN: Learning from Church History

An extremely important part of church history was the Reformation, which officially began in 1517. The Reformation was a sixteenth-century movement to reform the existing church in Western Europe—to reform wrong practices and distorted teachings within the church. One of the central issues was "How is a person justified?" All the Reformers believed that a person is justified by *faith alone*, and then out of justification flows sanctification. The Reformers understood the immensely important distinction between justification and sanctification. Justification is a legal status we are granted before God when he pronounces us righteous. Justification is the act of God, once for all declaring us righteous in his sight. This occurs at the moment when we place our faith in Christ—when we are converted. Sanctification is the lifelong work of the Spirit of God gradually changing us into the image of his Son. It is the continual process in which our moral condition is brought more and more into conformity with our righteous legal status before God. In other words, we are in the *process* of becoming more and more who we already are in Christ.

Prior to and during the Reformation, many of the church leaders confused the gospel by intermingling sanctification with justification. They taught that a person had to actually become holy before he or she could be pronounced righteous. This created a great distortion of the gospel because this meant that if you were ever to be saved, then you would have to reach that perfect goal of righteousness. Church leaders also taught that grace is infused into the soul by participating in the church sacraments to the extent specified by the authorities, and it is only when you achieve that required goal of complete holiness that God could ever pronounce you righteous. In other words, they were teaching that God *infuses* grace into you through church sacraments, such as baptism, the Eucharist, penance (including confession and special works), confirmation, marriage, holy orders, and anointing the sick. When enough grace is infused into a person's life, then that person has the possibility of reaching a level of complete holiness in which God can *then* pronounce him or her justified. The Reformers realized this approach confused sanctification with justification and undermined the teaching of Scripture that God justifies us by faith alone.[8] The Reformers taught that there are particularly clear passages in the Bible that describe how God justifies those who are "ungodly." The apostle Paul defends the truth that God does the unthinkable—he justifies the *ungodly*! God justifies the ungodly based on the crediting of Christ's righteousness to the ungodly person who has faith in Christ: "But to him who does not work but believes on Him *who justifies the ungodly*, *his faith is accounted for righteousness*" (Rom. 4:5).

In other words, while a person is *still ungodly*, God imputes righteousness to that person based on his or her faith in Christ. This same passage reveals that God actually imputes righteousness to the person who has been "lawless" not because of any "works" he has done (or because she reaches a level of actual righteousness) but because of the blessedness of God's forgiveness.

Romans 4:6–8 says, "Just as David also describes the blessedness of the man to whom God imputes righteousness apart from works: 'Blessed are those whose lawless deeds are forgiven, / And whose sins are covered; / Blessed is the man to whom the LORD shall not impute sin.'"

In other words—you are justified by faith alone. Because Christ's righteousness is judicially *imputed* to you, you are counted as righteous in God's sight. Sanctification is the process of our moral condition being brought into conformity with our righteous legal status before God. To reiterate: we are in the *process* of becoming more and more who we already are in Christ—we are *already* justified!

## ABSORB

*Justification* is an act of God, once for all declaring us righteous in his sight the moment we converted. *Sanctification* is then the lifelong work of the Spirit of God gradually changing us into the image of his Son. If you confuse *sanctification* with *justification*, you confuse the gospel.

## INTERACT

○ If one confuses sanctification with justification, what happens to the message of the gospel?

## LISTEN: What Happens When We Sin?

It is important to know that we do not lose our justification status of being declared righteous in God's sight when we sin. Notice what the apostle John wrote: "My little children, these things I write to you, so that you may not sin. And if anyone sins, we have an Advocate with the Father, Jesus Christ the righteous. And He Himself is the propitiation for our sins" (1 John 2:1–2).

This verse gives us clear insight into what happens when believers sin. It is important to acknowledge that believers do sin. But the Word is saying, on the one hand, don't sin! Sin is a great dishonor to God, and your Christian life is damaged. Don't think because you are justified that it really doesn't matter whether or not you sin. This warning guards us from attempting to presume on the grace of God. But on the other hand, we also don't have to despair because our Advocate (the opposite of a prosecuting attorney) is the Son of the Judge of the Universe.[9] And the Son of God makes his case for us *not* on the basis of *our perfection* but on the basis of *his sacrifice*, which removed the wrath of God from us. At the cross, God's wrath was removed from us. Remember the definition of propitiation? Propitiation is *the removal of God's wrath by providing a substitute offering.* Christ has already given his life as the propitiation for our sins. The wrath of God has been removed from those who are justified.

It is important to realize that when we sin as those who are already justified, our legal standing before God is not dissolved. Nowhere in the New Testament do we find someone having to be "re-justified" after they sin. We are still forgiven because Christ himself is the propitiation for our sins—his sacrifice *forever* satisfies the justice of God. So when we sin as Christians, our status (or standing) with God is not affected, but sin does affect our *fellowship* with God. The Westminster Confession of Faith explains what the Bible teaches concerning what happens when Christians sin and what our attitude toward sin should be: "Although they never can fall from the state of justification, yet they may, by their sins, fall under their God's fatherly displeasure, and not have the light of His countenance restored unto them, until they humble themselves, confess their sins, beg pardon, and renew their faith and repentance."[10]

Thomas Watson, seventeenth-century pastor and theologian, elaborates on what happens when we as God's children fall to temptation: "Though a child of God, after pardon, may incur His fatherly displeasure, yet His judicial wrath is removed. . . . Corrections may befall the saints, but not destruction."[11]

In other words, even though we who are justified may incur God's fatherly displeasure, we will never incur his judicial wrath where we are condemned or punished in hell. God will treat us as a father would and will discipline and correct us for our own good (Heb. 12:7–10).

When we sin, our union with Christ is not in jeopardy. But our communion is.

**—Kevin DeYoung,**
*The Hole in Our Holiness*

---

## ABSORB

**When we sin as Christians, we do not lose our justification status of being declared righteous in God's sight. But sin does break our fellowship with God, and our Father will discipline and correct us in order to restore that fellowship.**

## INTERACT

○ How does it make you feel to know that sin breaks your fellowship with God? Have you ever felt the disciplining hand of God on your life?

## LISTEN: How to Restore Our Fellowship with God

John R. W. Stott in his work *Basic Christianity* sets forth an excellent analogy of what occurs when we as God's own children sin against our Father:

> Suppose a boy is offensively rude to his parents. A cloud descends on the home. There is tension in the atmosphere. Father and son are not on speaking terms. What has happened? Has the boy ceased to be a son? No. Their relationship has not changed; it is their fellowship which has been broken. Relationship depends on birth; fellowship depends on behavior. As soon as the boy apologizes, he is forgiven. And forgiveness restores fellowship. Meanwhile, his relationship has stayed the same. He may have been temporarily a disobedient, and even a defiant son; but he has not ceased to be a son. So it is with the children of God. When we sin, we do not forfeit our relationship to Him as children, though our fellowship with Him is spoiled until we confess and forsake our sin. As soon as we "confess our sin, he is faithful and just to forgive us our sin and cleanse us from all unrighteousness" (1 John 1:9).[12]

Therefore when we sin, in order to restore our fellowship with God we need to confess and forsake our sin. The two verses below highlight this process:

> He who covers his sins will not prosper, / But whoever confesses and forsakes them will have mercy. (Prov. 28:13)

> If we confess our sins, He is faithful and just to forgive us our sins and to cleanse us from all unrighteousness. (1 John 1:9)

## ABSORB

**When we sin we are to confess and forsake our sin in order to have our fellowship restored with our Father.**

---

### INTERACT

---

○ If you had a child who disobeyed or disrespected you, what would you want his or her attitude to be in order to have the fellowship or closeness restored?

**Reflect:** We are actually called "saints" by God! But sometimes we do not feel holy because we do sin. One of the ways that we can put into practice what we learn from God's Word is to face up to the reality that when we sin, we should not suppress it or ignore it. If we are being judgmental, negative, lustful, prideful, angry, or if we lack patience, kindness, joy, or contentedness, then we must face up to it and confess and forsake the sin.

Do you feel that you have a clear understanding of the difference between justification and sanctification? Is there anything I can be praying about for you until we meet for the next session?

## CULTIVATING SPIRITUAL HABITS

**Read:** Psalm 119

**Journal:** Go back to sessions one and two and write down the definition of justification. Then write down the definition of sanctification. Meditate on the difference between justification and sanctification.

### Memorize

> *He who covers his sins will not prosper,*
> *But whoever confesses and forsakes them will have mercy.*
>
> P R O V E R B S   2 8 : 1 3

# The Power and Value of the Word

## The Importance of Scripture

**Purpose of Session Seven:** The power and value of the Word of God cannot be overestimated. This session is designed to highlight why the Scriptures are so valuable and to encourage you to make the Word a part of your daily life so that you will be constantly strengthened in the faith. This session presents five reasons why the Word of God is so important and powerful for our lives.

## LISTEN: Our Great Need for an Unchanging Reference Point

Admiral Richard Byrd was famous for his explorations at the South Pole. During an expedition in 1934 in Antarctica, he spent a polar winter all by himself and almost died in temperatures forty to sixty degrees below zero, but survived to write a book about the ordeal titled *Alone*. A short time after he settled in for the winter, some high winds and snowdrifts buried any traces of his hut (what he called his shack) under the snow. He recorded in his book: "North and south of the shack I marked a path about one hundred yards long, which I called the hurricane deck. Every three paces a two-foot bamboo stick was driven into the crust, and along these poles I ultimately strung a life line. By running my hand over this, blind-man fashion, I could feel my way back and forth in the worst weather."[1]

He would take walks beyond the hurricane deck during the dark polar days, and about every thirty yards he would place a bamboo stake in the snow to find his way back to the hurricane deck. One day his mind wandered, and he lost track of how long he had walked; he looked back and couldn't see the last bamboo stake he had stuck in the snow. He was shocked when it dawned on him—any step in the wrong direction could take him farther away from his hut, and he could very easily wander in a wilderness of nothing but frozen snow and never find his way back. It would be just a matter of time before he would freeze to death. The snow was so frozen that he left no footprints or tracks. He wrote: "It was scary. The first impulse was to run. I quelled that, and soberly took stock of my predicament. . . . I was lost, and I was sick inside."[2]

Instead of panicking he broke off some ridges of snow formed by wind on the snowfield and piled them up like a small tower, a "beacon of snow." So this beacon (or tower) of snow became his reference point, and standing behind his reference point, he lined up with the stars in a certain direction. Then he walked a hundred paces in that one direction. He shined his flashlight, looking for a bamboo stake. He didn't see anything. He turned around and walked straight back one hundred paces and found his reference point—the beacon of snow. Now lining up again with the same stars he swung his course thirty degrees to the left and set out again. He kept repeating the process until, finally, he started from the beacon again and walked one hundred paces and then piled up a small mound of snow and walked an additional thirty paces, shined the light, and was overjoyed—he saw a bamboo stick and was able to find his way back home. He writes: "No shipwrecked mariner, sighting a distant sail, could have been more overjoyed."[3]

The snow beacon had become his *reference point*—it was something that was a constant, something sure and certain on which he could count and could come back to again and again to find guidance and direction, something that eventually helped him discover his way home.

In this world, God knew that you and I would need a beacon because without a beacon—a constant, an unchanging reference point—we humans would wander into a blizzard of ideas not knowing how to get back home. So God gave us an *unchanging reference point*—the Scriptures, the Word of God. The Word of God is far more important and critical for finding direction and finding stabilization for our lives than we could ever imagine. When you lose sight of this unchanging reference point, you are in a frozen wilderness of solitude, random chaos, and subjective choices.

--- ABSORB ---

**In a world of competing and confusing ideas about the meaning of life and God, the only unchanging reference point to come back to for truth is the Word of God!**

--- INTERACT ---

○ Why would it be vitally important to have an unchanging reference point to come back to for ultimate answers, such as answers to the questions, why are we here and what is the meaning and purpose of life?

○ Most of us know people who reject the Bible as an unchanging reference point. What are some of the ways they decide what is the meaning and purpose of life?

## LISTEN: Jesus Values the Old Testament

John 10 describes Jesus speaking of his identity as being equal with God. Some of the religious people therefore accused him of blasphemy because he said he was the Son of God. Jesus then appealed to the Old Testament Scriptures for his authority. He said something very profound: "And the Scripture cannot be broken" (John 10:35). In other words, according to Christ, there is nothing strong enough to break the authority and power of Scripture—it is the final authority to which anyone can appeal. "Scripture cannot be emptied of its force by being shown to be erroneous."[4] Jesus had the highest respect for the authority of Scripture. According to Jesus, nothing can ever override its authority.

One of the significant things you will discover about Christ is that he had complete, absolute confidence that the Scriptures came from God. In the Sermon on the Mount Jesus gives one of the strongest statements anywhere concerning the reliability of the Bible: "Do not think that I came to destroy the Law or the Prophets. I did not come to destroy but to fulfill. For assuredly, I say to you, till heaven and earth pass away, one jot or one tittle will by no means pass from the law till all is fulfilled" (Matt. 5:17–18).[5]

A *jot* was the smallest letter in the Hebrew alphabet, and a *tittle* was a small pen stroke, something similar to the dotting of an *i* or a crossing of a *t*.[6]

**Jot** = smallest letter in the Hebrew alphabet, not much bigger than a comma.

**Tittle** = a small stroke of the pen—a very small projection, a little hook that distinguishes one Hebrew letter from another.

Resh = R   Dalet = D

Jesus was saying that the reliability of the Old Testament Scriptures, even down to every jot and tittle (down to its most minute particulars) is so sure and so certain that it will absolutely come to pass! Jesus had total confidence in the Scriptures and that everything in the Word would be fulfilled—everything would be carried out because he saw God as the source of the Scriptures! Jesus had complete confidence that the Old Testament was the unfailing Word of God.[7]

In Mark 12:36 Jesus quotes David's words from Psalm 110:1 and points out that David spoke "by the Holy Spirit." This reveals that Jesus saw David as a person who was inspired by the Holy Spirit when he wrote the psalm. This indicates that Jesus saw the writers of the Old Testament as inspired.

Jesus also classifies Old Testament laws (such as "Honor your father and your mother," and "He who curses father or mother, let him be put to death") as "the commandment of God" and "the Word of God." Jesus candidly told the Pharisees and Scribes: "All too well you reject the *commandment of God*, that you may keep your tradition . . . making the *Word of God* of no effect through your tradition which you have handed down" (Mark 7:9–13).

> If you wish to know God, you must know His Word. If you wish to perceive His power, you must see how He works by His Word. If you wish to know His purpose before it comes to pass, you can only discover it by His Word.
> —**Charles H. Spurgeon, English preacher**

## ABSORB

**The first reason the Word is important and powerful for our lives is because Jesus, the Son of God, had the highest respect for the Scriptures and saw them as totally reliable and authoritative.**

## INTERACT

○ Why do you think Jesus had such great confidence in the reliability of the Scriptures?

○ If Jesus accepted the Old Testament as fully reliable and trustworthy, then why should that give you confidence in the Bible?

○ Jesus was convinced that everything in the Word would absolutely come to pass. How could this motivate us to read and study more of the Old Testament?

## LISTEN: Jesus Preapproved the New Testament

Not only did Jesus affirm the complete authority of the Old Testament but he also preapproved the New Testament (which were not put in writing until after Jesus died). Because Jesus is the Son of God, he had no hesitation placing his own words on the same level with that of the Old Testament Scriptures. Jesus saw his own words as eternal and unfailing: "Heaven and earth will pass away, but *My words* will by no means pass away" (Mark 13:31).

Jesus also preapproved the authority of the writings of the apostles when he said the Holy Spirit would come and would guide the apostles to remember the truth Jesus had spoken and tell them of the "things to come."

> But the Helper, the Holy Spirit, whom the Father will send in My name, He will teach you all things, and bring to your remembrance all things that I said to you. (John 14:26)

> However, when He, the Spirit of truth, has come, He will guide you into all truth; for He will not speak on His own authority, but whatever He hears He will speak; and He will tell you things to come. (John 16:13)

Jesus also affirmed the future authority of the apostles' words:

> "A servant is not greater than his master. . . . If they kept My word, *they will keep yours also*." (John 15:20)

The primary test used by the early church to recognize which letters, Gospels, and books were to be considered part of the inspired New Testament (part of the "canon" of Scripture) was, "Does it have apostolic authority, approval, or sanction?"[8]

---

### ABSORB

**The second reason the Word is important and powerful for our lives is because Jesus's words are eternal and unfailing and he preapproved the writings of the New Testament.**

---

### INTERACT

○ What do you think Jesus meant when he said that his words would not pass away?

○ Think about all the things Jesus said and the stories he told in the Gospels—about forgiveness, love of enemies, prodigal sons,

Every word of God is pure; / He is a shield to those who put their trust in Him.

**—Proverbs 30:5**

repentance, belief, and heaven and hell. Knowing that his words are eternal and unfailing, how does that make you want to listen more carefully?

## LISTEN: The Scriptures Are "God-Breathed"

"All Scripture is given by inspiration of God," states 2 Timothy 3:16. The phrase "inspired by God" in the Greek New Testament is *theopneustos*, which literally means "God-breathed."[9] The biblical word "inspired" is unique and is not to be confused with the common way the word "inspired" is used. For example, an artist might say, "I was *inspired* to paint this picture," or a writer will claim that she was *inspired* to write a book. And it is true that gifted people are emotionally or intellectually moved to create great masterpieces. But the idea of inspiration in 2 Timothy 3:16 is that the Bible finds its source in the very breath of God—it is the product of God. The ideas in the Bible are not mere human ideas but God's will and the expression of his character: "holy men of God spoke as they were moved by the Holy Spirit" (2 Pet. 1:21). This means that God *used humans* to write the Bible, yet they were moved or guided by the Holy Spirit when they wrote it. This does not mean that God dictated his words to them or that God used people like a keyboard. But the Holy Spirit superintended the production of Scripture. He used their human personalities and styles of writing but so guided them that what they wrote is what he wanted written!

### ABSORB

**The third reason the Word is important and powerful for our lives is because all Scripture is inspired by God.**

### INTERACT

○ Picture in your mind God himself handing you a book and saying, "You can trust this book because it finds its very source in me; it is the Word of God. I'm giving this as a gift to you, and the more you read it and think about it and meditate on it, the more you will know what I am really like." If that happened, what would be your response? What would you do with that book?

## LISTEN: Faith Comes through the Word

The Word says that the depth of the wisdom and knowledge of God is so great that his ways are beyond searching out (Rom. 11:33). Yet in his vast wisdom, God tells us that he awakens and strengthens faith in us through the Word of God: "So then faith comes by hearing, and hearing by the word of God" (Rom. 10:17).

Through the centuries Christians have experienced a growing and strengthening of their faith as they have read or listened to the Word of God. This is the work of God's Spirit who empowers our hearts and minds to see the value of God and his Word. The Word will awaken and strengthen your faith.

### — ABSORB —

**The fourth reason the Word is important and powerful for our lives is because God instills faith in us through the Word.**

### INTERACT

○ What has been your own experience with reading and meditating on Scripture? Have you sensed God strengthening your faith?

---

### Studying the Bible for More than Half a Century

"The vigor of our spiritual life will be in exact proportion to the place held by the Bible in our life and thoughts. I solemnly state this from the experience of fifty-four years. . . . I have read the Bible through one hundred times, and always with increasing delight. Each time it seems like a new book to me. Great has been the blessing from consecutive, diligent, daily study. I look upon it as a lost day when I have not had a good time over the Word of God."

**George Mueller**[a]

[a]Quoted in Henry H. Halley, *Halley's Bible Handbook* (Grand Rapids: Zondervan, 1965), 2.

---

## LISTEN: The Word Is Filled with Promises

I prayed for faith, and thought that someday faith would come down and strike me like lightning. But faith did not seem to come. One day I read the tenth chapter of Romans, "Now faith cometh by hearing, and hearing by the Word of God." I had closed my Bible, and prayed for faith. I now opened my Bible, and began to study, and faith has been growing ever since.

**—Dwight L. Moody (1837–99), evangelist**

The famous and brilliant seventeenth-century French mathematician and philosopher Blaise Pascal astutely observed: "All men seek happiness. This is without exception. Whatever different means they employ, they all tend to this end. The cause of some going to war, and of others avoiding it, is the same desire in both, attended with different views. The will [that which chooses inside of us] never takes the least step but to this object. This is the motive of every action of every man, even of those who hang themselves."[10]

Most people would agree with Pascal that we make decisions based on what we think will give us the greatest happiness in life. The reality is that sin promises to give us happiness. The power of sin is the deceitful promise that we will get more happiness out of life if we choose sin. But the Word of God is filled with promises *from God himself* that there is more joy, more real and enduring happiness by following his will for our lives than by any other choices that we could ever make. As we believe God, that his promises are real and true, then the promises of sin lose their attracting power. The Word of God gives us great hope and leads us to true freedom. Listed below are just a few of the great promises of God.

In Your presence is fullness of joy; / At Your right hand are pleasures forevermore. (Ps. 16:11)

Eye has not seen, nor ear heard, / Nor have entered into the heart of man / The things which God has prepared for those who love Him. (1 Cor. 2:9)

And everyone who has left houses or brothers or sisters or father or mother or wife or children or lands, for My name's sake, shall receive a hundredfold, and inherit eternal life. (Matt. 19:29)

For I consider that the sufferings of this present time are not worthy to be compared with the glory which shall be revealed in us. (Rom. 8:18)

### ABSORB

**The fifth reason the Word is important and powerful for our lives is because the promises of the Word of God give us hope and joy.**

### INTERACT

○ Which one of the above promises captures your attention the most and why?

## LISTEN: Disciplines to Stimulate Your Spiritual Growth

Listed below are two spiritual disciplines that will consistently get you into the Word and get the Word into you.

### PLAN TO READ GOD'S WORD EACH DAY

Many Christians through the centuries have found it very beneficial to plan when and where they are going to read. Many noted Christian leaders chose to read first thing in the morning as a way to start each day. Once you pick a time and place, read slowly and seek to comprehend what you read. You may want to ask God two questions as you read: "God, what do you want me to learn about you?" And, "What do you want me to do as a result of what I have read?" If you are relatively new to Bible reading, the following are excellent places to begin:

- Gospel of Mark (found in the New Testament)
- Philippians (New Testament)
- Proverbs (Old Testament)
- Gospel of John (New Testament)
- Genesis (Old Testament)
- Gospel of Matthew (New Testament)
- James (New Testament)
- Romans (New Testament)

### MEMORIZE SCRIPTURE

Many Christians have greatly benefited from memorizing the Word. It is obvious from the Gospels that Christ, the Son of God, memorized much of the Scriptures. Pastor and author John Piper writes this concerning the value of memorizing the Word:

> I spend this much time on Bible memory because I believe in the power of the indwelling Word of God to solve a thousand problems before they happen, and to heal a thousand wounds after they happen, and to kill a thousand sins in the moment of temptation, and to sweeten a thousand days with the "drippings of the honeycomb" [Ps. 119:103]. I am jealous for you, my readers, that you would "let the word of Christ dwell in you richly" (Col. 3:16). This is the path to solid joy and all the service of love that it sustains. Christ will be seen as the fortune He is when we treasure His Word more than money, and when the joy it wakens overflows with sacrificial love (2 Cor. 8:2).[11]

The Bible was written not to satisfy your curiosity but to help you conform to Christ's image. Not to make you a smarter sinner but to make you like the Savior. Not to fill your head with a collection of biblical facts but to transform your life.

**—Howard Hendricks,** *Living by the Book*

Don't worry about what you do not understand. . . . Worry about what you do understand in the Bible but do not live by.

**—Corrie ten Boom, Holocaust survivor and author**

## ABSORB

### Reading and memorizing the Word are invaluable.

## INTERACT

○ Life in the twenty-first century is characterized by many time demands and much stress. Often when we do have free time we just want to relax and watch television or engage in some other form of entertainment. Over a period of time, external influences can erode our faith and create doubts. The primary means that God uses to fortify our faith is the Word of God. What can we do to make sure we carve out time for the Word?

**Reflect:** Ask yourself—"Am I reading the Word each day and am I memorizing the Word?" It is one thing to know it is a good idea to do so; it is another thing to do so.

Recall the story at the beginning of the session about Admiral Byrd's strategy to find his way home. Why is it so important to have an unchanging reference point for truth? How can I best pray for you? Where do you feel the most pressure in your life right now?

## CULTIVATING SPIRITUAL HABITS

**Read:** Isaiah 52:13–53:12

**Journal:** Go back and reread the section, "Listen: Disciplines to Stimulate Your Spiritual Growth." Evaluate your schedule to see how you can adjust it to make time to read the Word each day.

### Memorize

*All Scripture is given by inspiration of God, and is profitable for doctrine, for reproof, for correction, for instruction in righteousness.*

2 TIMOTHY 3:16

# LEVEL TWO

# Yesterday's Prophecies and Manuscript Evidence

## Evidence for the Inspiration of the Bible (Part 1)

**Purpose of Session Eight:** This session focuses on the trustworthiness of the Scriptures as the very Word of God. A question Christians often face is, "How do you know the Bible is the inspired Word of God and not just another book produced by humans?" This session will furnish you with reasoned answers and will help you share your faith in a culture of skepticism. Over two sessions we will cover four reasons to believe the Scriptures have a divine source.

## LISTEN: Loving God with Your Mind

When Jesus, the Son of God, was asked which was the most important commandment in Scripture, he was quick to respond: "You shall love the LORD your God with all your heart, with all your soul, with all your mind, and with all your strength" (Mark 12:30). In other words, we are to love God with the totality of our being. And notice, this includes our *minds*! God gave us minds to reason and use in order to love and glorify him. God created the mind! God does not ask us to dismiss clear thinking and logic in our relationship with him. We are actually *required* to love God "with our minds." Christian apologist Josh McDowell has often reiterated this and has said, "The heart cannot embrace what the mind rejects as false."[1] Faith does not abandon our reasoning processes in order to make a decision about whether or not something is true concerning God or the Christian faith.

## ABSORB

**Faith does not abandon our reasoning processes in order to make a decision about whether something is true concerning God or the Christian faith.**

## INTERACT

○ McDowell's statement, "The heart cannot embrace what the mind rejects as false," implies that we cannot fully accept with our heart, soul, and strength something we can't accept with our mind. Do you agree with his statement? Why?

## LISTEN: God Gives Us Reasons to Believe

Faith is not an invalidation of logic; it is a confirmation of it and a holding on to those compelling reasons to believe. C. S. Lewis comments about faith: "Now Faith . . . is the art of holding on to things your reason has once accepted, in spite of your changing moods."[2]

There are clear examples in the Scriptures where God grants to the human mind reasons to believe. A classic case is when God revealed himself to Moses. God appeared to Moses in a burning bush and said: "Thus you shall say to the children of Israel, 'I AM has sent me to you'" (Exod. 3:15). But Moses protested to God that the children of Israel might be skeptical of such a claim—why should they believe the Lord God sent him just because Moses claimed it was so? So the Lord granted to Moses the ability to perform three amazing signs: (1) turning his staff into a serpent, (2) causing his hand to become leprous, and (3) changing the Nile River into blood. When the people heard the testimony of Moses and saw the three signs with their own eyes, the Scriptures say, "So the people believed!" (Exod. 4:31). In other words, the signs that God worked through Moses were the objective evidence of why it was reasonable to believe that the *Lord God* sent Moses to them.

Jesus also points out that there is compelling evidence to believe that the Father sent him into the world: "The works [signs and miracles of healing, etc.] which the Father has given Me to finish—the very works that I do—bear witness of Me, that the Father has sent Me" (John 5:36); "The works that I do in My Father's name, they bear witness of Me. . . . If I do not do the works of My Father, do not believe Me; but if I do, though you do not believe Me, believe the works, that you may know and believe that the Father is in Me, and I in Him" (John 10:25, 37–38). In other words, the supernatural signs and miraculous healings are strong enough evidence to show that the Father sent Jesus into the world. God could have sent Jesus and simply demanded that people believe in the Son, but he didn't do that. He gave evidence to believe that Jesus was sent from above.

## ABSORB

**Christianity gives us tangible, historical, rational, and reasonable evidence to believe that Jesus is the Son of God and that the Bible is the Word of God.**

## INTERACT

○ What do you think Jesus meant when he said, "If I do not do the works [the miraculous works] of My Father, do not believe Me; but if I do, though you do not believe Me, believe the works, that you may know and believe that the Father is in Me, and I in Him"?

## LISTEN: Yesterday's Prophecies about Jesus's Birthplace and King Cyrus

*There are four key reasons* to believe that the Bible is the Word of God. In order to help you remember these four reasons, we are going to use the acronym YMCA, which usually stands for Young Men's Christian Association. For our purposes, YMCA will stand for the four reasons to believe that the Bible is the Word of God:

Yesterday's prophecies
Manuscript evidence
Christ's view of Scripture
Archaeological findings

In this session, we will discuss the first two reasons in detail; in the next session, we will conclude the discussion of manuscripts and discuss the last two reasons. Now we turn to the first reason, "yesterday's prophecies."

There are many prophecies in the Scriptures that have come to pass. The following are a select few that highlight the reality spoken of in the Bible that says: "I am God, and there is none like Me, / Declaring the end from the beginning, / And from ancient times things that are not yet done" (Isa. 46:9–10).

*Prophecy about the birthplace of the Messiah (Mic. 5:2).* About seven hundred years before Christ was born in Bethlehem, the prophet Micah made an astonishing prophecy concerning the background of the Messiah and the specific town in which he was to be born. Micah 5:2 reads: "But you, Bethlehem Ephrathah [the ancient name of the city in which Jesus was born], / Though you are little among the thousands of Judah, / Yet out of you shall come forth to Me / The One to be Ruler in Israel, / Whose goings forth are from of old, / From everlasting." This prophecy predicts that out of the small, obscure town of Bethlehem, a ruler in Israel would arise whose background is absolutely unique—his existence will be "from of old, / From everlasting"! Of course we sing today of that "little town of Bethlehem," celebrating that unique person—Jesus called Immanuel, "God with us"!

*Prophecy naming King Cyrus as liberator of the Jewish exiles (Isa. 44:28).* Isaiah spoke this prophecy more than one hundred fifty years before King Cyrus released the Jewish exiles to rebuild Jerusalem and the temple. Isaiah predicted: "Who says of Cyrus, 'He is My shepherd, / And he shall perform all My pleasure, / Saying to Jerusalem, "You shall be built," / And to the temple, "Your foundation shall be laid"'" (Isa. 44:28).[3]

The modern world detests authority but worships relevance. Our Christian conviction is that the Bible has both authority and relevance, and that the secret of both is Jesus Christ.

**—John R. W. Stott**

---

## ABSORB

**Jesus fulfilled the prophecy that the Messiah would be born in Bethlehem. Also, Isaiah accurately prophesied that a king named Cyrus would release the exiled Jews.**

---

## INTERACT

○ It is an impossible phenomenon to be able to truly predict the distant future apart from God being the source of that knowledge. In Isaiah 41:23 the Lord challenges the so-called "gods" to show the future. The Lord says: "Show the things that are to come hereafter, that we may know that you are gods." The authenticating sign of true divinity is the ability to foresee and predict the future. Why is it so difficult for people in our postmodern culture to believe that there is actual predictive prophecy in the Scriptures?

○ God reveals in his Word that he is omniscient: he has all knowledge—past, present, and future. What do you think it would be like to be able to look into the future?

## LISTEN: Yesterday's Prophecies about the Servant/Messiah

*Prophecy about the person and ministry of the Servant/Messiah (Isa. 53).* Isaiah 53 predicts, seven hundred years in advance, that God would send a special "servant" (the Messiah). The prophecy describes what happens to this servant with such specific detail that the prophecy could only fit Jesus Christ. The details of this prophecy include the following:

1. **Very few would initially believe in this servant.** When Christ came, the majority of religious leaders did not believe he was the Son of God, and then even incited the crowds to have Jesus crucified. Isaiah 53:1 reads: "Who has believed our report?" (The context implies very few.)

2. **This servant would be rejected, undergo great suffering, and even be pierced for the sins of others.** Such is the description of Christ's passion—his suffering and crucifixion. In the New Testament Jesus clearly states that he came to give his life as a ransom for many and that he would die as a sacrifice for the sins of others (Mark 10:45; John 3:16). Jesus was wounded—pierced through—when he was crucified for our sins. Isaiah 53:3–6, 10–12 reads: "He is despised and rejected by men, / . . . / Surely He has borne our griefs / And carried our sorrows; / . . . / But He was wounded [literally—"pierced through"][4] for our transgressions, / . . . / And the LORD has laid on Him the iniquity of us all. / . . . / When You make His soul an offering for sin, / . . . / For he shall bear their iniquities. / . . . / And He bore the sin of many."[5]

3. **This servant would be silent when accused.** He would not argue his case when he was oppressed, even though he had done no violence, and there was no deceit found in him. This describes Jesus, who did not defend himself when he was oppressed at his trial, even though he was totally innocent and had done only good. Isaiah 53:7 reads: "He was oppressed and He was afflicted, / Yet He opened not His mouth; / . . . And as a sheep before its shearers is silent, / So He opened not His mouth."

4. **This servant would be "cut off from the land of the living"; he would "pour out his soul unto death."** However, after this servant is made a sacrifice for the sins of others, something absolutely extraordinary happens—the prophecy states that God "shall prolong His days"! This is an enigma; after death this servant's life is prolonged! Such a prophecy can only be explained by the resurrection of Christ. Isaiah 53:8, 10, 12 reads: "For He was cut off from the land of the living; / . . . When You

make His soul an offering for sin / . . . He shall prolong His days, / And the pleasure of the LORD shall prosper in His hand. / . . . He poured out His soul unto death. . . ."

5. **This servant's death would be with the wicked and his grave with the rich.** Jesus was crucified between two wicked criminals. Criminals are normally assigned dishonorable burials; instead, Jesus was buried in a rich man's tomb. Isaiah 53:9 reads: "And they made His grave with the wicked— / But with the rich at His death."

---

### ABSORB

**The prophecies of Isaiah 53 were fulfilled by Christ with such precision that they provide us assurance that God is the source of these predictions. God furnishes us convincing reasons to believe!**

---

### INTERACT

○ Out of all the specific details of the prophecy of Isaiah 53, which one captures your attention the most and why?

---

## LISTEN: Yesterday's Prophecies about Resurrection, World Empires, and Destruction of the Temple

*Prophecy that God would not leave the soul of the Messiah in the grave nor allow him to see corruption.* The apostle Peter's first sermon announced that Psalm 16 was a prophecy of the Messiah's resurrection. David composed Psalm 16 and it is set in the first person ("I will bless the LORD," "My heart is glad"), but it is clear that David was foreseeing what would happen to the Messiah. Psalm 16:10 states, "For you will not leave my soul in Sheol, / Nor will You allow Your Holy One to see corruption," which means that his soul would not be left in the grave and his body would be resurrected. Peter points out that David died, was buried, and his tomb was present among them still, so therefore David was obviously not speaking about himself but of the coming Christ. Acts 2:27, which is quoting Psalm 16:10, reads, "For You will not leave my soul in Hades, / Nor will You allow Your Holy One to see corruption." Such a prophecy is uniquely designed to show that the resurrection of Christ was prophesied approximately a millennium before it occurred.

*Daniel's prophecy predicting the coming world empires and the time of the Messiah.* The book of Daniel records dreams and prophecies that describe history unfolding—the Babylonian Empire, the Medo-Persian Empire, the Grecian Empire (and the four Greek divisions), and the Roman Empire. This is most remarkable since Daniel recorded these prophecies around 539 BC, where he foretold the coming kingdoms of the next five centuries. The book of Daniel also includes the stunning prophecy that predicts the time of the Messiah: "Know therefore and understand, / That from the going forth of the command / To restore and build Jerusalem / Until Messiah the Prince, / There shall be seven weeks and sixty-two weeks" (Dan. 9:25). When we understand that the word "weeks" refers to a period of seven years, this prophecy puts the coming of the Messiah to specifically the time of Jesus of Nazareth.[6]

*New Testament prophecies about the destruction of the Jewish temple.* Jesus himself prophesied distinctly that the temple of Jerusalem would be completely destroyed within his generation: "Assuredly, I say to you, not one stone shall be left here upon another, that shall not be thrown down" (Matt. 24:2). This prophecy was very unpopular with the Jewish people, but it definitely came to pass in AD 70 when the Romans destroyed the temple in Jerusalem.

These are just a few of the many prophecies of the Bible. One of the distinguishing marks of the reality that the Lord is the living God is that he has spoken from the beginning things that would take place years later. This is compelling evidence that he is God: "I am God, and there is none like Me, / Declaring the end from the beginning, / And from ancient times things that are not yet done" (Isa. 46:9–10), and "I have declared the former things from the beginning; / They went forth from My mouth, and I caused them to hear it / . . . Before it came to pass I proclaimed it to you, / Lest you should say, 'My idol has done them'" (Isa. 48:3, 5). God is saying that a mark of divinity is being able to announce the future before it happens. True prophecy finds its source in God alone. The fulfilled prophecies of Scripture give us reasons to believe that God actually speaks in his Word.

--- ABSORB ---

**There are prophecies in the Scriptures that have been fulfilled with such accuracy that they present persuasive evidence that the source of Scripture is God.**

--- INTERACT ---

○ Do you think that there are a lot of people in our culture who do not know about these prophecies of the Bible that have been fulfilled?

○ Why would it be helpful for us who are followers of Christ to become very familiar with these prophecies?

○ Do you feel your faith being strengthened as you have looked closely at these prophecies?

## LISTEN: Manuscript Evidence

But sanctify the Lord God in your hearts, and always be ready to give a defense to everyone who asks you a reason for the hope that is in you, with meekness and fear.

**—1 Peter 3:15**

The second reason to believe that the Bible is the Word of God—the "M" of YMCA—is manuscript evidence. The manuscripts of Scripture are accurate reproductions of the original manuscripts and are reliable sources of historical information. In this session we will discuss evidence relating to the New Testament, and in the next session we will discuss evidence relating to the Old Testament.

Manuscript evidence does not "prove" that the Scriptures are the Word of God, but it does answer the critic's challenge: "How can you trust what is in the Bible since it has been copied and translated and obviously changed so many times through the centuries?"

The answer to the challenge is that the New Testament is one of the most reliable works from the ancient world. First of all, it has by far the greatest number of existing manuscripts compared to copies of other ancient classical works. For example, we have only seven manuscripts written by Plato, only eight by Herodotus, and ten by Caesar. But the number of existing manuscripts (complete or fragmented) for the New Testament that have been catalogued is over 5,800![7] Not only are there more copies, but the oldest copies of New Testament manuscripts are dated closely to the actual time they were first written. For example, the manuscripts from Plato, Aristotle, Herodotus, Caesar, Tacitus, and Homer all have a gap of time between the original writing of the manuscripts and the oldest existing copies that ranges from 500 to 1,400 years (most are at least a thousand years). This is a massive amount of gap time when you compare it to the New Testament. The oldest New Testament fragment of a papyrus (John 18:31–33; called the John Rylands manuscript [$\mathfrak{P}^{52}$]) is dated anywhere from 10 to 50 years after the original manuscript was written. John A. T. Robinson, critical scholar, writes about the manuscripts of the New Testament: "The wealth of manuscripts, and above all the narrow interval of time between the writing and the earliest extant copies, make it by far the best attested text of any ancient writing in the world."[8]

Not only are there more than 5,800 Greek manuscripts, but there are also hundreds of manuscripts of the New Testament that were translated into other languages (other versions include Latin, Syriac, Ethopic, Slavic, Armenian, etc.). The total number of early manuscripts in other languages is to date **19,284**.[9] On top of that, the first Christian leaders after the apostles (called early church fathers—Justin Martyr, Irenaeus, Clement of Alexandria, Origen, Tertullian, Hippolytus, Eusebius) quoted the Scriptures profusely in their writings. There are over **36,000 quotations** made by the early church fathers from the New Testament alone.[10] New Testament scholar Bruce Metzger writes: "*Indeed so extensive are these citations that if all the sources for our knowledge of the text of the New Testament were destroyed, they would be sufficient alone for the reconstruction of practically the entire New Testament.*"[11]

The New Testament, with this overwhelming number of copies and citations, yields a much stronger base than other ancient writings for establishing the original text of Scripture.[12] The internationally renowned Christian apologist Ravi Zacharias concludes, "In real terms, the New Testament is easily the best attested ancient writing in terms of the sheer number of documents, the time span between the events and the document, and the variety of documents available to sustain or contradict it. There is nothing in ancient manuscript evidence to match such textual availability and integrity."[13]

---

### ABSORB

**The manuscripts of Scripture are accurate reproductions of the original manuscripts and are reliable sources for historical information.**

---

### INTERACT

○ Do you think most people are aware that there is such an overwhelming number of New Testament manuscripts and such a small interval of time between the original writing and the oldest existing copies? Why do you think some critics have questioned the general integrity of the copies of manuscripts of the New Testament but have not done the same with ancient classical works that have far fewer copies?

## Your Word Is a Light

Psalm 119:105 says, "Your Word is a lamp to my feet / And a light to my path." The Word gives clear direction on how we are to live and what is truth. Not only is the Word of God described as a light, but Jesus himself said that he is the light of the world. And Christ reveals himself through the light of the gospel:

> The light has come into the world, and men loved darkness rather than light, because their deeds were evil. For everyone practicing evil hates the light and does not come to the light, lest his deeds should be exposed. But he who does the truth comes to the light, that his deeds may be clearly seen, that they have been done in God. (John 3:19–21)

## LISTEN: Comparing the Manuscripts

When scholars compare the thousands of Greek manuscripts of the New Testament with each other, there are sometimes variants (or differences). But the vast majority of these differences stem from unintentional errors, such as repeating a word or sentence, deleting a word or phrase, confusing similar letters, disordering words, changing the relationship between nouns and definite articles, revising spelling and grammar, or harmonizing similar passages.[14] After these variations are compared among the thousands of manuscripts, scholars are able to determine the original text with more than a 99 percent degree of accuracy. New Testament scholar D. A. Carson points out that "the purity of text is of such a substantial nature that nothing we believe to be true, and nothing we are commanded to do, is in any way jeopardized by the variants."[15]

And among the remaining questions, none affects any crucial element of the Christian faith. Also it is not as if we don't have the remaining fractional percent of the New Testament text—it simply is a matter of determining which remaining textual variants best reflect the original writings.

— ABSORB —

**After comparing all of the existing New Testament manuscripts, scholars are able to determine the original text with more than a 99 percent degree of accuracy.**

## C. S. Lewis on the Gospels and Legend

"If he [the biblical critic] tells me that something in a Gospel is legend or romance, I want to know how many legends and romances he has read, how well his palate is trained in detecting them by the flavor; not how many years he has spent on that Gospel. . . . Read the dialogues [in John's Gospel]: that with the Samaritan woman at the well, or that which follows the healing of the man born blind. Look at its pictures: Jesus (if I may use the word) doodling with his finger in the dust; the unforgettable η δε νυξ ["and it was night"—describing the scene right before Judas betrayed Jesus as recorded in John 13:30]. . . . I have been reading poems, romances, vision-literature, legends, myths all my life. I know what they are like. I know that not one of them is like this."

**C. S. Lewis[a]**

[a]*Christian Reflections* (Grand Rapids: Eerdmans, 1967), 154–55.

### INTERACT

○ Do you now feel more confident in the integrity of the Scriptures?

○ Why would it be important for Christians to be familiar with this information about manuscripts?

**Reflect:** Jesus said, "You shall love the LORD your God with all your heart, with all your soul, with all your mind, and with all your strength" (Mark 12:30). If you are not progressing in all areas, then take time to ask God why you are not. Think back on the prophecies that have been fulfilled and let that confirm your trust in the Bible as the Word of God. Is there anything I can be praying about for you until we meet for the next session?

## CULTIVATING SPIRITUAL HABITS

**Read:** Psalm 19 and Acts 22:1–21

**Journal:** If this chapter has helped strengthen your faith in the Scriptures, then write out any thoughts you have about that.

## Memorize

> *Do not think that I came to destroy the Law or the Prophets. I did not come to destroy but to fulfill. For assuredly, I say to you, till heaven and earth pass away, one jot or one tittle will by no means pass from the law till all is fulfilled.*

> MATTHEW 5:17–18

# Christ's View of Scripture and Archaeological Findings

## Evidence for the Inspiration of the Bible (Part 2)

**Purpose of Session Nine:** This session continues focusing on the trustworthiness of Scripture as the very Word of God. A question Christians often face is, "How do you know the Bible is the Word of God and not just another book produced by humans?" As we explored answers to this question in the last session, we covered "Y" and part of "M" in our YMCA acronym:

Yesterday's prophecies

Manuscript evidence

Christ's view of Scripture

Archaeological findings

In this session, we continue with "M" and look at more manuscript evidence, this time from Old Testament manuscripts. We also look at Christ's view of Scripture, as well as archaeological findings.

## LISTEN: The Masoretes

Until 1947 the oldest Hebrew (Old Testament) manuscript we possessed was copied about AD 925, called the Aleppo Codex ("codex" means a manuscript book). The Aleppo Codex along with the Leningrad Codex (copied in AD 1008) are part of what is known as the "Masoretic Text." The Masoretes were a group of Jewish scholars and scribes who lived and worked between AD 500 and 950. They were tasked with preserving and transmitting the Hebrew Old

Testament.[1] Biblical scholar F. F. Bruce describes how the Masoretes copied the Old Testament maintaining nearly perfect accuracy.

> The Masoretes were well disciplined and treated the text with the greatest imaginable reverence, and devised a complicated system of safeguards against scribal slips. They counted, for example, the number of times each letter of the alphabet occurs in each book; they pointed out the middle letter of the Pentateuch and the middle letter of the whole Hebrew Bible, and made even more detailed calculations than these. "Everything countable seems to be counted," says Wheeler Robinson, and they made up mnemonics by which the various totals might be readily remembered.[2]

— ABSORB —

**The Masoretes developed a sophisticated process of copying the Hebrew text of the Old Testament that ensured remarkable accuracy.**

INTERACT

○ What would you have liked most and least about being a Masoretic scribe who spent your days copying Scripture by hand?

## LISTEN: The Discovery of the Dead Sea Scrolls

An incredible discovery was made between 1947 and 1956: eleven caves by the Dead Sea in the Holy Land were found to contain a total of 227 biblical manuscripts (scrolls), some of them dating back to 175–150 BC. Up until then, the oldest Hebrew manuscripts were dated approximately nine hundred years after Christ, but these scrolls dramatically changed that. These manuscripts are called the Dead Sea Scrolls. Just a few scrolls were found in their entirety. One example is the *Isaiah Scroll*, which was found with all 66 chapters of the book of Isaiah (a second scroll of Isaiah was found with substantial portions of Isaiah 41–66).[3] Also, the *Great Psalms Scroll* contains a good portion of the Psalms (although the bottom third of each page has been lost).[4] For the other biblical books only fragments survived (some quite substantial but most of them small).[5] In the mid-twentieth century when scholars examined the copies of Isaiah from the Dead Sea Scrolls and compared them to the Isaiah text preserved by the Masoretes, they discovered that the Masoretic Hebrew

Bible, even though a thousand years later, agreed word-for-word more than 95 percent of the time! Gleason Archer writes: "The 5 percent of variation consisted chiefly of obvious slips of the pen and variations in spelling." In many cases, this is similar to how English spelling changes over the years—such as from "saviour" to "savior" and "judgement" to "judgment." Archer also records that even the scrolls that differ a bit more from the Masoretic text do not differ in any way that affects any crucial Jewish or Christian belief.[6]

William F. Albright, a distinguished professor at Johns Hopkins University, was one scholar who carefully weighed the significance of these new discoveries. Archer quotes Albright's conclusion that the text of the Hebrew Bible "has been preserved with an accuracy perhaps unparalleled in any other Near Eastern Literature."[7]

First-century Jewish historian Flavius Josephus testified to the high regard in which the Scriptures were held and the abiding commitment to keep them pure: "We have given practical proof of our reverence for our own Scriptures. For, although such long ages have now passed, no one has ventured either to add, or to remove, or to alter a syllable; and it is an instinct with every Jew, from the day of his birth, to regard them as the decrees of God, to abide by them, and, if need be, cheerfully to die for them."[8]

The discovery of the Dead Sea Scrolls is one of the amazing faith-building archaeological finds of the twentieth century. The Hebrew Scriptures from which scholars translate have been precisely preserved and transmitted so we can say with genuine confidence that we have the true Word of God.

## ABSORB

**The Dead Sea Scrolls demonstrate that the Hebrew Bible has been preserved with an accuracy that is unparalleled in any other Near Eastern literature.**

## INTERACT

○ How does it make you feel knowing that the Scriptures have been preserved with such accuracy?

○ How would you relay to a friend the significance of the Dead Sea Scrolls?

If Jesus rose from the dead, then you have to accept all that he said; if he didn't rise from the dead, then why worry about any of what he said? The issue on which everything hangs is not whether or not you like his teaching but whether or not he rose from the dead.

**—Timothy Keller,**
***The Reason for God***

## LISTEN: Christ's View of Scripture

The "C" in YMCA stands for Christ's view of Scripture. Jesus viewed the Scriptures as being the Word of God. If Jesus is the Son of God, then his view of Scripture is invaluable to us.

Two sessions ago we saw that Jesus clearly viewed the Scriptures as the final, reliable authority and the supreme source of truth. He was convinced that the Scriptures were the authoritative Word of God. He said, "The Scripture cannot be broken" (John 10:35), meaning that there is nothing strong enough to break the authority of Scripture because the source of authority is found in God. Jesus also said, "Till heaven and earth pass away, one jot or one tittle will by no means pass from the law till all is fulfilled" (Matt. 5:18), which means that the reliability and truthfulness of the Word of God, even down to the smallest stroke of the pen, is so sure and certain that it will absolutely come to pass. Jesus had total confidence that Scripture found its source in God himself. Also, we saw that Jesus "preapproved" the authority of the writings of the apostles for the New Testament, noting how the Spirit of God would bring to their remembrance all the things he said to them and would guide them into all truth (John 14:26; 16:13). (See session seven for a more detailed discussion of Jesus's view of Scripture.)

### ABSORB

**Jesus viewed the Scriptures as being the Word of God. If Jesus is the Son of God then his view of Scripture is invaluable!**

### INTERACT

○ Why do you think Jesus's view of Scripture carries a lot of weight in affirming that the Bible is the Word of God?

○ Hebrews 4:12 says, "For the word of God is living and powerful, and sharper than any two-edged sword." In what sense do you think the word of God is living, powerful, and sharp?

For the word of God is living and powerful, and sharper than any two-edged sword, piercing even to the division of soul and spirit, and of joints and marrow, and is a discerner of the thoughts and intents of the heart.

**—Hebrews 4:12**

## LISTEN: Solid Evidence That Jesus Is the Son of God

We have seen that Jesus held a high view of Scripture, but why does that matter? There is solid evidence that Jesus is the Son of God, therefore his view of Scripture is invaluable.

There are strong reasons to believe that Jesus is the Son of God:

**1. Jesus's character and teachings match his claim to be the Son of God.** Historian Will Durant, in his massive work *The Story of Civilization*, gives an insightful analysis of the portrait of Christ presented in the Gospels:

> No one reading these scenes can doubt the reality of the figure behind them. That a few simple men should in one generation have invented so powerful and appealing a personality, so lofty an ethic and so inspiring a vision of human brotherhood, would be a miracle far more incredible than any recorded in the Gospels. After two centuries of Higher Criticism the outlines of the life, character, and teachings of Christ remain reasonably clear and constitute the most fascinating feature in the history of Western man.[9]

**2. Jesus's miracles are significant in validating his claim to be the Son of God.** It is noteworthy that even the enemies of Christ did not question Christ's ability to perform miracles; they simply questioned his source of

---

## Historians Have No Qualms about Jesus

You may have read critics who have questioned the very existence of Jesus as a historical person. They may have suggested that he was simply a myth or legend made up by a group of religious people who wanted to perpetuate a religious system.

As F. F. Bruce, who was Rylands professor of biblical criticism and exegesis at the University of Manchester, wrote, "Some writers may toy with the fancy of a 'Christ-myth' but they do not do so on the ground of historical evidence. The historicity of Jesus Christ is as axiomatic for an unbiased historian as the historicity of Julius Caesar. It is not historians who propagate the 'Christ-myth' theories." German New Testament professor Otto Betz similarly concluded, "No serious scholar has ventured to postulate the non-historicity of Jesus."[a]

Jesus's existence is attested to outside the New Testament. There is credible corroborative evidence that a historical person (Christ) existed in the first century. Ancient sources such as Flavius Josephus, Tacitus, Pliny the Younger, and Thallus all corroborate the historical reality of Jesus Christ. For an interesting and concise summary of this corroboration I recommend Lee Strobel's interview with historian Edwin Yamauchi in Strobel's book *The Case for Christ*.[b]

[a]Quotes from Josh McDowell, *The New Evidence That Demands a Verdict* (Nashville: Thomas Nelson, 1999), 120.
[b]*The Case for Christ* (Grand Rapids: Zondervan, 1988), 75–86.

power. Because Christ challenged their traditions, they reacted by attributing Jesus's miracle-working powers to the dark powers of Satan (Mark 3:22; Matt. 12:24).

**3. The prophecies about Jesus are evidence that he was the Son of God.** In the last session we looked at many Old Testament prophecies that pertain to Jesus.

**4. Christ's resurrection confirms Jesus's claims to be the Son of God.** The enemies of Christ had no motives to perpetuate a resurrection story. The friends of Christ died for their belief that Jesus was resurrected, and they had the opportunity to know firsthand whether Jesus rose from the dead. People do not willingly die for what they know to be false.

But aren't the followers of Jesus just like countless people of other religions who have died for their beliefs? In his book *The Case for Christ*, Lee Strobel interacts with J. P. Moreland concerning just this question. Moreland puts forward a critical distinction that is often overlooked when comparing the first disciples of Christ to followers of other religions: the disciples of Jesus were able to verify *with their own eyes* the truthfulness or falsity of whether Jesus was really resurrected from the grave. Listen to Moreland's careful explanation and Strobel's response: "The apostles were willing to die for something they had seen with their own eyes and touched with their own hands. They were in a unique position not to just believe Jesus rose from the dead but to know for sure. And when you've got eleven credible people with no ulterior motives, with nothing to gain and a lot to lose, who all agree they observe something with their own eyes—now you've got some difficulty explaining that away." Lee Strobel responds:

> I knew he was right. In fact, this critical distinction was pivotal in my own spiritual journey. It had been put to me this way: People will die for their religious beliefs if they sincerely believe they're true, but people won't die for their religious beliefs if they know their beliefs are false. While most people can only have faith that their beliefs are true, the disciples were in a position to know without a doubt whether or not Jesus had risen from the dead. They claimed that they saw Him, talked with Him, and ate with Him. If they weren't absolutely certain, they wouldn't have allowed themselves to be tortured to death for proclaiming that the Resurrection had happened.[10]

Think about it: would you yourself undergo persecution, torture, and excruciating pain and death for retelling a story that you knew was not true? If you wouldn't do that, then why would anyone think the disciples would be willing to die for something they *knew* was a lie?

**5. The conversion of Paul, who had been one of the greatest antagonists of Christians, supports the claims of Jesus.** Paul (formerly called Saul) was a man whose sole passion was to stamp out Christianity (originally described as "the sect of the Nazarenes") once and for all. Paul belonged to a strict religious fraternity called the "Pharisees." He persecuted the church and was instrumental in the imprisonment and deaths of Christians. He did all this to defend the religious tradition he believed in. Yet he was transformed when the risen Christ appeared to him. The historian and New Testament scholar F. F. Bruce records the immense importance of the transformation of Paul in affirming the reality of Christ as the Son of God. Bruce asserts, "It is reasonable to believe that the evidence which convinced such a man of the out-and-out wrongness of his former course, and led him so decisively to abandon previously cherished beliefs for a movement which he had so vigorously opposed, must have been of a singularly impressive quality. The conversion of Paul has for long been regarded as weighty evidence for the truth of Christianity."[11] Paul's personal accounts of his conversion (Acts 22:1–21 and 26:1–29; see also 1 Cor. 15:8) are compelling evidence that he had seen the resurrected Christ.

Paul was so convinced that he had encountered Christ that he was willing to endure for the rest of his life unrelenting opposition and persecution. At great personal cost he unwaveringly preached the gospel in different cities of the Roman Empire. Eventually he was put to death as a result of preaching the gospel that Christ was the resurrected Son of God.

## ABSORB

There is solid evidence to make the case that Jesus is the Son of God. Some may say, "I want a watertight argument to prove beyond all doubt that Christ is who he says he is." The reality is that there *is* enough evidence to make a solid rational decision. Tim Keller often remarks that God doesn't give watertight arguments but rather gives a watertight person.

## INTERACT

○ There was a dramatic life change in Paul after he encountered the resurrected Christ. In 1 Timothy 1:13, 16 he says: "Although I was formerly a blasphemer, a persecutor, and an insolent man . . . I obtained mercy. . . . And the grace of our Lord was exceedingly abundant. . . ." Do you feel in any way like the apostle Paul—that God has shown you much patience, mercy, and grace? In what way?

○ What is it about the teachings of Jesus that most fascinates you?

## You Lie, You Die

"As a journalist I've come across a fair number of liars. In my experience, people usually lie because they figure it will get them something they want—or get them out of something they definitely don't want.

"I might be tempted to lie to you about making a winning touchdown if I think it will get me respect. (Of course, this backfires as soon as you discover that I wasn't even on the football team.) You might lie about cheating on an exam if you think it will get you out of a failing grade. But what was in it for the disciples if they were lying about Jesus? Their claims that he was God got them criticism, persecution, and ultimately death.

"What do you think? Would all those eyewitnesses risk their lives for a lie?"

**Lee Strobel[a]**

[a]*The Case for Christ: Student Edition* (Grand Rapids: Zondervan, 2001), 56.

○ The disciples of Jesus had the opportunity to know firsthand whether he rose from the dead. Why does this make Christianity unique among all other religions?

## LISTEN: Archaeological Findings

The "A" in YMCA stands for archaeological findings. Archaeological findings contribute to confirming the historical accuracy and trustworthiness of the events recorded in the Bible.

Just as manuscript evidence does not "prove" that the Bible is the Word of God, the same is true with archaeological evidence. But archaeology does answer the critic's charge that the Bible consists of legendary tales that have no historical basis. When an ancient writer of Scripture mentions geographical, cultural, artifactual, and historical details, and these details are confirmed as accurate time after time, this increases our confidence in the writer.[12] Archaeology in the twentieth and twenty-first centuries has increased confidence in the biblical writers. Throughout the years critics of the Bible have questioned it as a source of history. Yet one of the foremost biblical archaeologists of the twentieth century, William F. Albright, points out:

> Until recently it was the fashion among biblical historians to treat the patriarchal sagas of Genesis [chaps. 11–50] as though they were artificial creations of Israelite scribes of the Divided Monarchy or tales told by imaginative rhapsodists around the Israelite campfires during centuries following their occupation of the

country. . . . Archaeological discoveries since 1925 have changed all this. Aside from a few die-hards among older scholars, there is scarcely a single biblical historian who has not been impressed by the rapid accumulation of data supporting the substantial historicity of patriarchal tradition.[13]

From the chaos of prehistory, the Bible was projected as though it were a monstrous fossil, with no contemporary evidence to demonstrate its authenticity and its origin in a human world like ours. . . . Discovery after discovery has established the accuracy of innumerable details, and has brought increased recognition of the value of the Bible as a source of history.[14]

Many of the discoveries in the last century confirm the historicity of names and places found in the Scriptures. One dramatic example is the attestation of King David. Although David is the most prominent king of the Old Testament, up until 1993 there was no evidence outside the Bible directly attesting to his existence. Therefore critics had argued that he was mere legend. Then a stunning discovery was made by Avraham Biram and his team at the foot of Mount Hermon. They discovered a black stone slab containing Aramaic inscriptions that included the phrases "The King of Israel" and "House of David." Hershel Shanks, the editor of *Biblical Archaeological Review*, summed up the significance of the discovery, saying, "The stele [stone slab] brings to life the biblical text in a very dramatic way. It also gives us more confidence in the historical reality of the biblical text."[15]

The Tel Dan stone

---

ABSORB

---

## Archaeological findings contribute to confirming the historical accuracy and trustworthiness of the events recorded in the Bible.

---

INTERACT

---

○ After reading these last two sessions, which have presented four key reasons to believe that the Bible is the Word of God (YMCA: yesterday's prophecies, manuscript evidence, Christ's view of Scripture, and archaeological findings), which of these four have given you a greater sense of confidence in the Scriptures being the Word of God and why?

**Reflect:** Think deeply about the connection that exists between how you view the reality of Christ and how passionate you are about carrying out his mission for us.

Think back to how God has guided the transmission of the biblical manuscripts in history. He has preserved the copies in such a way that we can know that we hold in our hands today the true Word of God. How might that knowledge affect your reading of Scripture this week? Is there anything I can be praying about for you until we meet for the next session?

## CULTIVATING SPIRITUAL HABITS

**Read:** Matthew 5:5–15; Mark 11:20–26; and Psalm 51

**Journal:** Write out why Christ's high view of Scripture would motivate you to spend more time reading and meditating upon the Word.

### Memorize

*Your Word is a lamp to my feet*
*And a light to my path.*

PSALM 119:105

# Jesus's Model Prayer

## The Great Value of Prayer (Part 1)

---

**Purpose of Session Ten:** Prayer is one of the most essential elements for growing in your Christian life. In this session we discuss the Lord's Prayer, the model prayer Jesus taught his disciples. In the next session, we focus on six important elements of prayer.

---

## LISTEN: The Lord's Prayer

Prayer is such a vast subject that volumes have been written about it. Yet there are certain observations and features about prayer that most biblical scholars agree form the basis for understanding the true nature of prayer. If you understand these things and live them out, then you can experience prayer as God intended.

Prayer is talking to God. Jesus gave the disciples (which include us) a special prayer that is often referred to as the Lord's Prayer. Before he communicated this model prayer, Jesus first told his disciples what *not* to do. He warned them to be aware of wrong motives: do not pray to be seen by people (Matt. 6:5). In other words, prayer is not to be used as a means to draw attention to yourself so that others will think you are spiritual. Jesus also said, "And when you pray, do not use vain repetitions as the heathen do. For they think that they will be heard for their many words. Therefore do not be like them. For your Father knows the things you have need of before you ask Him. In this manner, therefore, pray: Our Father in heaven, / Hallowed be Your name" (Matt. 6:7–9). Jesus's prayer is a model or pattern that is intended to give us insight into the important parts of prayer.

## ABSORB

**In the Lord's Prayer, Jesus provides a window on the true nature of prayer. The Lord's Prayer serves as a model or pattern to help us know how to pray.**

## INTERACT

○ Can you remember a time when praying the Lord's Prayer in a group was very meaningful to you? Why was it a meaningful experience?

○ Have you ever prayed, asking God for something, and when it was answered you sensed it really was God who answered your prayer? Can you remember some of the details of your answered prayer?

## LISTEN: Addressing God as "Our Father"

Jesus begins this model prayer with "Our Father in heaven." Jesus is teaching his followers that God is our heavenly Father. The idea of "relationship" is the very first thing Jesus teaches regarding prayer. It is an amazing thought that God chooses to reveal himself as "Our Father."

Although the Lord's Prayer is often prayed precisely as recorded in the New Testament, it appears that Christ is giving us more than a single prayer to pray. He is teaching us the most important things of life to pray about. Throughout this prayer important issues or ideas are mentioned, and we can expand on these ideas as we pray. For example, in our prayer to God we might expand on the idea of God being our heavenly Father by praying:

Our Father in heaven, I am eternally grateful that you are my Father in heaven. To be a child of yours is a privilege beyond description. You created me, and then you adopted me into your family through faith in Christ. I thank you, Father, that it is true what your Word says—that every good and perfect gift comes from you. I thank you that, as my Father in heaven, you know how to give good things to your children. Father, thank you for being my Father. In the Psalms it says that as a father has compassion on his children, so the Lord has compassion on those who fear him. Thank you that you are the kind of Father that comes running to meet the prodigal son!

---

## ABSORB

### Recognizing God as "Our Father in heaven" is an important aspect of prayer.

---

## INTERACT

○ How does it strike you that God reveals himself to us as a father? How would it be an encouragement to pray knowing that God looks at you as one of his children whom he deeply loves?

## LISTEN: God's Name, Kingdom, and Will

Jesus teaches us to pray, "Hallowed be Your name." He is instructing us to pray that God's name would *be treated as holy*. The name of God represents God himself! When we are asking that his name be treated as holy, we are asking that God would be believed, loved, trusted, and respected with a healthy, holy fear. It is a request that people would take God and his Word seriously.[1]

Next, Jesus instructs us to pray: "Your kingdom come. / Your will be done / On earth as it is in heaven" (Matt. 6:10). When we pray that the kingdom of God would come, we are praying for both the present and the future. In one sense, when people believe in Christ they are conveyed (or transferred) into the present kingdom of God. Colossians 1:13 plainly spells this out: "He [the Father] has delivered us from the power of darkness and conveyed us into the *kingdom* of the Son of His love." Therefore, when we pray this way, we are asking God to bring more and more people to faith in Christ so that they become a part of his kingdom. Yet there is also the future glorious aspect of the kingdom when Christ returns again: "I charge you therefore before God and the Lord Jesus Christ, who will judge the living and the dead at His *appearing* and His *kingdom*" (2 Tim. 4:1). So when we pray that his kingdom will come, we are not only asking God to rule and reign in our lives, but we are asking that the kingdom of God will come in all of its glory: we look and pray "for the blessed hope and glorious appearing of our great God and Savior Jesus Christ" (Titus 2:13). We are to pray for that glorious day!

Then, we are to pray that "Your will be done / On earth as it is in heaven," which means that we are also praying that Christ's followers would live in such a way that they bring heaven to earth. The will of God is always done in heaven by the angels—they always choose good and choose to obey God. But on earth, people disregard the will of God—there is slander, arrogance, stealing, lying, hurtful words, adultery, murder, selfishness, and so on. Jesus

---

## Moody the Pray-er

"Out of a very intimate acquaintance with D. L. Moody, I wish to testify that he was a far greater pray-er than he was preacher. Time and time again, he was confronted by obstacles that seemed insurmountable, but he always knew the way to overcome all difficulties. He knew the way to bring to pass anything that needed to be brought to pass. He knew and believed in the deepest depths of his soul that nothing was too hard for the Lord, and that prayer could do anything that God could do."

**R. A. Torrey**[a]

[a]*Why God Used D. L. Moody* (Chicago: Fleming H. Revell, 1923), 13.

---

is highlighting the importance of praying for God's will to be done. The will of God in this sense means the prescriptive will of God (also called God's "moral will" or "will of command" or "will of desire"), which is what God commands of us. The prescriptive will of God also describes what his disposition is toward good and evil: God despises evil and loves what is right and good. It is always best to start praying with yourself and your responsibilities and then move to a wider circle. This is a way of bringing our priorities into line with his. The wise theologian Robert Law once wrote: "Prayer is a mighty instrument, not for getting man's will done in heaven but for getting God's will done on earth."

### ABSORB

**Some valuable features of prayer are praying that God's name be hallowed and his kingdom come and his will be done.**

### INTERACT

○ Why do you think God wants his name to be hallowed (treated as holy)?

○ What are some things that you know are definitely God's will that you could pray be done on earth?

## LISTEN: The Basic Needs of Life

The Lord's Prayer also addresses the basic needs of our lives. When Jesus teaches us to pray, "Give us this day our daily bread" (Matt. 6:11), he wants us to see that even our daily food comes from God. "Daily bread" is a notion that includes all things necessary to sustain our lives. Martin Luther, a reformer in the sixteenth century, caught the fuller intent of this request when he wrote, "Everything necessary for the preservation of this life is bread—including food, a healthy body, good weather, house, home, wife, children, good government, and peace."[2]

### ABSORB

**Praying for the basic needs of life is vital to our prayer lives.**

### INTERACT

○ Have you ever thought about how much God has already given us in our country (compared to many other countries)? How should God's goodness affect the way we think and pray?

## LISTEN: Forgiveness, Temptation, and Praise

The focus of forgiveness is also embedded in the Lord's Prayer. Because Jesus never sinned (as it clearly states in Heb. 4:15), he never needed forgiveness. So when Jesus prayed, "And forgive us our debts, / As we forgive our debtors" (Matt. 6:12), he wasn't praying that prayer for himself but was teaching *the disciples* what to pray. Consequently, the Lord's Prayer could be called more correctly the Disciples' Prayer. Jesus is teaching us, who sin, to ask for God's forgiveness. One aspect of sin is debt. Debt arises when you owe someone something. If you do someone wrong, then you owe them whatever it takes to make it right. When we wrong God we incur a debt we cannot pay, so we are asking him to let our debt go—to forgive our debt of sin. God forgives us on the basis of Christ paying our sin-debt on our behalf. When we sin (perhaps every day), we should come to God to ask for that continual forgiveness. Jesus assumes that because we have already been forgiven so much by God we will naturally forgive others who have done us wrong. One of the chief marks of a real follower of Christ is that he or she will have a disposition to forgive the debt of others who have done him or her wrong.

The Lord also teaches us to pray for deliverance from temptation. Jesus directs us to pray: "And do not lead us into temptation, / But deliver us from the evil one" (Matt. 6:13).[3] And James 1:13 states: "Let no one say when he is tempted, 'I am tempted by God'; for God cannot be tempted by evil, nor does He Himself tempt anyone." Immediately a question arises: If God does not tempt anyone, then what does Jesus mean when he teaches us to pray to the Father: "do not lead us into temptation"? The answer is that God does not tempt us, but he does at times allow "the Tempter"—the devil—to tempt his people. The intent of this prayer may be that we are to recognize our weakness and vulnerability so that we cry out to God, "Father, please do not lead us into circumstances where we will be tempted by the Evil One (the devil) but deliver us from his deceitful power." Or Jesus may be simply saying: "Do not allow us to be so led into temptation that it overwhelms us, but rescue us from the evil one."[4] It is an acknowledgment of our weakness and God's ability to deliver us from the power of the Tempter. Luther's famous hymn *A Mighty Fortress Is Our God* captures the power and craftiness of the enemy we face:

> For still our ancient foe
> doth seek to work us woe;
> his craft and power are great,
> and armed with cruel hate,
> on earth is not his equal.
>
> Did we in our own strength confide,
> our striving would be losing,
> were not the right man on our side,
> the man of God's own choosing.
> Dost ask who that may be?
> Christ Jesus, it is He;
> Lord Sabaoth [Lord of Hosts] His name,
> from age to age the same,
> and He must win the battle.

The final emphasis of the Lord's Prayer is on God's sovereign power and glory. It ends with the words, "*For Yours is the kingdom and the power and the glory forever. Amen*" (Matt. 6:13), which are very similar to the ancient prayer of King David in 1 Chronicles 29:11: "Yours, O LORD, is the greatness, / *The power* and *the glory*, / The victory and the majesty; / For all that is in heaven and in earth is Yours; / Yours is *the kingdom*, O LORD."

This is a major theme throughout the Bible—God reigns supreme with absolute power and blazing glory. God is our King, and when we grasp even a small amount of his greatness and majesty, we instinctively want to praise him for being the sovereign, omnipotent King that he is!

## ABSORB

**Prayer for forgiveness and deliverance from temptation, and praise for God's kingdom, power, and glory are all vital features of prayer.**

## INTERACT

○ As you pray to God concerning forgiveness, why do you think it is important not to hold a grudge against anyone?

○ Why is it important that we ask God to deliver us from the tempting power of the devil? How can we learn from the mistakes of others who have fallen to temptation?

○ Does knowing that the kingdom and the power and the glory belong to God forevermore give you confidence as you pray? Why?

**Reflect:** Ask yourself, "If I am going to be used of God to have an impact in a significant way, am I willing, like Jesus, to spend time each day in prayer to our Father?"

Think back through the Lord's Prayer and reflect on the different categories of the prayer and why each is important. Is there anything I can be praying about for you until we meet for the next session?

## CULTIVATING SPIRITUAL HABITS

**Read:** John 17 (This is the long prayer that Jesus prayed for his disciples right before he was arrested and crucified.)

Beware in your prayers, above everything else, of limiting God, not only by unbelief, but by fancying that you know what He can do. Expect unexpected things, "above all that we ask or think." Each time, before you intercede, be quiet first, and worship God in His glory. Think of what He can do, and how He delights to hear the prayers of His redeemed people. Think of your place and privilege in Christ, and expect great things!
—**Andrew Murray (1828–1917), South African Dutch Reformed pastor**

**Journal:** Spend time reading the Lord's Prayer, and write a prayer to God based on the elements of that prayer.

### Memorize

*Our Father in heaven, hallowed be Your name. Your kingdom come. Your will be done on earth as it is in heaven. Give us this day our daily bread. And forgive us our debts, as we forgive our debtors. And do not lead us into temptation, but deliver us from the evil one. For Yours is the kingdom and the power and the glory forever. Amen.*

MATTHEW 6:9–13

# A Life of Prayer

## The Great Value of Prayer (Part 2)

---

**Purpose of Session Eleven:** There are many important aspects of prayer. After looking in depth at Jesus's model prayer, we now explore six significant truths of prayer: we pray in faith, sin hinders our prayers, our prayers are ultimately answered by God in accordance with his wisdom and plan, we should pray in accordance with God's will, we can always go to God for grace and mercy, and we should persevere in prayer.

---

## LISTEN: Promises and Faith

There are many passages of Scripture that explain the importance of praying in faith. For example, Jesus said to his disciples: "Have *faith* in God. For assuredly, I say to you, whoever says to this mountain, 'Be removed and be cast into the sea,' and does not doubt in his heart, but *believes* that those things he says will be done, he will have whatever he says. Therefore I say to you, whatever things you ask when you pray, *believe* that you receive them, and you will have them" (Mark 11:22–24).

Throughout the Gospels, Jesus commends people for their faith in him. Notice that the key phrase in this passage of Scripture is "faith *in God*." The faith is not in "faith," and the faith is not in "ourselves," but it is faith *in God*. This means that we are to expect that God *will* carry out his promises. This is the essence of faith—taking God at his word. When God promises something, he wants us to believe him. There are certain conditions, or "qualifiers," that are spelled out in other passages of the Bible, such as 1 John 5:14–15: "Now this is the confidence that we have in Him, that if we ask anything according to His will, He hears us. And if we know that He hears us, whatever we ask, we know that we have the petitions that we have asked of Him." These qualifiers help us understand that the will of God must also be factored in as we exercise faith in God. But the truth is that Christians sometimes simply fail to take God at his word. The Scriptures indicate that a lack of faith is why we are sometimes sadly lacking in our walk with Christ: "You do not have because you do not ask" (James 4:2). One of the best ways to pray is to take some particular promise of God and hold it vividly in your heart and mind as you pray to God. For example, here are a few of the *many* promises of God in the Bible:

- **The promise that God will work all things together for good for us.** Romans 8:28 gives us the promise: "And we know that all things work together for good to those who love God, to those who are the called according to His purpose." This is a promise that no matter how bad a situation may become, God is still working all things together for good. Even when we receive the worst of news, this promise gives us unimaginable hope.
- **The promise that God will give us wisdom when we ask in faith.** James 1:5 states, "If any of you lacks wisdom, let him ask of God, who gives to all liberally and without reproach, and it will be given to him."
- **The promise that God will give us peace.** In Isaiah 26:3 we have the promise: "You will keep him in perfect peace, / Whose mind is stayed on You, / Because he trusts in You."
- **The promise that God will provide a way of escape when you are tempted.** The Lord promises in 1 Corinthians 10:13, "No temptation has overtaken you except such as is common to man; but God is faithful, who will not allow you to be tempted beyond what you are able, but with the temptation will also make the way of escape, that you may be able to bear it."

## ABSORB

**The first significant element of prayer is to pray in faith, believing God's promises as we pray.**

## INTERACT

○ Why do you think believing God's promises is important as we pray?

## Comparing the Promises of God to Cashing a Check

"A promise from God may very instructively be compared to a check payable to order. It is given to the believer with the view of bestowing upon him some good thing. It is not meant that he should read it over comfortably, and then have done with it. No, he is to treat the promise as a reality, as a man treats a check. He is to take the promise, and endorse it with his own name by personally receiving it as true. He is by faith to accept it as his own. He sets to his seal that God is true, and true as to this particular word of promise. He goes further, and believes that he has the blessing in having the sure promise of it, and therefore he puts his name to it to testify to the receipt of the blessing."

**Charles Spurgeon**[a]

[a]*Faith's Checkbook: A Devotional* (New Kensington, PA: Whitaker House, 1992), 5.

○ Take a couple of minutes to scan some of the promises of God listed in the appendix to this session. Pick out one or two promises that capture your attention and talk about why they are encouraging.

## LISTEN: Sin Hinders Our Prayers

Psalm 66:18 states, "If I regard iniquity in my heart, / The Lord will not hear." The writer of the psalm understood that sin can hinder our prayers. When we know something is wrong between us and God—when he points out some particular sin in our hearts, and we choose to hold on to it instead of confessing it and turning from it—then we cannot expect that the Lord will answer our prayers. God doesn't demand perfection before he answers prayer, but our attitude and willingness to turn from sin does play a definite role in how our prayers are answered.

— ABSORB —

**The second significant element of prayer is to know that failure to deal with sin in our hearts can hinder prayer.**

## Prayer and the Acronym "ACTS"

Although the Lord's Prayer is the pattern for prayer that Jesus gave to his disciples, another structure that many Christians have used is given by the acronym "ACTS," which represents adoration, confession, thanksgiving, and supplication (making requests). All four of these are listed in the Bible as important aspects of prayer. Including these four elements in prayer can also be beneficial to make sure that our prayers become "God-focused" rather than simply giving God a "wish list."

- **Adoration.** Adoration is to adore God, to praise, bless, honor, and worship him—to "love the LORD your God with all your heart, with all your soul, with all your mind, and with all your strength" (Mark 12:30).
- **Confession.** Proverbs 28:13 says, "He who covers his sins will not prosper, / But whoever confesses and forsakes them will have mercy."
- **Thanksgiving.** "In everything give thanks; for this is the will of God in Christ Jesus for you" (1 Thess. 5:18).
- **Supplication.** This is making requests of God; it includes intercession, prayer on behalf of others. The apostle Paul says, "Therefore I exhort first of all that supplications, prayers, intercessions, and giving of thanks be made for all men, for kings and all who are in authority, that we may lead a quiet and peaceable life in all godliness and reverence" (1 Tim. 2:1–2).

### INTERACT

○ Imagine yourself as a parent; you ask your child to pick up his toys so that he can go to the store with you to buy a new toy truck that he has been asking for. Your child responds, "No, I don't want to pick them up." You reason with your son, but he still refuses—he simply ignores you. Would you take him immediately to buy the truck or would you wait? Why? Can you see reasons why God would not answer our prayers if we hold on to sin in our hearts?

## LISTEN: Prayer and God's Sovereign Wisdom and Plan

Remember Mark 11:24, which says, "Therefore I say to you, whatever things you ask when you pray, believe that you receive them, and you will have them." As important as faith is to our prayers, there is an even more important factor regarding how our prayers are answered—namely, God's great wisdom and plan. Jesus prayed the night before he was to be crucified, and he asked that it might pass from him. Mark 14:35–36 states, "He went a little farther, and fell on the ground, and prayed that if it were possible, the hour might pass from Him. And He said, 'Abba, Father, all things are possible for You. Take this cup away from Me; nevertheless, not what I will, but what You will.'" The cup Jesus was talking about was the bitter cup of the crucifixion (the violent death on the cross) and even more the sacrifice he was about to make—the wrath of God being poured out on him. Even Jesus, the Son of God, who had unlimited faith in his Father, prayed to his Father to "take this cup away from Me; nevertheless, not what I will, but what You will." Even Jesus was willing to submit to the ultimate will of his Father. This is perfect humility and a perfect example of what our attitude should be when we ask God to answer our prayers.

A common question that Christians ask is, "Why does God seem to not answer some of my prayers?" There are several passages in the Bible that promise that when we bring a real need before God he will answer the prayers of his children. For example, Psalm 50:15 says, "Call upon Me in the day of trouble; / I will deliver you, and you shall glorify Me." Charles Spurgeon gives an excellent analysis of such promises:

> God may . . . subject us to many trials. Yet, if He says, "*I will deliver you,*" you can be sure that He will keep His word. When you get God's "*I will,*" you may always cash it by faith. God's promise for the future is a bona fide offer for the present, if you simply have faith to use it. "*Call upon me in the day of trouble: I will deliver you*" is tantamount to deliverance already received. It means, "*If I do not deliver you now, I will deliver you at a time that is better than now. You would prefer to be delivered at this future time rather than now if you were as wise as I am.*"
>
> Promptness is implied in God's promise of deliverance, for a late deliverance is not truly deliverance. "Ah," someone says, "I am in such trouble that if I do not get deliverance soon I will die of grief." Rest assured that you will not die of despair. You will be delivered before you die that way. God will deliver you at the best possible time. The Lord is always punctual. You never were kept waiting by Him. You have kept Him waiting many times, but He is prompt to the instant. He never keeps His servants waiting one single tick of the clock beyond His own appointed, fitting, wise, and proper moment. "*I will deliver you*" implies that His delays will not be too long, lest the spirit of man should fail because of hope deferred. The Lord rides on the wings of the wind when He comes to the rescue of those who seek Him. Therefore, be courageous![1]

— **ABSORB** —

**The third significant element of prayer is to know that the ultimate determining factor as to how our prayers are answered is the sovereign wisdom and plan of God.**

─── **INTERACT** ───

○ Spurgeon points out that if God does not deliver you at the very time when you call out to him, then he will deliver you at a time that is better than now; and you would actually prefer to be delivered at this future time rather than now if you were as wise as God. Is Spurgeon's explanation helpful to you? Why?

○ If Jesus himself was willing to say, "Nevertheless, not what I will, but what You will," then how should we approach our Father with our deep desires when we pray?

## LISTEN: Pray in Accordance with God's Will

Christ gives us a great open invitation: "Whatever things you ask when you pray, believe that you receive them, and you will have them" (Mark 11:24). As you compare Scripture with Scripture you discover that there is an underlying qualification that Christ taught in John 14:13: "And whatever you ask in My name, that I will do, that the Father may be glorified in the Son."

This verse says that in some way, what we ask for should have as its aim *to glorify God*. To pray in Jesus's name means more than just attaching the phrase "in Jesus's name" to the end of our prayers. To pray in Jesus's name means that we understand who Jesus is and have faith and confidence in him as the Son of God whom the Father sent. It means we are confident that God will answer our prayers because Jesus is our mediator. Again, we must remember that God never intended prayer to be a kind of Aladdin's magic lamp. Prayer has a purpose—to bring honor and glory to God. If we use prayer in a way that does not tie into God's glory, then we should not be surprised when such prayers go unanswered. James 4:2–3 helps us to understand this: "You do not have because you do not ask. You ask and do not receive, because you ask amiss, that you may spend *it* on your pleasures." John reiterates that when we pray, we should ask in accordance with his will: "Now this is the confidence that we have in Him, that if we ask anything *according to His will*, He hears us" (1 John 5:14).

## ABSORB

**The fourth significant element of prayer is to pray in accordance with God's will for your life. Also, answered prayer is for the glory of God.**

## INTERACT

○ What do you think would happen if God answered every prayer of every Christian at all times?

## LISTEN: Praying When You Need Grace and Mercy

One of the reasons why we as Christians sometimes stop praying for a time is because we feel shame for failing God and conclude that we have no right to ask him for anything. However, notice what the New Testament says about coming before the Lord in prayer: "Let us therefore come boldly [with confidence] to the throne of grace, that we may obtain mercy and find grace to help in time of need" (Heb. 4:16). A humble attitude allows us to receive God's grace and mercy.

> The prayer power has never been tried to its full capacity. If we want to see mighty wonders of divine power and grace wrought in the place of weakness, failure and disappointment, let us answer God's standing challenge, "Call unto me, and I will answer thee, and show thee great and mighty things which thou knowest not!"
>
> —**J. Hudson Taylor (1832–1905), missionary to China**

## ABSORB

**The fifth significant element of prayer is to know that when we do not feel deserving we can still go to God in prayer and receive grace and mercy.**

## INTERACT

○ When do we need mercy? In this passage, "grace" refers to God's kind favor that we don't deserve. How would it help you to pray, knowing that God is ready to grant to you grace even when you have fallen short of how he wants you to think and live?

## LISTEN: Perseverance in Prayer

I never prayed sincerely and earnestly for anything but it came at some time; no matter at how distant a day, somehow, in some shape, probably the least I would have devised, it came.

**—Adoniram Judson, missionary to Burma**

Jesus told the disciples a parable to help them (and us) think deeply about the importance of persevering in prayer:

> Then He [Jesus] spoke a parable to them, that men always ought to pray and not lose heart, saying: "There was in a certain city a judge who did not fear God nor regard man. Now there was a widow in that city; and she came to him, saying, 'Get justice for me from my adversary.' And he would not for a while; but afterward he said within himself, 'Though I do not fear God nor regard man, yet because this widow troubles me I will avenge her, lest by her continual coming she weary me.'"
>
> Then the Lord said, "Hear what the unjust judge said. And shall God not avenge His own elect who cry out day and night to Him, though He bears long with them? I tell you that He will avenge them speedily. Nevertheless, when the Son of Man comes, will He really find faith on the earth?" (Luke 18:1–8)

The point of the parable is not to say that God is like the unjust judge, but that if an uncompassionate and unjust judge would respond to persistent pleas, how much more will our compassionate and just God respond to those who do not give up in prayer? This is a parable to teach that God does not want us to become discouraged when our prayers are not immediately answered. He does not want us to give up. In the Sermon on the Mount, Jesus taught us to keep asking, keep seeking, and keep knocking:

> Ask, and it will be given to you; seek, and you will find; knock, and it will be opened to you. For everyone who asks receives, and he who seeks finds, and to him who knocks it will be opened. Or what man is there among you who, if his son asks for bread, will give him a stone? Or if he asks for a fish, will he give him a serpent? If you then, being evil, know how to give good gifts to your children, how much more will your Father who is in heaven give good things to those who ask Him! (Matt. 7:7–11)

### — ABSORB —

**The sixth significant element of prayer is to persevere in prayer. Do not give up—do not lose heart!**

### — INTERACT —

○ What is it about Jesus's parable of the unjust judge that motivates you to want to be strong and steadfast in prayer?

○ If you had one prayer that you desire God to answer, what would that prayer be?

## LISTEN: Practical Advice for Spiritual Apathy

John Piper, in his book *When I Don't Desire God*, gives some practical advice that may help when we feel apathetic toward prayer (and reading the Word) or when we become "mechanical" in prayer and simply pray about things that are not very important. Piper candidly reveals that as he looks at his own prayer life he can see how easy it is to focus primarily on peripherals, such as asking God to make his day go well or asking God for a safe trip. He points out that circumstances are not unimportant but that God wants to change our hearts, not necessarily give us a life of ease. Piper says that almost every day he prays that God would give him desires for God and his Word:

> I follow the acronym myself that I have given to many people to help them fight for joy. The acronym is *IOUS*. . . . Here's the way I pray over the Word in my fight for joy.
>
> **I—(Incline!)** The first thing my soul needs is an inclination toward God and his Word. Without that, nothing else will happen of any value in my life. I must want to know God and read his Word and draw near to him. Where does that "want to" come from? It comes from God. So Psalm 119:36 teaches us to pray, "Incline my heart to your testimonies, and not to selfish gain!" Very simply we ask God to take our hearts, which are more inclined to breakfast and the newspaper, and change that inclination. We are asking that God create desires that are not there.
>
> **O—(Open!)** Next I need to have the eyes of my heart opened so that when my inclination leads me to the Word, I see what is really there, and not just my own ideas. Who opens the eyes of the heart? God does. So Psalm 119:18 teaches us to pray, "Open my eyes, that I may behold wondrous things out of your law." So many times we read the Bible and see nothing wonderful. Its reading does not produce joy. So what can we do? We can cry to God: "Open the eyes of my heart, O Lord, to see what it says about you as wonderful."
>
> **U—(Unite!)** Then I am concerned that my heart is badly fragmented. Parts of it are inclined, and parts of it are not. Parts see wonder, and parts say, "That's not so wonderful." What I long for is a united heart where all the parts say a joyful Yes! to what God reveals in his Word. Where does that wholeness and unity come from? It comes from God. So Psalm 86:11 teaches us to pray, "Unite my heart to fear your name." Don't stumble over the word fear when you thought we were seeking joy. The fear of the Lord is a joyful experience when you renounce all sin. A thunderstorm can be a trembling joy when you know you can't be destroyed by lightning. "O Lord, let your ear be attentive to . . . the prayer of your servants who delight to fear your name" (Neh. 1:11 ESV).

It is not enough to begin to pray, nor to pray aright [correctly]; nor is it enough to continue for a time to pray; but we must patiently, believingly, continue in prayer until we obtain an answer. And further, we have not only to continue in prayer unto the end, but we have also to believe that God does hear us, and will answer our prayers. Most frequently we fail in not continuing in prayer until the blessing is obtained and in not expecting the blessing.

**—George Mueller**

"His delight shall be in the fear the LORD" (Isa. 11:3). Therefore pray that God would unite your heart to joyfully fear the Lord.

S—(**Satisfy!**) What I really want from all this engagement with the Word of God and the work of his Spirit in answer to my prayers is for my heart to be satisfied with God and not with the world. Where does that satisfaction come from? It comes from God. So Psalm 90:14 teaches us to pray, "Satisfy us in the morning with your steadfast love, that we may rejoice and be glad all our days."[2]

## ABSORB

### When you don't feel like praying, you can pray that God would give you desires for him and his Word.

## INTERACT

○ The famous missionary to China, Amy Carmichael, said: "Learn to live in your will, not your feelings." What did she mean, and how does this apply to praying and seeking God?

**Reflect:** Are you actually living life in the face of God's promises? Consider going through the promises of God listed in the appendix to this session, picking out some of them, and praying those promises to God. Remember that when you pray for the salvation of a loved one or friend, that could be one of the most significant activities you could do.

There are many elements to prayer. The more we understand what the Scriptures have to say about prayer, the more we will be prepared to live a sustained life of fervent prayer. What is the most pressing thing in your life that I can be praying for you until we meet for the next session?

## CULTIVATING SPIRITUAL HABITS

**Read:** Proverbs 2:1–3:5

**Journal:** Write out a prayer to God based on ACTS or IOUS.

## Memorize

*Be anxious for nothing, but in everything by prayer and supplication, with thanksgiving, let your requests be made known to God; and the peace of God, which surpasses all understanding, will guard your hearts and minds through Christ Jesus.*

PHILIPPIANS 4:6–7

# Key Promises of God to Know and Memorize

Knowing some of the key promises of the Bible will be especially helpful in strengthening your faith. Utilizing God's promises when you pray will add a stunning dynamic to your prayer life. Memorizing these verses will benefit you for the rest of your life.

**Joshua 1:9** Have I not commanded you? Be strong and of good courage; do not be afraid, nor be dismayed, for the Lord your God is with you wherever you go.

**Psalm 30:5** For His anger is but for a moment, / His favor is for life; / Weeping may endure for a night, / But joy comes in the morning.

**Psalm 31:24** Be of good courage, / And He shall strengthen your heart, / All you who hope in the Lord.

**Psalm 33:18** Behold, the eye of the Lord is on those who fear Him, / On those who hope in His mercy.

**Psalm 34:10** The young lions lack and suffer hunger; / But those who seek the Lord shall not lack any good thing.

**Psalm 34:17** The righteous cry out, and the Lord hears, / And delivers them out of all their troubles.

**Psalm 34:19** Many are the afflictions of the righteous, / But the Lord delivers him out of them all.

**Psalm 46:1–2** God is our refuge and strength, / A very present help in trouble. / Therefore we will not fear, / Even though the earth be removed, / And though the mountains be carried into the midst of the sea.

**Psalm 50:15** Call upon Me in the day of trouble; / I will deliver you, and you shall glorify Me.

**Psalm 84:11** For the Lord God is a sun and shield; / The Lord will give grace and glory; / No good thing will He withhold / From those who walk uprightly.

**Psalm 103:8** The Lord is merciful and gracious, / Slow to anger, and abounding in mercy.

**Psalm 103:17** But the mercy of the LORD is from everlasting to everlasting / On those who fear Him, / And His righteousness to children's children.

**Psalm 145:18–19** The LORD is near to all who call upon Him, / To all who call upon Him in truth. / He will fulfill the desire of those who fear Him; / He also will hear their cry and save them.

**Isaiah 41:10** Fear not, for I am with you; / Be not dismayed, for I am your God. / I will strengthen you, / Yes, I will help you, / I will uphold you with My righteous right hand.

**Isaiah 54:17** "No weapon formed against you shall prosper, / And every tongue which rises against you in judgment / You shall condemn. / This is the heritage of the servants of the LORD, / And their righteousness is from Me," / Says the LORD.

**Jeremiah 32:40** And I will make an everlasting covenant with them, that I will not turn away from doing them good; but I will put My fear in their hearts so that they will not depart from Me.

**Jeremiah 33:3** Call to Me, and I will answer you, and show you great and mighty things, which you do not know.

**Matthew 6:33** But seek first the kingdom of God and His righteousness, and all these things shall be added to you.

**Matthew 7:11** If you then, being evil, know how to give good gifts to your children, how much more will your Father who is in heaven give good things to those who ask Him!

**Luke 6:38** Give, and it will be given to you: good measure, pressed down, shaken together, and running over will be put into your bosom. For with the same measure that you use, it will be measured back to you.

**John 14:13–14** And whatever you ask in My name, that will I do, that the Father may be glorified in the Son. If you ask anything in My name, I will do it.

**John 14:27** Peace I leave with you, My peace I give to you; not as the world gives do I give to you. Let not your heart be troubled, neither let it be afraid.

**Philippians 4:6–7** Be anxious for nothing, but in everything by prayer and supplication, with thanksgiving, let your requests be made known to God; and the peace of God, which surpasses all understanding, will guard your hearts and minds through Christ Jesus.

**Philippians 4:19** And my God shall supply all your need according to His riches in glory by Christ Jesus.

**2 Timothy 1:7** For God has not given us a spirit of fear, but of power and of love and of a sound mind.

**1 John 5:14–15** Now this is the confidence that we have in Him, that if we ask anything according to His will, He hears us. And if we know that He hears us, whatever we ask, we know that we have the petitions that we have asked of Him.

# Understanding God's Will

## The Guidance of God (Part 1)

**Purpose of Session Twelve:** This session and the next focus on how God guides us as his children. While there is no secret technique to determining God's plan, there are a number of things we can do to be guided by God. In these two sessions, we first clarify what the "will of God" means (and doesn't mean), then we look at seven specific ways God guides us (three in this session, four in the next). In this session we look at reading the Word, praying, and delighting in the Lord.

## LISTEN: A Life Filled with Choices

Every day we are faced with choices and decisions. Sometimes the choices seem insignificant, such as what to eat for lunch or which route to take to work. At other times the choices seem much larger, such as whom to marry or what job to pursue. We all have big questions in our lives: What college should I attend? What life goals should I pursue? Should I buy or rent a home? Should I trust that person? Should I make a particular costly investment? This session and the next will help you understand how to follow God's guidance in all your plans, decisions, and choices in life. God offers us sufficient guidance so that we can make choices that are in sync with his good pleasure—his will. Paul prays for Christians that we would be filled with the knowledge of his will, with the goal to live in such a way as to be fully pleasing to him. Colossians 1:9–10 states: "For this reason we also, since the day we heard it, do not cease to pray for you, and to ask that you may be filled with the knowledge of His will in all wisdom and spiritual understanding; that you may walk worthy of the Lord, fully pleasing Him." The goal of these sessions is to offer biblical answers about how to be filled with the knowledge of God's will and how to be fully pleasing to him.

---

## ABSORB

### God offers us sufficient guidance so that we can make choices that are pleasing to the Lord.

---

## INTERACT

○ What have been some of the most important decisions that you have made in your life? Choose one of those important decisions and try to think back to how you came to the decision you made.

The will of God is one of the most confusing phrases in the Christian vocabulary.

—**Kevin DeYoung,**
***Just Do Something***

## LISTEN: Clarifying the Meaning of the "Will of God"

There are few things more confusing than when people talk about the will of God. If there ever was a need for clarity, it is in defining what is meant by the "will of God." Good theologians have been very precise in their definitions.

The phrase "the will of God" is sometimes used in Scripture to refer to God's eternal plan or what theologians call the "sovereign will" of God. This "sovereign will" is mentioned in Ephesians 1:11: "In Him also we have obtained an inheritance, being predestined according to the purpose of Him who works all things according to the counsel of *His will*." The *sovereign will* is God's all-inclusive plan in which he makes all things conform to his will. The "all things" include even the evil, disobedient acts of his creatures. For example, in the Old Testament, Joseph's brothers treated him cruelly and sinfully, and they intended evil against Joseph. Even though the brothers violated the moral law of God and were responsible for their own disobedience, the Lord had a higher plan (a higher purpose or will) and used their treacherous behavior for good. Joseph clearly understood that God had an ultimate *sovereign will* when he said to his brothers, "But as for you, *you meant evil against me; but God meant it for good*" (Gen. 50:20). No one can stop or thwart the sovereign will of God: "For I am God, and there is no other; / I am God, and there is none like Me, / Declaring the end from the beginning, / And from ancient times things that are not yet done, / Saying, 'My counsel shall stand, / And I will do all My pleasure'" (Isa. 46:9–10). The Scriptures are clear that God's

Sometimes God allows what He hates to accomplish what He loves.

**—Joni Eareckson Tada,** *The God I Love*

sovereign will rules over all: "For I know that the LORD is great, / And our Lord is above all gods. *Whatever the LORD pleases He does*, / In heaven and in earth" (Ps. 135:5–6). The sovereign will of God rules and overrules all the plans and actions of mankind! Some theologians also call God's sovereign will *God's will of decree* because it is immutable and fixed.

## ABSORB

The sovereign will of God is his all-inclusive plan in which he works all things according to the counsel of his will. God's sovereign plan is greater than the disobedient choices of his creatures and the consequences of those evil choices. Nothing happens without his direction or active permission. God's sovereign will is what he ordains to come to pass. It ultimately rules and overrules everything and brings him the highest glory.

## INTERACT

○ If God was not in ultimate control over everything, then who would be ultimately ruling in the end? Are you glad that God rules and overrules the evil acts of his creatures?

## LISTEN: God's "Sovereign Will" versus God's "Prescriptive Will"

Even though God has an all-inclusive sovereign will, which is referred to as "his will," there is another sense in which the Bible uses the term "will of God." Sometimes the term "will of God" is used in the sense of what could be called the "prescriptive will" of God (also called God's "moral will" or "will of command" or "will of desire").[1] God's prescriptive will is what God commands of us. God's prescriptive will is like a doctor's *prescription* that, if taken, has beneficial effects, but it can be refused. For example, the New Testament clearly states: "For this is the *will of God*, your sanctification: that you should abstain from sexual immorality" (1 Thess. 4:3). We know it is God's will (his prescriptive will) that we abstain from sexual immorality. It is obvious that God's will in this sense is often not obeyed by people. When Jesus taught us to pray "Your will be done / On earth as it is in heaven" (Matt. 6:10), Christ was assuming that God's will (his *prescriptive will*) is not always obeyed here on earth. This prescriptive will of God would not only include the clear commands and instructions from the Word but also the wise discernment and wisdom that is the outworking of knowing his Word and having a close relationship with God. God desires for his children to make wise decisions, and he wants us to know, as it says in Proverbs 2:9, "every good path" to take in the choices before us in life. This prescriptive will would also include God's *disposition* or *attitude* toward good and evil.

Therefore when we seek to know how God guides us, we are seeking to know how God brings our hearts and minds into harmony with his heart, his desires, and his good pleasure. God wants us to follow and acquire wisdom and discernment so that we make choices that fully please him.

So throughout these two sessions we will focus on how to understand the *prescriptive will* of God—which includes any directions and decisions that God desires for us to choose. Whenever God intends for us to know what path to choose in a particular decision in his guidance of us, then because it is "knowable," it falls within the prescriptive will of God.

## — ABSORB —

> God's prescriptive will is what God desires for us to choose in his guidance for our lives. God's prescriptive will is like a doctor's prescription that, if taken, has beneficial effects but also can be refused. This prescriptive will of God not only includes the clear commands and instructions from the Word but also the wise discernment and wisdom that is the outworking of knowing his Word and having a close relationship with him.

The *sovereign will* of God is how things are; the *prescriptive will* of God is how things ought to be.

## — INTERACT —

○ Can you see why there is confusion if you don't clarify the difference between the *sovereign will* and the *prescriptive will* of God? How would you help a ten-year-old understand the difference?

## LISTEN: Questionable Techniques to Finding God's Will

Old Testament scholar Bruce Waltke makes an excellent observation when he writes in his book *Finding the Will of God*:

If we accept the fact that our heavenly Father loves us, and that we are His children, does it make sense that He would hide His will from us? Many Christians talk about "the will of God" as though it were a version of the old con man's ruse, the three-shell game. You remember the game: A pea is hidden under a walnut shell; two other walnut shells are placed on either side of the first, then all three are quickly moved around the table. The con man then asks you, the spectator or "mark," to guess which shell the pea is under. No matter which shell you guess, you are always wrong. . . .

When I hear Christians talking about the will of God, they often use phrases such as "If only I could find God's will," as though He is keeping it hidden from them, or "I'm praying that I'll discover His will for my life," because they apparently believe the Lord doesn't want them to find it, or that He wants to make it as hard as possible for them to find so that they will prove their worth. . . .

God guides His people to do His pleasure. It is imperative that we grasp the fact that the Lord guides us rather than hides from us. He doesn't sit back and play games with His children. Instead, He offers us clear guidance for living our lives to please Him.[2]

Although God wants his people to know his will—his desires for our lives—oftentimes Christians will engage in unusual ways to try to determine the will of God.

Author and pastor Charles Swindoll writes about a college student who needed a car:

He didn't know which one God would have him purchase, but as a Christian, he was determined to find God's will before he bought anything. One night, he had a series of dreams. Everything in his dreams was yellow. He had his answer. After checking out several used car lots the next day, he finally found the one he was sure the Lord would have him buy. You guessed it. Yellow inside and out. He didn't bother to check it out. He didn't even give it a trial run around the block. It was yellow, so he bought it. Appropriately, it turned out to be a lemon."[3]

Waltke tells the fictional story of Douglas, a teenager who was active in his church youth group and who wanted to discern God's will for his social life:

So Douglas has worked out a system for Friday nights.

First he makes a list of the girls he wants to take out on a date. Then he begins phoning, starting at the top of the list. If the line is busy, he takes that as God's sign that he is not to date that girl. If no one answers, he is to wait and try again later. If the phone rings and the gal he's interested in answers, that means God has given His blessing for Douglas to ask her out.[4]

As you study the New Testament, you discover that the way God normally[5] guides his new covenant people as they seek him for guidance is not by questionable techniques, signs, hunches, fleeces, and so on, but by believers "answering the call to walk close to the Lord and be conformed to his likeness. Only then will we have the heart of God to know what pleases him."[6]

God's prescriptive will includes the discerning application of the Scriptures to new situations in life by having our minds renewed (as described in Romans 12:1–2).[7] The rest of these two sessions will focus on seven key ways God guides us.[8]

---

### ABSORB

**The way God normally guides his new covenant people as they seek him for guidance is not by questionable techniques, signs, hunches, fleeces, and so on, but by believers answering the call to walk close with the Lord and be conformed to Christ's likeness. Only then will we have the heart of God to know what pleases him.**

---

### INTERACT

○ Do you think that these methods (paying attention to the colors in our dreams and assuming busy signals were meaningful) were good ways to seek and follow the guidance of God?

○ In Proverbs 2, the personification of wisdom gives a challenge: "If you receive my words, / And treasure my commands within you, / So that you incline your ear to wisdom, / And apply your heart to understanding; / Yes, if you cry out for discernment, / . . . / If you seek [understanding] as silver, / And . . . hidden treasures; / . . . / Then you will understand righteousness and justice, / Equity and every good path" (vv. 1–4, 9). What do you think is the main point of wisdom's challenge?

## LISTEN: Explicit Instructions from God

God has *already* told us in his Word much of what his will is for our lives. In fact, there are passages that even explicitly tell us that certain things *are the will of God*:

Rejoice always, pray without ceasing, in everything give thanks; for this is the *will of God* in Christ Jesus for you. (1 Thess. 5:16–18)

For this is the *will of God*, your sanctification: that you should abstain from sexual immorality. (1 Thess. 4:3)

Therefore do not be unwise, but understand what the *will of the Lord* is. And do not be drunk with wine, in which is dissipation; but be filled with the Spirit. (Eph. 5:17–18)

For this is the *will of God*, that by doing good you may put to silence the ignorance of foolish men. (1 Pet. 2:15)

According to these verses, God's will for your life is to be joyful, to pray, to give thanks in everything, to abstain from sexual immorality, to not get drunk but be filled with the Spirit, and to do good. You can know for sure that these things are the will of God for your life. In fact, whenever God gives instructions to us or tells us to refrain from doing something, then we can know with clarity that God is telling us that this is his will for our lives! Therefore, the more we read his Word, the more potential we have to understand the will of God for our lives.

God gives us guidance throughout the Word. He tells us to "love your enemies," "to forgive those who have trespassed against you," "to seek first the kingdom of God," to "judge not, that you be not judged," to "not worry about tomorrow," to "love the Lord Your God with all your heart . . . and to love your neighbor as yourself," and so on. All Scripture helps us to know God's will (2 Tim. 3:16)!

## — ABSORB —

### Much of the will of God for our lives has already been spelled out in detail in the Scriptures.

## INTERACT

○ If Christians simply followed the will of God in all the obvious things that God reveals to us in his Word, do you think our lives would have a much greater impact for good in this world?

○ Why is it that we can become fixated on trying to discover the will of God concerning what car to buy but miss out on the importance of God's will as to how we are to treat people, or how joyful we should be, or how we should be passionate about sharing the gospel with a dying world?

## LISTEN: Interpreting and Applying the Word Accurately

An important part of reading the Scriptures is knowing how to interpret the Word according to the original way that God intended it to be understood. Second Timothy 2:15 highlights the importance of "rightly dividing the word of truth": "Be diligent to present yourself approved to God, a worker who does not need to be ashamed, rightly dividing [correctly explaining] the word of truth." The more we understand God's Word, the more we will understand his will for our lives.

Romans 12:1–2 are key verses in understanding the process of how we begin to experience the will of the Lord: "I beseech you therefore, brethren, by the mercies of God, that you present your bodies a living sacrifice, holy, acceptable to God, which is your reasonable service. And do not be conformed to this world, but be transformed by the renewing of your mind, that you may prove what is that good and acceptable and perfect will of God."

---

### Romans 12:1—Dedicating Our Lives

"Paul Little wrote, 'So many of us see God as a kind of celestial Scrooge who peers over the balcony of heaven trying to find anybody who is enjoying life. And when he spots a happy person, he yells, "Now cut that out!" That concept of God should make us shudder because it's blasphemous!'

"God is not some cosmic kill-joy who delights in taking advantage of people who are foolish enough to submit their wills to His. The one who loved us enough to sacrifice His Son to save us when we were His enemies (Rom. 5:8–10) is certainly worthy of our trust now that we are His children. 'He who did not spare His own Son, but delivered Him up for us all, how will He not also with Him freely give us all things?' (Rom. 8:32). We don't need to 'surrender to God's will' as though we were resigning ourselves to a somber and joyless existence. Instead, we can say with David, 'I delight to do Your will, O my God' (Ps. 40:8), knowing that He loves us enough to desire a destiny for us that is beyond our highest hopes."

**Kenneth Boa[a]**

[a]"Discerning the Will of God," http://www.kenboa.org/text_resources/free_articles/5335.

---

The process goes like this:

For Christians, discovering God's will begins with the dedication of our lives to God. This dedication must involve two continual actions: Renunciation and Renewal. As we continually *renounce* the norms of behavior typical of pagan culture (see Gal. 5:19–20 and Lam. 3:13–16), and *renew* our minds, our lives will be ordered consistent with our dedication to God.

In these verses *dedication* leads to *discernment*. By dedicating ourselves, we ". . . may prove what the will of God is, that which is good and acceptable and perfect." [Everett Harrison states,] "It appears from the context that the believer is not viewed as ignorant of the will of God, but as needing to avoid blurring its outline by failure to renew the mind continually."[9]

John Piper says, "What is necessary is that we have a renewed mind, that is so shaped and so governed by the revealed will of God in the Bible, that we see and assess all relevant factors with the mind of Christ, and discern what God is calling us to do. This is very different from constantly trying to hear God's voice saying do this and do that. People who try to lead their lives by hearing voices are not in sync with Romans 12:2."[10]

As we *read* (and interpret accurately) and *meditate* on God's Word, we begin to grow close to God so that we can live out his good and perfect will—we begin to live to please him. As we know his Word, it is only then that we will have the heart of God to know what pleases him.

Also, there are a great many giants of the faith who have stressed not just reading the Word but reading it and praying about it—that is, talking with God about what you are reading. It keeps reading from being just an intellectual or academic exercise.

### ABSORB

**The first way God guides us is through our reading and meditating on his Word.**

### INTERACT

○ Have you ever known someone who claimed he or she was being led by God to do something, but you knew that what he or she was doing was not the will of God? How did you know?

○ What is the best way to renew your mind?

## LISTEN: Prayer and the Guidance of God

In the New Testament James talks about the importance of *asking* God for wisdom: "If any of you lacks wisdom, let him *ask of God*, who gives to all liberally and without reproach, and it will be given to him. But let him ask in faith" (James 1:5–6).

When God promises to give wisdom to those who ask in faith, we can know that it is an important means to follow the guidance of God! However, there needs to be a word of caution. Sometimes Christians pray about something, and because they have prayed about it they assume their decision is the right one. Prayer alone does not make our choices infallible. There are other factors involved (as these two sessions demonstrate). But prayer and spending time with God can temper our hearts to be more open and ready to make decisions that are sometimes hard to make. A willing spirit to do whatever God wants us to do is valuable in the sight of God. And passages such as James 1:5–6 do mean something. God does give his people wisdom to make good decisions!

### ABSORB

**The second way God guides us is through our praying and asking God for wisdom.**

### INTERACT

○ When you ask God for wisdom, how do you know when you receive it?

---

## Just Do Something!

"Obsessing over the future is not how God wants us to live, because showing us the future is not God's way. His way is to speak to us in the Scriptures and transform us by the renewing of our minds (Rom. 12:1–2). His way is not a crystal ball. His way is wisdom. We should stop looking for God to reveal the future to us and remove all risk from our lives. We should start looking to God—His character and His promises—and thereby have confidence to take risks for His name's sake."

**Kevin DeYoung**[a]

[a]*Just Do Something: A Liberating Approach to Finding God's Will* (Chicago: Moody, 2009), 41.

## LISTEN: Delight Yourself in the Lord

In the fourth and fifth centuries there was a famous Christian leader—Augustine of Hippo—who gave a sermon on 1 John in which he made a statement that is often quoted: "Love and do what you please." His intent behind this statement was that if you have God-saturated love guiding your motives, you will be making good choices. In other words, "Love God and do what you please." Augustine's words are a reflection of the important truth in Psalm 37:4, which tells us that as we delight in God then we are able to begin to love what he loves, and our very desires are being shaped by him: "Delight yourself also in the LORD, / And He shall give you the desires of your heart."

Bruce Waltke captures the application of this verse when he writes:

> One way I know God's will is by the desires of my heart. The Holy Spirit puts my desires into me, so I am convinced that I am pleasing God by doing what He would have me do.
>
> So often it seems that Christians are not sure what they should do in a particular situation, or they become flustered waiting for God to "give them a sign," when all they really need to consider is the desire of their heart. You see, if you are walking close to the Lord, and He shapes your character and influences your life, then He also is shaping your desires. . . .
>
> This does not mean that God is a genie, granting you magic wishes whenever you come before Him, but that He shapes your heart after He has cleansed it of all sin, so that your desires correspond to His. . . . The things you long for in your heart are put there by the Holy Spirit.

Instead of focusing on divining a detailed road map for our every decision, God calls us into a relationship with him, a relationship that will then shape the decisions we make. Waltke helpfully summarizes this when he says, "Within the framework of loving God and your fellow man, you are free to follow the desires of your heart."[11]

Augustine was essentially on target—Love God and do as you please! Of course there are other key factors (discussed in the next session) to confirm your decisions as you seek to follow God's guidance.

---

#### ABSORB

**The third way God guides us is our delighting in God: "Delight yourself also in the LORD, / And He shall give you the desires of your heart" (Ps. 37:4).**

========== **INTERACT** ==========

○ Does Waltke's point above make sense to you? How can following your desires help you to make future decisions in your life?

**Reflect:** Think about how much more your life could benefit this world by simply carrying out Christ's golden rule ("whatever you want men to do to you, do also to them") in a more consistent way!

This session teaches in part how to be filled with the knowledge of God's will. Three indispensable factors are the Word, prayer, and delighting yourself in the Lord. The Lord is amazing in how he guides us in this world. What is something for which you need wisdom that I can be praying for you until we meet for the next session?

## CULTIVATING SPIRITUAL HABITS

**Read:** Romans 12:1–2; Philippians 1:9–10; Colossians 1:9–10; Ephesians 5:15–17; Proverbs 9:10; 15:33; Job 28:28; 1 Peter 1:17

**Journal:** Read through the appendix to this session and write down your thoughts and prayers concerning confessing, yielding, asking, and believing.

### Memorize

> *Delight yourself also in the LORD,*
> *And He shall give you the desires of your heart.*

> PSALM 37:4

# The Will of God and the Holy Spirit

God's Word reveals that it is *his will* that we be filled with the Spirit; Ephesians 5:17–18 states: "Therefore do not be unwise, but understand what the *will of the Lord* is. And do not be drunk with wine, in which is dissipation; but *be filled with the Spirit.*" When a person is filled with wine it controls his or her behavior; instead of wine controlling us we are to be controlled by the Holy Spirit. *To be filled with the Spirit includes being empowered and emboldened for service, passionate about what the Holy Spirit is passionate about, full of joy, and submissive to God, with the Word of Christ richly dwelling in your heart.* There has been much discussion among churches and denominations about how to be filled with the Spirit, but there remains a consensus among diverse Christian leaders that four elements are foundational to be filled with the Spirit:

1. **Confess all known sin.** Psalm 66:18 says: "If I regard iniquity in my heart, / The Lord will not hear." If we are to ask the Lord to fill us with his Spirit then we must let go of any sin that we are holding on to. Confession and repentance are recurring themes throughout both the Old and New Testaments for returning and drawing near to God.

2. **Yield your life to God.** Romans 6:13 says: "Present yourselves to God as being alive from the dead, and your members as instruments of righteousness to God." Also Romans 12:1 says: "I beseech you therefore, brethren, by the mercies of God, that you present your bodies a living sacrifice, holy, acceptable to God, which is your reasonable service."

3. **Ask God to fill you with his Spirit.** "Asking" is a requirement to make sure we understand that we are totally dependent on God and so that we realize the glory belongs to him. Jesus himself taught us to ask: "Ask, and it will be given to you; seek, and you will find; knock, and it will be opened to you. For everyone who asks receives, and he who seeks finds, and to him who knocks it will be opened. Or what man is there among you who, if his son asks for bread, will give him a stone? Or if he asks for a fish, will he give him a serpent? If you then, being

evil, know how to give good gifts to your children, how much more will your Father who is in heaven give good things to those who ask Him!" (Matt. 7:7–11).[12]

4. **Believe and trust God that he will answer your prayer.** Jesus clearly encourages us that when we pray and ask God for things within his will, then we are to believe that we receive them: "Therefore I say to you, whatever things you ask when you pray, believe that you receive them, and you will have them" (Mark 11:24). This act of asking to be filled with the Spirit involves faith: "The just shall live by faith" (Rom. 1:17; Gal. 3:11). Also we know this is the will of God to be filled with the Spirit; therefore we can confidently ask of God. Remember 1 John 5:14–15: "Now this is the confidence that we have in Him, that if we ask anything according to His will, He hears us. And if we know that He hears us, whatever we ask, we know that we have the petitions that we have asked of Him."

Because we oftentimes give in to the desires of the flesh, we must come back to this command frequently: "be filled with the Spirit." John Piper presents a candid picture of reality when he says: "Nobody stays full of the Spirit all the time—no one is always totally joyful and submissive to God and empowered for service. But this should still be our aim, our goal, our great longing."[13] This is a lifestyle process where we regularly ask God to fill us with his Spirit. The Scriptures tell us: "Draw near to God and He will draw near to you" (James 4:8).

The value of being filled with the Holy Spirit is that it allows our hearts to be humble and open to following the guidance of God.

# Knowing God's Will

## The Guidance of God (Part 2)

**Purpose of Session Thirteen:** This is a continuation of the last session, where we focus on how God guides us. While there is no secret technique to determining God's plan, there are a number of things we can do to be guided by God.[1] In this session we look at seeking wise counsel, evaluating circumstances, using sound judgment, and experiencing divine intervention.

## LISTEN: The Will of God Is Good

God is most glorified in us when we are most satisfied in Him.

**—John Piper,** *God's Passion for His Glory*

One of the most important things to understand about the will of God is simply that the will of God is good! Unless we are convinced that what God commands of us and desires for us to choose is good, we will struggle with wanting to search out God's will for our lives. Genesis records that the very first temptation was when the Tempter enticed Eve to doubt that God's will was good when God commanded her not to eat from the forbidden tree. The Tempter implanted the insidious doubt in Eve's mind: "For God knows that in the day you eat of it your eyes will be opened, and you will be like God, knowing good and evil" (Gen. 3:5). Yet God explains in great detail that his will for us is always what will give us the greatest ultimate happiness for our lives. He doesn't want to withhold anything from us that is good: "No good thing will He withhold / From those who walk uprightly" (Ps. 84:11). The apostle Paul describes the will of God as good in Romans 12:2: "that you may prove what is that *good* and acceptable and perfect *will of God*."

## — ABSORB —

### God is good, and his will for us is good.

## — INTERACT —

○ The very first temptation of Adam and Eve dealt with the devil's deception that God wanted to keep from them the very best—that God's will was not good. Do you think the enemy still uses that tactic today? Can you give an example?

## LISTEN: The Value of Wise Counsel

God has not left us alone in this world. There are people available in our lives whom God can use to give us wise counsel at strategic decision-making times. The Bible instructs us to seek out counsel:

- "Without counsel, plans go awry, / But in the multitude of counselors they are established." (Prov. 15:22)
- "A man of understanding will attain wise counsel." (Prov. 1:5)
- "With the well-advised is wisdom." (Prov. 13:10)
- "He who heeds counsel is wise." (Prov. 12:15)
- "Plans are established by counsel; / By wise counsel wage war." (Prov. 20:18)
- "Listen to counsel and receive instruction, / That you may be wise in your latter days." (Prov. 19:20)
- Leaders of the ancient Christian church sought out counsel and advice. When there was a debate over theology and customs that would affect the church in Antioch, the apostle Paul and Barnabas went to seek wise counsel from the apostles and elders in Jerusalem (Acts 15:1–21).

Sometimes Christians will say: "I felt *called* to the ministry" or "God *called* me to serve in this capacity." Bruce Waltke gives a practical definition of the concept of God's "call": "A call is an inner desire given by the Holy Spirit, through the Word of God, and confirmed by the community of Christ."[2] In other words, when the Holy Spirit gives you an inner desire to serve in a particular ministry, the desire will also be in alignment with the Word of God and normally confirmed by the body of Christ.

Will God ever ask you to do something you are not able to do? The answer is yes—all the time! It must be that way, for God's glory and kingdom. If we function according to our ability alone, we get the glory; if we function according to the power of the Spirit within us, God gets the glory. He wants to reveal Himself to a watching world.

**—Henry and Melvin Blackaby,** *Experiencing the Spirit*

### The fourth way God guides us is through our seeking wise counsel.

○ What was one of the most difficult decisions you have had to make?

○ Is there an important decision you have to make in the near future that would be helped if you would seek out wise counsel?

○ Have you ever felt God wanted you to do something (such as forgive someone or seek reconciliation) but you were hesitant to seek wise counsel because you were afraid they too might confirm that you should take that difficult step?

## LISTEN: The Encouragement of Circumstances

When you are seeking the guidance of God through (1) reading and meditating on God's Word, (2) praying to God for wisdom, (3) delighting in the Lord, and (4) seeking wise counsel, *then* circumstances can be very helpful in knowing what choices to make. When all the above converge on one decision, that might become an indicator to move ahead in the decision. The Bible uses the "providence" of God to mean that "God has not abandoned the world that He created but works within that creation to manage all things according to the 'immutable counsel of His own will.'"[3] Nothing happens by pure chance. Jesus said: "Are not two sparrows sold for a copper coin? And not one of them falls to the ground apart from your Father's will" (Matt. 10:29). Even a small bird falling in the forest cannot occur without the governing permission or direction of our heavenly Father. Therefore, the providence of God guiding the circumstances of the events of life can serve to help give you direction as you seek to make godly decisions. Reading the circumstances can be of great encouragement in confirming the desires of your heart.

There should be a caution, however: we must not put circumstances above God's Word.

For example, in 1 Samuel 26, the innocent young man David (who is described as a "man after God's own heart") was being chased by King Saul. The king was obsessively jealous of David and wanted to kill him. But as the king was searching to kill David, the tables were suddenly turned—at night David and one of his best soldiers, named Abishai, sneaked into Saul's camp and found the king asleep on the ground: "Then Abishai said to David, 'God has delivered your enemy into your hand this day. Now therefore, please, let me strike him at once with the spear, right to the earth; and I will not have to strike him a second time!' But David said to Abishai, 'Do not destroy him; for who can stretch out his hand against the LORD's anointed, and be guiltless?'" (1 Sam. 26:8–9).

Abishai read the circumstances in such a way that he thought it was God's will to dispose of King Saul. But David knew the Word of the Lord was clear that he (David) was not to touch the Lord's anointed king (Saul). David understood that God had spoken warnings about touching those whom he had anointed—"Do not touch My anointed ones" (1 Chron. 16:22). Even though the circumstances looked like this would be the perfect opportunity to get justice and defeat Saul, David was willing to wait on God and not go against the Word of God. We must never put circumstances above God's Word.

## ABSORB

**The fifth way God guides us is through our evaluation of our circumstances (reading God's providence).**

## INTERACT

○ Have you ever seen circumstances come together in such a way that you sensed that God was definitely guiding you to do something?

○ If you were David, would it have been tempting to think God was delivering Saul into your hands? What would you have done?

## Discernment

"Most of the decisions we make are not spelled out specifically in the Bible. Discernment is how we follow God's leading through the process of spiritually sensitive application of biblical truth to the particularities of our situation. Romans 12:2 describes this: 'Do not be conformed to this world, but be transformed by the renewing of your mind, that you may prove what the will of God is, that which is good and acceptable and perfect.' In this case God does not declare a specific word about what to do. But his Spirit shapes the mind and heart through the word and prayer so that we have inclinations toward what would be most glorifying to him and helpful to others."

**John Piper[a]**

[a]*A Godward Life* (Portland: Multnomah,1997), 217–18.

## LISTEN: God's Guidance and Our Minds

Proverbs 18:1 states: "A man who isolates himself seeks his own desire; / He rages against all wise judgment [ESV, sound judgment]." Sound judgment is portrayed in the Bible as a good thing! Human reasoning is a gift from God and can be a very good thing if it is in alignment with the Word of God. Sound judgment is something God expects us to use. When the leaders of the early church found that there was an issue of setting their priorities, they used good, sound judgment to make the decision that the twelve apostles should devote their time to ministering the Word instead of administering the food program. In simple terms it is recorded: "Then the twelve summoned the multitude of the disciples and said, 'It is not desirable that we should leave the word of God and serve tables'" (Acts 6:2). In light of the apostles' giftedness and calling, it was simply sound judgment that they would do what they were most gifted to do. When sound judgment is lacking, then there often arises confusion and disorder. Again, wise counsel will help us determine whether or not our judgment is sound in a particular decision.

### —— ABSORB ——

**The sixth way God guides us is through our use of sound judgment.**

═══════ **INTERACT** ═══════

○ Can you think of a time when you made a decision and later looked back and saw that you had not used sound judgment?

## LISTEN: God's Freedom to Guide

*God is God!* He can do anything he desires: "Our God is in heaven; / He does whatever He pleases" (Ps. 115:3). We shouldn't be surprised that on different occasions God led his people in miraculous ways. The apostle Paul was dramatically converted as Christ personally appeared to him on the road to Damascus. When God transitioned his people from the old covenant to the new covenant (changing the dietary laws, and so on), he gave to the apostle Peter guidance through a special vision (Acts 10). God also changed Paul's missionary plans through a dream—Paul saw a man from Macedonia in his dream calling out for help (Acts 16:9–10). Again, because God is God, when he so chooses, he still divinely intervenes to give us guidance; this is at his sovereign discretion. However, some Christians seem to imply that if there is not some sort of dramatic or miraculous sign, word, or intervention, then you are not really experiencing the full expression of God's guidance. *But that is not what the Scriptures teach.* You have already seen six key ways from the Bible that God *does* give clear guidance: through reading and meditating on his Word, praying to God for wisdom, delighting yourself in the Lord, seeking wise counsel, evaluating circumstances/providence, and also using sound judgment. It is freeing to know that God's Word tells us that we can clearly discern the guidance of God for our lives even when he chooses to not give a dramatic, miraculous-type sign or word. Knowing this helps us to keep from moving into unbiblical/unbalanced extremes as we make dozens of decisions in our everyday lives.

═══════ **ABSORB** ═══════

### The seventh way God guides us is through divine intervention.

═══════ **INTERACT** ═══════

○ Have you ever experienced what could be labeled as an obvious, visible miracle in your life?

## Prayer, Fasting, and Guidance

"Monday, April 19 [1742] I set apart this day for *fasting and prayer* to God for his grace, especially to prepare me for the work of the ministry; *to give me divine aid and direction*, in my preparations for that great work, and in his own time to send me into his harvest. Accordingly, in the morning, endeavored to plead for the divine presence for the day, and not without some life. In the forenoon, I felt a power of intercession for precious immortal souls, for the advancement of the kingdom of my dear Lord and Saviour in the world; and withal, a most sweet resignation, and even consolation and joy in the thoughts of suffering hardships, distresses, and even death itself, in the promotion of it; and had special enlargement in pleading for the enlightening and conversion of the poor heathen. . . . I enjoyed great sweetness in communion with my dear Saviour. I think I never in my life felt such an entire weanedness from this world, and so much resigned to God in everything. Oh! that I may always live to and upon my blessed God! Amen, Amen."

**David Brainerd[a]**

[a]*Life and Diary of David Brainerd*, ed. Jonathan Edwards (New York: Cosimo, 2007), 80–81; emphasis added.

## LISTEN: A Mentor from History—George Mueller

Sometimes it is helpful to observe how deeply committed Christians of the past sought out the guidance of God. George Mueller (1805–98) lived in Bristol, England, and is noted in church history for founding orphanages and for trusting God to provide for the orphans. "He built five large orphan houses and cared for 10,024 orphans in his lifetime. When he started in 1834 there were accommodations for 3,600 orphans in all of England and twice that many children under eight were in prison. One of the great effects of Mueller's ministry was to inspire others so that 'fifty years after Mr. Mueller began his work, at least one hundred thousand orphans were cared for in England alone' [quoting Pierson's biography of Mueller]."[4] He recorded hundreds of answers to prayers. "He had prayed in millions of dollars (in today's currency) for the Orphans and never asked anyone directly for money." Mueller wrote, "*The first and primary object* of the work was, (and still is) that God might be magnified by the fact, that the orphans under my care are provided, with all they need, only by prayer and faith, without any one being asked by me or my fellow-laborers, whereby it may be seen, that God is FAITHFUL STILL, and HEARS PRAYER STILL."[5]

People of all denominations have admired Mueller for his spiritual and social activism mixed with his strong confidence that God guides his people. Perhaps there is something to be gained from George Mueller's practical advice in following the guidance of God. Here are Mueller's own words:

1. I seek at the beginning to get my heart into such a state that it has no will of its own in regard to a given matter. Nine-tenths of the trouble with people is just here. Nine-tenths of the difficulties are overcome when our hearts are ready to do the Lord's will, whatever it may be. When one is truly in this state, it is usually but a little way to the knowledge of what His will is.
2. Having done this, I do not leave the result to feeling of simple impression. If I do so, I make myself liable to great delusions.
3. I seek the will of the Spirit of God through, or in connection with, the Word of God. . . . The Spirit and the Word must be combined. If I look to the Spirit alone without the Word I lay myself open to great delusions also. If the Holy Spirit guides us at all, He will do it according to the Scriptures and never contrary to them.
4. Next I take into account providential circumstances. These often plainly indicate God's will in connection with His Word and Spirit.
5. I ask God in prayer to reveal His will to me aright.
6. Thus, through prayer to God, the study of the Word, and reflection, I come to a deliberate judgment according to the best of my ability and knowledge, and if my mind is thus at peace, and continues so after two or three more petitions, I proceed accordingly.

In trivial matters, and in transactions involving most important issues, I have found this method always effective.[6]

## ABSORB

**George Mueller's radical life of faith demonstrates the high value of combining the Word of God with prayer, along with sound judgment and a heart yielded to God.**

## INTERACT

○ What stands out to you in George Mueller's approach in receiving guidance from God?

**Reflect:** Mueller's social activism was supported by his unwavering faith in the promises of God. Be open to how God might use your radical faith to help others who are in desperate need. God may be stirring you up to do something that will glorify his name.

Think about how good the will of God is for your life. God wants us to know his will; therefore he helps us make the very best choices to please him. Is there an important decision you need to make for which I can be praying for you until we meet for the next session?

## CULTIVATING SPIRITUAL HABITS

**Read:** John 1:1–14; Colossians 1:9–18

**Journal:** Write down in your journal the seven ways in which God guides us; jot down a verse and some thoughts for each one.

### Memorize

*I beseech you therefore, brethren, by the mercies of God, that you present your bodies a living sacrifice, holy, acceptable to God, which is your reasonable service. And do not be conformed to this world, but be transformed by the renewing of your mind, that you may prove what is that good and acceptable and perfect will of God.*

ROMANS 12:1–2

# The Mystery of the Trinity

## The Trinity (Part 1)

---

**Purpose of Session Fourteen:** The Bible teaches that there is only one God, and he exists in three persons. Theologians describe this mystery of God's existence as "the Trinity." In this session and the next we will clear up common misconceptions and misunderstandings concerning the Trinity and will focus on what the Bible teaches about the Trinity.

---

## LISTEN: Misconceptions

In one sense, the biblical teaching about the Trinity is a mystery that we will never be able to fully understand, but at the same time we *can* grasp what God has chosen to reveal about himself in the Holy Scriptures. In church history certain groups and sects have wandered from the historic truths concerning the Trinity. These sessions will give you a biblical foundation so that you can be aware of the historical errors concerning the nature of the Trinity in order to avoid making the same errors.

We should not be surprised to think that it would be very difficult to fully comprehend the greatness and complexity of God. John Wesley, who led a major revival in England in the eighteenth century, made a statement that helps us to approach this subject with humility: "Bring me a worm that can comprehend a man, and then I will show you a man that can comprehend the triune God."[1] Although the term "Trinity" is not found in the Bible, historically it has been an extremely helpful word to describe what the Bible reveals when it teaches that there is only one God who eternally exists as three persons.[2] The word "Trinity" has the meaning of "tri-unity," which expresses the idea of

**153**

"three-in-oneness." The term is used to summarize the teaching of Scripture that God is three persons yet one God.[3] Some theologians and pastors like to refer to God as the "Triune God." There is an ancient creed (the Athanasian Creed) that highlights the fact that there is a diversity of three persons yet the unity of one God: "We worship one God in the Trinity, and the Trinity in unity; we distinguish among the persons, but we do not divide the substance. The entire three persons are co-eternal and co-equal with one another, so that . . . we worship complete unity in Trinity and Trinity in unity."

### — ABSORB —

**"Trinity" is a term used to describe how God reveals himself as one God who eternally exists as three distinct persons—the Father, Son, and Holy Spirit. God is one in essence and three in person.**

### — INTERACT —

○ Up to this point, what is your biggest question about the Trinity?

○ Why is it difficult for us to grasp the idea that there is only one God but at the same time three different persons?

## LISTEN: Three Persons

The Bible describes the Father as God (Phil. 1:2), and Jesus as God (Titus 2:13), and the Holy Spirit as God (Acts 5:3–4). The Scriptures indicate that the Father, Son, and Holy Spirit are distinct persons. Jesus said in John 12:49, "For I have not spoken on My own authority; but *the Father who sent Me* gave Me a command, what I should say and what I should speak."

This means that Jesus was sent by the Father, and the Father communicated to the Son. The Father is not the same person as the Son. Also you will discover in the Bible that after the Son returned to the Father, both the Father and the Son sent the Holy Spirit into the world: "But the Helper, *the Holy Spirit, whom the Father will send* in My name, He will teach you all things, and bring to your remembrance all things that I said to you" (John 14:26).

And, "It is to your advantage that I go away; for if I do not go away, the Helper will not come to you; but if I depart, *I will send Him* to you" (John 16:7).

Therefore, the Holy Spirit, who is a person, must be distinct from the Father and the Son. When Jesus was baptized, we see the Father speaking from heaven and the Spirit descending from heaven in the form of a dove as Jesus comes out of the water (Mark 1:10–11). This means that the Father is not the Son, the Son is not the Holy Spirit, and the Holy Spirit is not the Father. Jesus is called God, but he is not the Father or the Holy Spirit. The Holy Spirit is described as God, but he is not the Son or the Father. They are different *persons*, not just three different ways of looking at God. They communicate to each other personally, such as: "*The Father loves the Son*, and has given all things into His hand" (John 3:35).

## ABSORB

**God is three persons. Each person is fully God. There is one God.[4]**

## INTERACT

○ There are many people in our society who say they believe in a God but not in a personal God. To them, God is an impersonal force behind everything. What kind of picture do you get of God

---

### The Trinity and Love

"Christianity, alone among the world faiths, teaches that God is triune. . . . The life of the Trinity is characterized not by self-centeredness but by mutually self-giving love. When we delight and serve someone else, we enter into a dynamic orbit around him or her, we center on the interests and desires of the other. That creates a dance, particularly if there are three persons, each of whom moves around the other two. So it is, the Bible tells us. Each of the divine persons centers upon the others. . . . Each voluntarily circles the other two, pouring love, delight and adoration into them. Each person of the Trinity loves, adores, defers to and rejoices in the others. That creates a dynamic, pulsating dance of joy and love. . . . When people say, 'God is love,' I think they mean that love is extremely important, or that God really wants us to love. But in the Christian conception, God really has love as his essence. If he was just one person he couldn't have been loving for all eternity."

**Timothy Keller[a]**

[a]*The Reason for God* (New York: Dutton, 2008), 214–16.

as you read such passages in the paragraphs above—personal or impersonal?

○ Are you glad God is personal? Why?

## LISTEN: Each Person of the Trinity Is Fully God

You will notice in the following verses that each person of the Trinity is referred to as God. It is highly significant that each is identified as God.

- Jesus is called "the Word" in John 1, and it states that the Word was God: "In the beginning was the Word, and the Word was with God, and *the Word was God*" (John 1:1). Clearly Jesus, the Son, is God.
- The Bible also equates the Holy Spirit with God: "But Peter said, 'Ananias, why has Satan filled your heart to *lie to the Holy Spirit*. . . . You have not lied to men but *to God*'" (Acts 5:3–4). Notice that Ananias lied to the Holy Spirit who is God!
- The Father is God. Several of the New Testament letters begin with this introduction: "Grace to you and peace from *God our Father*" (for example, Eph. 1:2; Col. 1:2; Phil. 1:2).
- It is clear from these verses and many others that each person of the Trinity is fully God.

### ABSORB

**The Bible teaches that Jesus is fully God, the Holy Spirit is fully God, and the Father is fully God.**

### INTERACT

○ At the trial of Jesus, the high priest asked him this question: "I put You under oath by the living God: Tell us if You are the Christ, the Son of God!" Jesus said to him, "It is as you said" (Matt. 26:63–64). If you had been there that day and heard Jesus, under oath, agreeing that he was the Son of God, what would have been going through your mind?

## LISTEN: There Is One God

Jesus clearly affirms the truth that there is only one God when he quotes Deuteronomy 6:4 and agrees with the most fundamental premise of the Law—"the Lord is One": "Jesus answered him, 'The first of all the commandments is: "Hear, O Israel, the Lord our God, the Lord is one"'" (Mark 12:29). Jesus fully agrees that there is only one God.

### — ABSORB —

**The mystery of the Trinity is that there is only one God, and this one God exists as one essence in three persons—God the Father, God the Son, and God the Holy Spirit.**

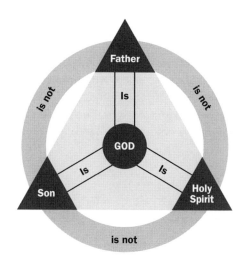

If there be one God subsisting in three persons, then let us give equal reverence to all the persons in the Trinity. There is not more or less in the Trinity; the Father is not more God than the Son and Holy Ghost. There is an order in the Godhead, but no degrees; one person has not a majority or super eminence above another, therefore we must give equal worship to all the persons.

**—Thomas Watson (1620–86), Puritan pastor**

### — INTERACT —

○ Ancient Christians drew a diagram to help explain the Trinity (one version is shown above).[5] You will notice that the Father is God, the Son is God, and the Holy Spirit is God. But the Father is not the Son, the Son is not the Holy Spirit, and the Holy Spirit is not the Father. Is this diagram helpful to your understanding of the Trinity? Why is the Trinity a mystery?

## LISTEN: C. S. Lewis's Analogy

The most difficult part of understanding the Trinity is trying to picture how there could be only *one being* (God) yet at the same time *three distinct persons*. C. S. Lewis, who was a brilliant thinker, gives a fascinating discussion in his book *Mere Christianity* as to why it is so difficult for us as humans to fully comprehend the Trinity. He illustrates this by showing that in our three-dimensional world we are limited to the directions that we can physically move. We can go up or down, sideways, or forward and backward. Our three-dimensional world has length, width, and height. Now suppose you live in a totally one-dimensional world. You can only draw a straight line. But if you lived in a two-dimensional world, you could connect four lines together to form a square. And in our real, three-dimensional world you can actually connect six squares together to form a cube (like a cardboard box). Now, if you lived in a two-dimensional world, you could draw six squares next to each other, but you could not grasp how it would be possible to connect the six squares together to form a cube. In that two-dimensional world you would have all the lines necessary for a cube, but you still could not imagine the concept of what a cube looks like. So there is an analogy here in explaining why it is difficult for us to understand the makeup of the Trinity. We now live in a three-dimensional world where we can only perceive a single being existing as one person. But in another dimension, God tells us that he is a single being but he exists in three persons. Such an idea is incomprehensible to us because we do not live on the divine level.[6]

### ABSORB

**Lewis's analogy helps us to see why it is difficult to comprehend how a single being could exist in three persons. Because God is so great, we shouldn't be so surprised to find out that there is a mystery concerning his existence and being.**

### INTERACT

○ What is helpful to you in Lewis's analogy?

○ As you think about the Trinity there are a lot of things in this world of a much lesser scale that are also difficult to understand. We cannot really comprehend how light can be both a particle and a wave. There are aspects of quantum mechanics that are very difficult to figure out. So why would we think that God, who created this intricately complex universe, would not have something about him that would be difficult to fathom? Talk about some things in this world that are very difficult to understand.

## LISTEN: An Attitude of Humility Is Reasonable

James R. White in his book *The Forgotten Trinity* makes this observation:

The Trinity is a truth that tests our dedication to the principle that God is smarter than we are. As strange as that may sound, I truly believe that in most instances where a religious group denies the Trinity, the reason can be traced back to the founder's unwillingness to admit the simple reality that God is bigger than we can ever imagine. That is really what Christians have always meant when they use the term "mystery" of the Trinity. The term has never meant that the Trinity is an inherently irrational thing. Instead, it simply means that we realize that God is completely unique in the way He exists, and there are elements of His being that are simply beyond our meager mental capacity to comprehend. The fact that God is eternal is another facet of His being that is beyond us. We cannot really grasp eternity, nor how God exists eternally rather than in time. Yet this truth is revealed to us in Scripture, and we believe it on the logical basis that God is trustworthy. It is a "mystery" that we accept on the basis of faith in God's revelation.[7]

## The Trinity Is Not Like an Egg

"I have heard the Father, Son, and Holy Spirit described like the three parts of an egg: the shell, the white stuff, and the yolk. I have also heard people say that God is like a three-leaf clover: three 'arms,' yet all are a part of the one clover stalk. Another popular comparison is to the three forms of $H_2O$ (water, ice, and steam). While these serve as cute metaphors for an unexplainable mystery, the fact is that God is not like an egg, a three-leaf clover, or the three forms of water. God is not like anything. He is incomprehensible, incomparable, and unlike any other being. He is outside our realm of existence and, thus, outside our ability to categorize Him. While analogies may be helpful in understanding certain aspects of Him, let's be careful not to think that our analogies in any way encapsulate His nature."

**Francis Chan[a]**

[a]*Forgotten God: Reversing Our Tragic Neglect of the Holy Spirit* (Colorado Springs: David C. Cook, 2009), 66.

The Bible teaches that there are not three Gods but one God. Is the Trinity a complete contradiction of logic? No. In order for something to be a real contradiction of logic, it must violate the law of noncontradiction. The law of noncontradiction states that A cannot be both A (what it is) and non-A (what it is not) at the same time and in the same relationship. For example, if I say that I am sitting in this wooden chair right at this moment, and then I say at the same moment that I am not sitting in this chair, then there is a true contradiction. R. C. Sproul[8] gives the illustration of Charles Dickens's famous line, "It was the best of times, it was the worst of times." This would be a contradiction if Dickens means that it was the best of times in the same way that it was the worst of times. But Dickens wasn't violating the law of noncontradiction because he meant that in one sense it was the best of times, but in another sense it was the worst of times. The Trinity is not an illogical concept because it is not a contradiction for God to be both three and one since he is not three and one in the same way. The doctrine of the Trinity does not say that there are three Gods and there is one God. It says that God is three in a different way than he is one. God is one in essence, but he is three in person. *Essence* and *person* are not the same thing.

## ABSORB

**The Trinity is a mystery; it goes *beyond* reason without going *against* reason. We may not be able to fully comprehend the Trinity, but we can grasp that the Scriptures teach that God is one in essence but three in person.**

## INTERACT

○ Have you ever communicated something that made total sense to you but someone didn't understand some of the details, and therefore you were misunderstood?

○ Why is it difficult for some people to acknowledge that the Scriptures teach that there is one God but who at the same time eternally exists in three persons?

## LISTEN: The Person of the Holy Spirit

Theologian R. C. Sproul succinctly explains why it is important to understand that the Holy Spirit is a *person*:

> The night my wife was converted to Christ she exclaimed, "Now I know who the Holy Spirit is." Prior to that time she had thought of the Holy Spirit as an "it" rather than a personal "who." When we speak of the personality of the Holy Spirit, we mean that the Third Member of the Trinity is a person and not a force. This is clear from Scripture, where only personal pronouns are used when referring to the Spirit. In John 16:13, Jesus said, "When He, the Spirit of truth, has come, He will guide you into all truth; for He will not speak on His own authority, but whatever He hears He will speak; and He will tell you things to come."
>
> Because the Holy Spirit is a real and distinct person and not an impersonal force, it is possible for us to enjoy a personal relationship with Him. Paul gives a benediction to the Corinthian church that highlights this, "The grace of the Lord Jesus Christ, and the love of God, and the communion of the Holy Spirit be with you all. Amen" (2 Cor. 13:14). To have communion with someone is to enter a personal relationship with him. In addition, we are called not to sin against, resist, or grieve the Holy Spirit. Impersonal forces cannot be "grieved." Grief can only be experienced by a personal being.
>
> Because the Holy Spirit is a person, it is appropriate to pray to Him. His role in prayer is to assist us in expressing ourselves adequately to the Father. As Jesus intercedes for us as our High Priest, so the Holy Spirit intercedes for us in prayer.
>
> Finally, the Bible speaks of the Holy Spirit performing tasks that only persons can perform. The Spirit *comforts*, *guides*, and *teaches*. . . . These activities are done in a manner that involves intelligence, will, feeling, and power. He searches, selects, reveals, comforts, convicts, and admonishes. Only a person could do these things. The response of the Christian, then, is not mere affirmation that such a being exists, but rather, to obey, love, and adore the Holy Spirit, the Third Person of the Trinity.[9]

Tell me how it is that in this room there are three candles and but one light, and I will explain to you the mode of the divine existence.

**—John Wesley**

---

### ABSORB

**The Holy Spirit is a person, not merely an influence, force, energy, or power.**

---

### INTERACT

○ How does it make you feel to know that the Holy Spirit is a person rather than some sort of energy or force?

○ Have you ever experienced the Holy Spirit working in your heart and mind concerning what he wanted you to do or not do?

**Reflect:** Tim Keller says that the life of the Trinity is characterized not by self-centeredness but by mutually self-giving love. As followers of Christ let us ask ourselves quite often: "Is my life characterized by the trinitarian example of self-giving love?" Love can be a powerful visual aid to let the world get a glimpse of God's love—"By this all will know that you are My disciples, if you have love for one another" (John 13:35).

The Trinity is a mystery that we are not fully able to understand, but we can begin to grasp what God has chosen to reveal about himself in the Holy Scriptures. It is exciting to discover that our God truly is an awesome God! How can I pray for you until we meet next time?

## CULTIVATING SPIRITUAL HABITS

**Read:** Genesis 1:26–27; John 14 and 16

**Journal:** Scan through this session and write down the main points that help you to better understand the Trinity.

### Memorize

*In the beginning was the Word, and the Word was with God, and the Word was God. He was in the beginning with God.*

JOHN 1:1–2

# The Ministry of the Holy Spirit

The more we understand the ministry of the Holy Spirit in our lives the more we will want to love, obey, and enjoy him as the Third Person of the Trinity. The following is a summary of some of the works of the Holy Spirit.

**The Holy Spirit works to bring us to salvation and to regenerate us.** In John 16:8 Jesus says of the Holy Spirit: "And when He has come, He will convict the world of sin, and of righteousness, and of judgment." That means that we come to understand our desperate need of Christ and salvation through the work and ministry of the Holy Spirit. Also Jesus explains that we are born again (regenerated) by the unique and mysterious work of the Holy Spirit in our lives: "The wind blows where it wishes, and you hear the sound of it, but cannot tell where it comes from and where it goes. So is everyone who is born of the Spirit" (John 3:8). And Titus 3:5 states: "He saved us, through the washing of *regeneration and renewing of the Holy Spirit*." Salvation is a work of God and is experienced in our lives through the ministry of the Holy Spirit.

**The Holy Spirit indwells every believer.** An incredible truth is that the Holy Spirit indwells every Christian. The apostle Paul explains in 1 Corinthians 6:19: "Do you not know that your body is a temple of the Holy Spirit who is in you, whom you have from God?" The distinguishing mark of belonging to Christ is to have the indwelling of the Holy Spirit: "But you are . . . in the Spirit, if indeed the Spirit of God dwells in you. Now if anyone does not have the Spirit of Christ, he is not His" (Rom. 8:9).

○ How does it make you feel to know that your body is the temple of the Holy Spirit? What are the implications of knowing that the Holy Spirit indwells us?

**The Holy Spirit is our "*Parakletos*"** [Greek, pronounced para-clay-tos; "Paraclete" in English]. Jesus promised his disciples that when he returned to his Father, his Father would send the *parakletos* in his (Christ's) name. This Greek term *parakletos* means "one who is called to someone's aid."[10] This word is translated variously as "Helper," "Advocate," "Comforter," or "Counselor." Actually the Holy Spirit is all those things to us!

○ Jesus told his disciples that when the Holy Spirit (the Helper) comes, "He [the Holy Spirit] will glorify Me [Jesus]" (John 16:14). What do you think it means that the Holy Spirit will glorify Jesus?

**The Holy Spirit baptizes us and also fills us.** It is recorded by the apostle Paul in 1 Corinthians 12:13: "For by one Spirit we were all baptized into one body—whether Jews or Greeks, whether slaves or free—and have all been made to drink into one Spirit." We are made members of the body of Christ, incorporated into the spiritual organism called the church. We are immersed and submerged in him and forever enjoy his presence and power.[11]

Also, as we saw in the appendix to session twelve, God's Word reveals that it is his will that we be filled with the Spirit. Ephesians 5:17–18 states: "Therefore do not be unwise, but understand what the *will of the Lord* is. And do not be drunk with wine, in which is dissipation; but *be filled with the Spirit*." When a person is filled with wine it controls his or her behavior; instead of wine controlling us, we are to be controlled by the Holy Spirit. The book of Acts records various manifestations of people filled with the Spirit. There are nine passages that mention what occurred when the disciples were filled with the Holy Spirit:

1. The disciples spoke in languages they had not previously learned (Acts 2:4, 6).
2. They boldly testified about Jesus (Acts 4:8, 13).
3. They "spoke the word of God with boldness" (Acts 4:31).
4. The apostles appointed men full of the Holy Spirit to become official servants of the church because they had such obvious zeal and faith (Acts 6:3).
5. Stephen had courage to preach boldly to a hostile crowd and even face stoning (Acts 7:55).
6. Paul was converted and filled with the Holy Spirit and immediately preached Christ in the synagogues (Acts 9:17–20).
7. Paul was filled with the Holy Spirit and was given discernment, and he pronounced judgment on an overt enemy of the gospel (Acts 13:9–10).
8. They were filled with joy (Acts 13:52).
9. They spoke in other languages and prophesied (Acts 19:6).

Therefore to be filled with the Holy Spirit may result in various manifestations—especially being empowered for service with boldness and joy and being passionate about what the Holy Spirit is passionate about. We are commanded to be filled with the Spirit. Because we often sin and grow spiritually empty, we need to seek God for fresh fillings of the Holy Spirit!

○ What do you think is the most attractive thing about a Christian being filled with the Holy Spirit?

**The Holy Spirit seals us and intercedes for us.** Ephesians reveals that the Lord even goes so far as to seal his own with the special seal of the Holy Spirit to keep us. This seal guarantees us all the further blessings of eternal life: "In Him you also trusted, after you heard the word of truth, the gospel of your salvation; in whom also, having believed, you were sealed with the Holy Spirit of promise, who is the guarantee of our inheritance until the redemption of the purchased possession, to the praise of His glory" (Eph. 1:13–14).

Not only are all true believers sealed with the Holy Spirit, but the Holy Spirit at key and critical junctures in our lives also prays and intercedes for us. Romans 8:26 gives us a glimpse behind the curtain: "Likewise the Spirit also helps in our weaknesses. For we do not know what we should pray for as we ought, but the Spirit Himself makes intercession for us with groanings which cannot be uttered."

**The Holy Spirit teaches us** (1 Cor. 2:13), **guides us** (Rom. 8:14), **and gives us spiritual gifts** as he sovereignly decides, "distributing to each one individually as He wills" (1 Cor. 12:11).

**The Holy Spirit is holy.** Humans are warned not to "blaspheme" the Holy Spirit. Jesus spoke this warning after he was accused of having an unclean spirit: "Assuredly, I say to you, all sins will be forgiven the sons of men, and whatever blasphemies they may utter; but he who blasphemes against the Holy Spirit never has forgiveness, but is subject to eternal condemnation" (Mark 3:28–30).

"Blaspheming the Holy Spirit" has been often understood either as a public statement that uses the name of the Holy Spirit in a profane way or as persistent unbelief and dying in that unbelief. While it is certainly true that if you die in unbelief then you will die unforgiven, this passage speaks to something more specific. When you consider the surrounding verses you will see that the religious group at that time known as the Pharisees were basically attributing the miracles of Jesus to the works of the devil. For the Pharisees to have Jesus himself in their midst, to see his miracles, his works, and his life and to still attribute them to be works of the devil is unpardonable. There is literally no clearer way that Christ could reveal himself to humankind, and if you were to reject him while he is right in front of you, it's as if nothing more could be done. Theologian Wayne Grudem appears to be right when he observes that the sin of blaspheming the Holy Spirit is not general unbelief in Christ: "A better possibility is that this sin consists of *unusually malicious, willful rejection and slander against the Holy Spirit's work attesting to Christ, and attributing that work to Satan.*"[12] The Pharisees clearly had the unmistakable opportunity to see who Jesus claimed to be. They had irrefutable evidence of his works, and their last judgment was to say that it was the work of the devil. The sin of blaspheming the Holy Spirit involves this type of extraordinary rejection and slander against the Holy Spirit that grows out of a totally hardened unrepentant heart. Therefore anyone who has a sensitive heart that worries he has committed this sin can have the assurance that he or she has not committed the unpardonable sin.

John Piper gives this definition of the unpardonable sin: "The unforgivable sin of blasphemy against the Holy Spirit is an act of resistance which belittles the Holy Spirit so grievously that he withdraws forever with his convicting power so that we are never able to repent and be forgiven."[13]

Charles Spurgeon's insight helps us to approach this subject with a degree of humility:

> If you have committed the unpardonable sin, I should really like to know what it is; for, after reading, I think, as much of sound divinity as anybody, I have never yet been able to discover what it is; nor have I ever met with any divine [biblical scholar] who has even seemed to me to approximate to any sure and certain description of what the unpardonable sin may be. . . . Whatever the unpardonable sin may be, and perhaps it is different in every person—perhaps it is a point of sin in each one, a filling up of his measure, beyond which there is no more hope of mercy—whatever it is, there is one thing that is sure, that no man who feels his need of Christ, and sincerely desires to be saved, can have committed that sin at all.[14]

**The Holy Spirit sanctifies us.** The New Testament describes how the Holy Spirit is specifically involved in our sanctification. Recall the meaning of sanctification: *Sanctification is the lifelong process after we are saved of growing more and more conformed to the likeness of Christ.* It is the work of the Holy Spirit to cause us to grow more conformed to the likeness of Christ: "But we are bound to give thanks to God always for you, brethren beloved by the Lord, because God from the beginning chose you for salvation through *sanctification by the Spirit* and belief in the truth" (2 Thess. 2:13).

○ The apostle Paul in Ephesians 4:30 admonishes us: "And do not grieve the Holy Spirit of God, by whom you were sealed for the day of redemption." What do you think it means "to grieve" the Holy Spirit?

# Eternally One God in Three Persons

## The Trinity (Part 2)

**Purpose of Session Fifteen:** This session continues our focus on the Trinity, which we began in the last session. The Trinity is a great mystery regarding God's existence. The Bible teaches that there is only one God, and he exists in three persons. We will delve more deeply into what the Trinity is and is not.

## LISTEN: The Eternal Relationship within the Trinity

From all eternity, before the universe existed, God (the Father) existed: "Before the mountains were brought forth, / Or ever You had formed the earth and the world, / Even from everlasting to everlasting, You are God" (Ps. 90:2). When Jesus (the Son) declares these words, "I am the Alpha and the Omega, the First and the Last" (Rev. 1:11), he is stating that he is eternal, just like the Father. Also, the Holy Spirit is referred to in Hebrews 9:14 as the "eternal Spirit." From all eternity God has existed, but this eternal ever-living God has never been "alone." The fellowship within the Trinity has always existed. And if the fellowship of the Trinity has always existed, and if the Son is said to be begotten by the Father, then this mysterious, seemingly contradictory idea is simply beyond our rational intellect.

— ABSORB —

It is beyond our intellect to envision how the Son is
begotten by the Father, yet has eternally existed.

○ What is most difficult for you in trying to picture eternity past?

## LISTEN: Further Light on the Eternity of the Trinity

The following quotes can bring some light and clarity as we contemplate the eternal, Triune God.

> The Son is eternally begotten by the Father. The Father is begotten by no one. Automatically we place this relationship within time and think of the Father originating the Son at a point in time. Most definitely not. The term ["begotten"] as we use it here speaks of an eternal, timeless relationship. It had no beginning, it will have no ending. It has always been. C. S. Lewis likened it to a book that is lying on top of another. We say the top book owes its position to the bottom one. It wouldn't be where it is without the one on the bottom. Now, if you can, imagine this relationship as *always having been*. There never was a time when the top book was not where it was, never a time when the bottom book was alone. This is what we mean when we speak of the Father *begetting* the Son. The relationship of the first person of the Trinity to the second person is that of *begetting*.[1]

John Piper, drawing on Jonathan Edwards's "An Essay on the Trinity," gives a concise and rich description of the eternal persons of the Trinity:

> The Son of God is the eternal idea or image that God has of Himself. And the image that He has of Himself is so perfect and so complete and so full as to be the living, personal reproduction (or begetting) of God the Father. And this living, personal image or radiance or form of God is God, namely, God the Son. And therefore God the Son is coeternal with God the Father and equal in essence and glory.[2]

Historically there has been significant discussion of the Holy Spirit's relationship with the Father and the Son. "The relationship of the Holy Spirit to the Father and the Son is described by the term *procession*. He is said to "proceed" from the Father and the Son on the basis of such passages as John 15:26 and John 16:7."[3]

From all eternity the one eternal God—this "ever-existing, never-becoming, always-perfect God"[4]—has existed in the infinite happiness of the fellowship of the Trinity. There was never a time when God was lonely. He has always existed as One-in-Three. God did not create humans because he was lonely or needed company. There has never been any deficiency in the blessed Trinity. Everything God does revolves around his glory.

God created his people *for His glory* (that his glory might be displayed and magnified): "Everyone who is called by My name, / Whom I have created for My glory" (Isa. 43:7). Everything that God created is from his fullness, and we can never add anything to him. That is what it means to be God; and it should humble us.[5]

## — ABSORB —

**From all eternity the one eternal God—this "ever-existing, never-becoming, always-perfect God"—has existed in the infinite happiness of the fellowship of the Trinity.**

## — INTERACT —

○ Does C. S. Lewis's example of the two books existing for eternity help you picture how the Son of God is eternally begotten with no beginning?

○ How does it make you feel to know that we were created to glorify God, and by doing so we will experience never-ending happiness? (Or how does it make you feel to know that "heaven will be a never-ending, ever-increasing discovery of more and more of God's glory with greater and ever-greater joy in Him"?)[6]

Passages such as Isaiah 55:8–9 remind us that compared to God our thinking is quite limited: "'For My thoughts are not your thoughts, nor are your ways My ways,' says the LORD. 'For as the heavens are higher than the earth, so are My ways higher than your ways, and My thoughts than your thoughts.'"

## LISTEN: What the Trinity Is and Is Not

When Christians describe the Trinity they say, "We believe in one God in three persons." It is important to know what this does *not* mean. This *does not* mean that

we believe in one God in three Gods.
we believe in one person in three Gods.
we believe in three persons in three Gods.
we believe in three persons in one person.

Rather—we believe in one God in three persons![7]

When it is said that there is "one God" or that "God is one," what the Bible means in saying that God is one can be described using the following terms:

**being**

essence

essential nature

substance (the stuff of God)

*ousia* (Greek) and *essentia* (Latin) (both mean all of the above and are key terms used in the historic creeds of the church)

that which makes God, God

In plain English it could be said that *ousia* and *essentia* describe the "stuff of God"—*that which makes God, God*. A problem immediately arises because when we think of "substance" or "essence" or "being," we tend to think of a physical being. Yet it is clear from the words of Christ that "*God is Spirit, and those who worship Him must worship in spirit and truth*" (John 4:24). This means that God is not physical like us; he is not limited to a spatial location. God is not made up of matter like created things are.[8] Whatever God's existence is, it is in some sense spiritual—God is spirit. Whatever makes God, God in his essential nature is not something physical. God is of one pure essence (substance, essential nature) that makes him pure deity. We have to humbly admit that this concept stretches our intellect. We cannot deny that this mystery is taught in the Bible, and we must not minimize this mystery just because our finite minds cannot understand an infinite God.

There is no subject where error is more dangerous, research more laborious, and discovery more fruitful than the oneness of the Trinity of the Father, the Son, and the Holy Spirit.

**—Augustine of Hippo**

### ABSORB

To say that there is one God, or that God is one, means that God is one being. It also means that God is of one essence, or one substance, or one essential nature. There are not three Gods in the Trinity, but one.

### INTERACT

○ Why is it so difficult for us to grasp the "three-in-one" concept?

○ Why is it difficult for us to comprehend Jesus's words: "God is Spirit"? What do you find most astonishing about the uniqueness of God?

## LISTEN: Pre-revelation of the Trinity in Genesis

Although God is most often depicted as "one" in the Old Testament, even in the first chapter of Genesis there is a revelation of the Trinity (albeit in kernel form). In Genesis 1:26–27 there is an implied plurality of persons: "Then God said, 'Let *Us* make man in *Our image*, according to *Our likeness*; let them have dominion over the fish of the sea, over the birds of the air, and over the cattle, over all the earth and over every creeping thing that creeps on the earth.' So God created man in His own image; *in the image of God* He created him; male and female He created them." Scripture shows a pattern of God revealing himself to humans by granting them, through the ages, an increasing knowledge of who he is. The most glorious revelation of God was the coming of the Son of God! Jesus made it clear: "He who has seen Me has seen the Father" (John 14:9).

Some people reject the notion that Genesis 1:26 refers to the Trinity and suggest that God was using the royal "we." Theologian Wayne Grudem responds:

> What do the plural verb ("let us") and the plural pronoun ("our") mean? Some have suggested they are plurals of majesty, a form of speech a king would use in saying, for example, "We are pleased to grant your request." However, in Old Testament Hebrew there are no other examples of a monarch using plural verbs or plural pronouns of himself in such a "plural of majesty," so this suggestion has no evidence to support it.[9]

Others suggest that in this passage God is speaking to angels. Yet we find no evidence in Scripture that angels participated in the creation of humans. John 1:3 says specifically of Christ: "All things were made through Him, and without Him nothing was made that was made." There is no mention anywhere in the Bible that humans were made in the image of angels. Throughout church history, church fathers and earlier theologians have almost unanimously accepted and affirmed that God was already revealing himself as a plurality of persons in the beginning pages of Genesis. In addition, Genesis 3:22 includes these words from God, "Behold, the man has become like one of Us, to know good and evil." In the first pages of the Bible we aren't told yet how many persons are within the Godhead, but it's apparent that there is more than one.[10]

It was the whole Trinity, which at the beginning of creation said, "Let us make man." It was the whole Trinity again, which at the beginning of the Gospel seemed to say, "Let us save man."

—**J. C. Ryle,**
***Commentary on Matthew 3***

In the first pages of Genesis there is a subtle
revelation of the plurality of the one God.

○ How does it make you feel that you are made in the image of the
Trinity? In what way do you think you are made in the image of
the Trinity?

## LISTEN: Clarification of "Three Persons"

When the Bible presents each member of the Trinity as a separate person,
theologians often phrase it like this: there is one God who eternally exists as
three *distinct persons*—the Father, Son, and Holy Spirit.

Theologians sometimes use the phrase *individual subsistences* (*individual
persons*) to refer to the Father, Son, and Holy Spirit. The following are the
different ways scholars refer to this separate personhood:

**persons**
individual subsistences (not to be confused with "substance")
personal distinctions in the divine being: "I, You, He"
distinct in personhood

When the Bible presents God as three persons, this means that the Father
is not the Son, the Son is not the Holy Spirit, and the Holy Spirit is not the
Father—all are distinct persons. They are distinct in personhood, and they
have had a personal relationship through all eternity.

What we are talking about are *personal distinctions* of the divine Being. We are
talking about the "I, You, He" found in such passages as Matthew 3, where the
Father speaks from heaven, the Son is being baptized, and the Spirit descends as
a dove. While trying to avoid the idea of separate individuals, we are speaking of
the personal self-distinctions God has revealed to exist within the one, indivisible
essence. . . . What we mean is that you can tell the Father from the Son, and the
Son from the Spirit, by how they are related to each other, and by what actions
they take in working our creation, salvation, etc. . . . My being is shared by only
one *person*: me. My being, since it is limited, cannot be distributed among two,

three, or any more *persons*. One being, one person: that's what it is to be a human. . . . What we are saying about God is that His being is not limited and finite like a creature's. His Being is infinite and unlimited, and hence can, in a way completely beyond our comprehension, be shared fully by three persons, the Father, Son, and Holy Spirit. The divine Being is one; the divine persons are three. . . . Unless we recognize the difference between the terms *being* and *person*, we will never have an accurate or workable understanding of the Trinity.[11]

— ABSORB —

There is one God who eternally exists as three *distinct persons*—the Father, Son, and Holy Spirit. They are distinct in personhood, and they have had a personal relationship through all eternity. God's being (essence) is infinite and unlimited and can be shared fully by three persons.

INTERACT

○ Why is this quote so important: "Unless we recognize the difference between the terms *being* and *person*, we will never have an accurate or workable understanding of the Trinity"?

## LISTEN: Different Roles but Equal in Value

The persons of the Trinity are of equal value but assume different roles and functions. Within the Trinity, no person is inferior to another. Theologians label the relationships between members of the Trinity *relational subordination* or *economic subordination*. "Relational subordination" does not mean that some members are "below" another member but that the roles are "ordered." Within the ordered relationships, it is understood that the Son and the Holy Spirit follow the will of the Father (and do not give commands to the Father), and so their roles can be seen as "subordinate" to the Father. However, the persons of the Son and the Holy Spirit are not inferior to the Father. Also, there is a distinction between the members in the ways they relate to each other and to the creation. For example, the Son relates to the Father in the role of a son to his father; that is, the Son obeys the Father. And, while there are different roles within the Trinity, none of the roles are considered superior. We see that the Father *sends* the Son (John 3:16) and *initiates* creation and redemption; the Son *redeems* fallen humankind; and the Holy Spirit *regenerates* and *sanctifies* people. But none of these tasks are considered more important than the others. Listen to 1 Corinthians 15:23–28:

> Then comes the end, when He [the Son] delivers the kingdom to God the Father, when He puts an end to all rule and all authority and power. For He must reign till He has put all enemies under His feet. The last enemy that will be destroyed is death. For "He has put all things under His feet." But when He says "all things are put under Him," it is evident that He who put all things under Him is excepted. Now when all things are made subject to Him, then the Son Himself will also be subject to Him who put all things under Him, that God may be all in all.

We can understand this concept even in the realm of human relationships. It could be compared with three people who jointly own a company. One of the owners assumes the role of chairperson of the board in order to focus on certain government regulations. Another owner oversees the finances. The third owner is out in the field enhancing public relations. All three have equal ownership and are equally paid, but each has a different role. They are equal in ownership but each has a distinct role and function.[12]

### ABSORB

**The uniqueness of the Trinity is that the persons are coequal, yet each person functions in his own role in perfect unity and love with each other. There is blessed oneness and happiness within the Trinity.**

### INTERACT

○ Imagine what would happen in human relationships—church, family, marriage, work—if each member functioned in perfect unity and harmony with each other. How can understanding the Trinity help us to live more harmoniously within our human relationships?

## LISTEN: Trinitarian Errors in History

Historically, errors have arisen in the church when one or more of the biblical foundations concerning the Trinity—God is three persons, each person is fully God, and there is one God—have been denied. The historic creeds have condemned such errors as heretical and harmful to having a true knowledge of God. We are grateful that we can learn from the errors of history. Here are a few examples.

**Error of Modalism.** Modalism claims that within God there are not three persons but only one person who can appear to humans in three different forms. This error is also called Sabellianism or "Oneness." This view of God purports that there is one person (God) who appears in three different manifestations—Father, Son, and Holy Spirit. This is like an actor changing costumes. This idea fails to take into account the actual, distinct persons of the Trinity. While Jesus was being baptized, the Father spoke about his love for his Son: "And the Holy Spirit descended in bodily form like a dove upon Him, and a voice came from heaven which said, '*You are My beloved Son*; in You I am well pleased'" (Luke 3:22). This is clearly evidence of a real and personal relationship between the Father and Son.

**Error of Tritheism.** This view holds that there are three Gods. This is an error because it denies the obvious teaching of Scripture that there is only one God. Jesus himself said: "The first of all the commandments is: 'Hear, O Israel, the Lord our God, the Lord is *one*'" (Mark 12:29).

**Error of Arianism.** The term "Arianism" comes from the views of Arius, a bishop of Alexandria whose views were condemned at the Council of Nicea in AD 325. Arius taught that at a point in time, God created the Son, but before that time the Son did not exist, nor did the Holy Spirit—only the Father. Arius denied that Jesus was of the same essence (*ousia*) as the Father. This view denies the biblical teaching that Jesus is fully God: "In the beginning was the Word, and the Word was with God, and the *Word was God*" (John 1:1).

Understanding these errors is extremely important because when there is error there also arises a distorted picture of the gospel. For example, the Bible says: "The Father loves the Son, and has given all things into His hand. He who believes in the Son has everlasting life; and he who does not believe the Son shall not see life, but the wrath of God abides on him" (John 3:35–36). The question then becomes, do you believe in the Son—that he is the eternal Son of God, or do you simply believe that he is just a man? What you believe about Christ makes an enormous difference. Jesus himself said: "He who does not honor the Son does not honor the Father who sent Him" (John 5:23). If we do not honor the Son as the eternal Son of God, then we do not honor the Father who sent him. If we do not honor either the Son or the Father, can we have a true saving relationship with God?

If you deny the Trinity you lose your soul; if you try to explain the Trinity you shall lose your mind.

**—Augustine**

## ABSORB

**The historic creeds of the church have affirmed the biblical, orthodox view of the Trinity. (You can read the Nicene Creed in the appendix to this session.)**

## INTERACT

○ Why is having a biblical view of the Trinity of immense importance?

**Reflect:** Each member of the Trinity functions in perfect unity and harmony with each other. Think about how you as a person can better function in unity and harmony with those whom God has placed in your life. Getting along with others can be a substantial advantage to reaching out to others with the message of the gospel.

Think about the greatness and the majesty of our Lord: "God in three persons, blessed Trinity!" How can I pray for you until we meet next time?

## *CULTIVATING SPIRITUAL HABITS*

**Read:** John 14:1–21 and Revelation 1

**Journal:** Read the appendix to this session (the Nicene Creed), then write down different aspects of the Trinity that you didn't know.

### Memorize

*All should honor the Son just as they honor the Father. He who does not honor the Son does not honor the Father who sent Him.*

JOHN 5:23

# The Nicene Creed

The Nicene Creed was written in AD 325 by leaders of the church and was later expanded. It was written to defend the biblical view of the Trinity and to reject formally the teachings of Arius, who claimed that Jesus was *created* and was not of the same nature as God. Read through the Nicene Creed and pick out things you have learned about the Trinity from this session. See if you understand why the leaders worded this creed the way they did.

We believe in one God, the Father, the Almighty, maker of heaven and earth, of all that is, seen and unseen.

We believe in one Lord, Jesus Christ, the only son of God, eternally begotten of the Father, God from God, Light from Light, true God from true God, begotten, not made, of one being [*ousia*] with the Father. Through him all things were made. For us and for our salvation he came down from heaven: by the power of the Holy Spirit he became incarnate from the Virgin Mary, and was made man. For our sake he was crucified under Pontius Pilate; he suffered death and was buried. On the third day he rose again in accordance with the Scriptures; he ascended into heaven and is seated at the right hand of the Father. He will come again in glory to judge the living and the dead, and his kingdom will have no end.

We believe in the Holy Spirit, the Lord, the giver of life, who proceeds from the Father and the Son. With the Father and the Son he is worshipped and glorified. He has spoken through the Prophets. We believe in one holy catholic* and apostolic Church. We acknowledge one baptism for the forgiveness of sins. We look for the resurrection of the dead, and the life of the world to come.

---

* The term "catholic" is used here in the sense of "universal": there is only one true body of Christ.

# LEVEL THREE

# Jesus's Divinity

## The Uniqueness of Christ (Part 1)

**Purpose of Session Sixteen:** This session (and the next) focuses on the nature of Christ, who is both fully God *and* fully man. In this session we look at Christ's divine nature, and in the next session we look at his human nature. The goal of this session is to give you a sound, biblical understanding of the unique person of Christ, especially his deity.

## LISTEN: Christ—In a Class All by Himself

Some basic questions arise for many Christians: How can Jesus be both God and man? What happened when the Son of God became a man? Did the Son of God stop being God when he became a man? How did his becoming a man affect his relationships within the Trinity? The answers to these questions lie in the unique nature of Jesus: Jesus, unlike anyone else who has ever existed, has two natures—*he is fully God and fully man*. Some theologians refer to Christ as "the God-man," and here are a few of his claims:

"I am the Son of God." (John 10:36)

"He who has seen me has seen the Father." (John 14:9)

"He who believes in me has everlasting life. I am the bread of life." (John 6:47–48)

"I am the way, the truth and the life. No one comes to the Father except through Me." (John 14:6)

These would appear to be outlandish statements except that Jesus's life, character, teachings, and miracles (the ultimate miracle being his resurrection) validated his claims! Christ is in a class all by himself. One of the most amazing facts about Jesus is that he is God the Son.

## ABSORB

**Jesus is in a class all by himself. His claims would appear to be outlandish except that Jesus's life, character, teachings, and miracles substantiate his claims.**

## INTERACT

○ Can you imagine a person walking into an auditorium and announcing: "I am the Son of God," and "He who believes in me has everlasting life," and "He who has seen me has seen the Father"? What would be your initial assessment of someone making such claims?

## LISTEN: Jesus's Divine Nature—Fully God

Who is Jesus? He claimed to be the Son of God, declaring himself equal with God. Because this is such a radical claim, some critics seek to redefine the clear teachings of Scripture, trying to make Jesus out to be only a man or something less than God himself. The following passage shows that Jesus equated himself with God: "But Jesus answered them, 'My Father has been working until now, and I have been working.' Therefore the Jews sought all the more to kill Him, because He not only broke the Sabbath, but also said *that God was His Father, making Himself equal with God*" (John 5:17–18).

The Jews clearly understood Jesus's claim even though it was slightly veiled, and it angered them so much that they wanted him dead. Jesus's claim—that God is his father—is controversial and profound. It angered the Jews tremendously, and yet it is what Jesus offered his disciples as proof of his divinity. One of the things you discover about the teachings of Jesus is that instead of just blatantly telling the crowds: "I am God," he often spoke in veiled words and parables about God's kingdom and about his own identity. Yet to clearly get this message, Jesus said they needed to have "ears to hear"—they needed to have spiritually receptive hearts. When he performed astounding miracles, it was evident that he was more than a mere human, but a hardened heart could always find some excuse not to believe! Jesus's miracles and statements invited those who were truly pursuing God to follow him and discover the truth about who he was. On the night of the Last Supper, Jesus was with his disciples and said, "If you had known Me, you would have known My Father also; and from now on you know Him and have seen Him." Immediately this raised questions, so "Philip said to Him, 'Lord, show us the Father, and it is sufficient for us.' Jesus said to him, 'Have I been with you so long, and yet you have not known Me, Philip? *He who has seen Me has seen the Father*'" (John 14:8–9).

Listen carefully to C. S. Lewis's famous challenge concerning our response to Jesus's claim:

> I am trying here to prevent anyone saying the really foolish thing that people often say about Him: 'I'm ready to accept Jesus as a great moral teacher, but I don't accept His claim to be God.' That is the one thing we must not say. A man who was merely a man and said the sort of things Jesus said would not be a great moral teacher. He would either be a lunatic—on the level with a man who says he is a poached egg—or he would be the devil of hell. You must take your choice. Either this was, and is, the Son of God, or else a madman or something worse. You can shut Him up for a fool or you can fall at His feet and call Him Lord and God. But let us not come with any patronizing nonsense about His being a great human teacher. He has not left that open to us.[1]

## ABSORB

**From Lewis's quote has come the old challenge concerning our response to who Christ claimed to be: "You have three basic choices: he was either a liar, a lunatic, or Lord."**

## INTERACT

○ Explain why those are our only real options.

## LISTEN: Why Jesus Called Himself the "Son of Man"

At strategic points, Jesus clearly identified himself as the Messiah, the Son of God. But one of his favorite terms for himself was the "Son of Man." On one level this title points to truth that he was truly human. But it is important to note that this phrase was used in Daniel 7:13–14, where it describes a vision of a special heavenly person who appears with the clouds of heaven, who instead of being like one of the "beast-like" kings described in Daniel's former visions, was like a Son of Man (a human). And to this Son of Man was given exalted, universal, absolute authority to rule over the everlasting kingdom of God.

> I was watching in the night visions,
> And behold, One like the *Son of Man*,
> Coming with the clouds of heaven!
> He came to the Ancient of Days,
> And they brought Him near before Him.
> Then to Him was given dominion and glory and a kingdom,
> That all peoples, nations, and languages should serve Him.
> His dominion is an everlasting dominion,
> Which shall not pass away,
> And His kingdom the one
> Which shall not be destroyed. (Dan. 7:13–14)

By using the title "Son of Man" for himself, Jesus was inferring that *he* is the Son of Man that was prophesied by Daniel.

John Piper, in his book *What Jesus Demands from the World*, analyzes why Jesus favored this title:

> The reason Jesus favored the title *Son of Man* for himself was that the terms *Messiah* and *Son of God* were loaded with popular political pretensions. They would give the wrong impression about the nature of his messiahship. They could easily imply that he fit in with the conceptions of that day that the Messiah would conquer Rome and liberate Israel and set up his earthly kingdom. But Jesus had to navigate these political waters by presenting himself as truly the Messiah, even the divine Son of God with universal authority, but also reject the popular notion that the Messiah would not suffer but immediately rule.
>
> The term *Son of Man* proved most useful in this regard because though it did carry exalted claims for those who had ears to hear, on the face of it he was not making explicit claims to political power. Under this favorite title (while not rejecting the others), Jesus was able to make his claims that the long-awaited messianic kingdom of God had come in his ministry.[2]

## ABSORB

**It appears that Jesus preferred calling himself the "Son of Man" because he actually was the fulfillment of the person in the vision found in Daniel 7:13–14. The term "Son of Man" provided Jesus the opportunity to use a divine messianic title and at the same time express what the Messiah would be and do. The title also serves to emphasize his dual nature—fully God and fully man.**

## INTERACT

○ Jesus was very creative in revealing who he was and the divine mission that his Father sent him to do. Why do you think the title "Son of Man" would help communicate more clearly what that was?

## LISTEN: Jesus—One with the Father

Jesus clearly taught that he came from heaven, and he made astonishing claims, such as "I and My Father are one." At certain points in Jesus's teaching, his inferences were so clear that even his critics could not miss his point: he was making himself out to be God. Jesus said, "'I and My Father are one.' Then the Jews took up stones again to stone Him. Jesus answered them, 'Many good works I have shown you from My Father. For which of those works do you stone Me?' The Jews answered Him, saying, 'For a good work we do not stone You, but for blasphemy, and because you, being a man, *make yourself God*'" (John 10:30–33).

Also, as you read the Old Testament account of God revealing himself to Moses, you discover that God identifies himself by the name "I AM" (which suggests that he has eternally existed as God!):

> Then Moses said to God, "Indeed, when I come to the children of Israel and say to them, 'The God of your fathers has sent me to you,' and they say to me, 'What is His name?' what shall I say to them?" And God said to Moses, "I AM WHO I AM." And He said, "Thus you shall say to the children of Israel, 'I AM has sent me to you.'" (Exod. 3:13–14)

As you read the New Testament and observe what Jesus said about himself, you discover in John 8 that "Jesus said to them, 'Most assuredly, I say to you, before Abraham was, I AM.' Then they took up stones to throw at Him" (John 8:58–59).

Jesus identified himself as the very same "I AM" who appeared to Moses. The Jewish opponents knew exactly what Jesus was asserting, and they wanted to stone him because, in their eyes, this claim was blasphemy (a demeaning slander against God, deserving the death penalty).

─── **ABSORB** ───

### There was no question that critics of Christ understood that he made himself out to be God.

─── **INTERACT** ───

○ If you had been there that day and heard Jesus say, "Before Abraham was, I AM," what would have been going through your mind?

## LISTEN: Peter and Thomas Affirm the Deity of Christ

At a strategic point in his ministry, Jesus asks his disciples what they think of his identity:

> He asked His disciples, saying, "Who do men say that I, the Son of Man, am?" So they said, "Some say John the Baptist, some Elijah, and others Jeremiah or one of the prophets." He said to them, "But who do you say that I am?" Simon Peter answered and said, "You are the Christ, the Son of the living God." Jesus answered and said to him, "Blessed are you, Simon Bar-Jonah, for flesh and blood has not revealed this to you, but My Father who is in heaven." (Matt. 16:13–17)

Peter gives Jesus a stunning answer: Jesus is the Christ the Son of the living God. The term "Christ" (Greek: *Christos*, Χριστος) means "the Anointed One" or "the Messiah."[3] Peter was saying that Jesus is the promised Messiah who the Old Testament prophets predicted would come. And Peter added, "the Son of the living God." Jesus not only accepts and confirms Peter's confession but tells Peter that this clear revelation has come from Jesus's Father in heaven! Here Jesus is clearly affirming his own deity—that he is the Son of God!

Later, after Jesus had risen from the dead, Thomas (a disciple of Jesus) was skeptical when he first heard that Jesus had risen from the dead. He said he would not believe unless he could see the risen Christ for himself. About a week later, when the resurrected Jesus appeared to Thomas face-to-face and showed him the scars on his hands and side, Thomas was overwhelmed and said, "My Lord and my God!" (John 20:28).

## ABSORB

### The close disciples of Jesus testified to his divine nature.

## INTERACT

○ What do you think the other disciples were thinking when Peter spoke up and said, "You are the Christ, the Son of the living God"?

○ If you had been with Thomas that day and had seen the resurrected Christ (recall that Jesus had been violently flogged, brutally crucified, and stabbed in his side with a spear), what do you think your first response would have been?

---

## The Meaning of "Christ"

When Jesus is referred to as "Jesus Christ," many think that "Christ" is Jesus's last name. It is not. The word "Christ" is a title and comes from the Greek word *Christos*, which means "Messiah." The English word "Messiah" comes from the Hebrew word *mashiach*, which means "Anointed One." So "Jesus Christ" means "Jesus the Messiah" (or "Jesus the Anointed One"). In the Old Testament, when God chose David to be king, he had the prophet Samuel anoint David with oil to designate David as God's anointed king. Consequently David became God's "anointed one"—the prototype of the ultimate coming king who would be the "Anointed One" who would restore the great kingdom of David. And he would be the son (a descendant) of David. As R. C. Sproul observes:

> This aspect greatly excited the Jews and fanned the flames of their hope for a political ruler who would free them from their bondage to Rome. . . .
> The Messiah would also be a heavenly being (Son of Man) and would be uniquely related to God the Father (Son of God). He would be both priest and prophet as well. The more we realize how complex the concept of Messiah was, the more amazed we are at the intricate way in which all these strands were woven together in the person and work of Jesus.[a]

[a]R. C. Sproul, *Essential Truths of the Christian Faith* (Wheaton: Tyndale, 1992), 104.

## LISTEN: Scripture Affirms the Deity of Christ

Remember the error of Arianism that denied that Jesus was of the same essence (*ousia*) as the Father. This view denies the biblical teaching that Jesus is fully God. Forms of Arianism are still present today in cults, sects, and even in some circles of "higher criticism" in theological academic settings. Listed below are a few of the many biblical passages that demonstrate that the Bible teaches that Jesus is fully God.

**The Word was God.** Jesus is identified as "the Word" in John 1:14. Therefore when "the Word" is equated with God in John 1:1, it is referring to Jesus: "In the beginning was the Word, and the Word was with God, and the Word was God." The text not only says that Jesus was *with* God but that he *was* God!

**Purchased with Christ's blood.** There is an interesting passage in Acts 20 in which Paul exhorts the leaders of the churches in Ephesus to shepherd faithfully the church of God that "He" (God) purchased with his own blood: "Therefore take heed to yourselves and to all the flock, among which the Holy Spirit has made you overseers, to shepherd the church of God which He purchased with His own blood" (Acts 20:28). Paul saw such a unity between God the Father and the Son that he could speak of Christ's death as shedding the blood of God!

**Christ our God and Savior.** The apostle Paul writes about when Christ will return from heaven. Christians are to look for that blessed hope of Christ's return: "looking for the blessed hope and glorious appearing of our great God and Savior Jesus Christ" (Titus 2:13). Paul describes the appearing of Jesus as the appearing of "our great God and Savior."

**Christ who is God over all.** The apostle Paul also describes Christ as God who is over all in Romans 9:5: "To them [the Jewish people] belong the patriarchs, and from their race, according to the flesh, is the Christ, who is God over all, blessed forever. Amen" (ESV).

**God's throne identical to Christ's throne.** Psalm 45:6 refers to the throne *of God* being forever and ever: "Your throne, O God, is forever and ever; / A scepter of righteousness is the scepter of Your kingdom." Notice however that the writer of Hebrews specifically points out that this passage refers to the Son of God: "But *to the Son* He says: 'Your throne, O God, is forever and ever; / A scepter of righteousness is the scepter of Your kingdom'" (Heb. 1:8). Here the Scriptures teach once again the unity of God—both the Father and the Son. Notice in Hebrews 1:8 that the Son is addressed as God himself! Matthew 1:23 quotes Isaiah 7:14 and describes Jesus as the fulfillment of this ancient prophecy; Jesus is called "Immanuel," which means "God with us": "'Behold, the virgin shall be with child, and bear a Son, and they shall call His name Immanuel,' which is translated '*God with us*.'" Jesus was literally "God with us" upon this earth!

In 1 Timothy 3:16 we have the words used in one of the first inspired hymns of the early church: "God was manifested in the flesh." This means God was

Emmanuel. God with us. He who resided in Heaven, co-equal and co-eternal with the Father and the Spirit, willingly descended into our world. He breathed our air, felt our pain, knew our sorrows, and died for our sins. He didn't come to frighten us, but to show us the way to warmth and safety.

—**Charles Swindoll,**
***The Finishing Touch***

found in the form of a human. The word "manifest" means "to make evident or certain by showing or displaying." God was made evident by displaying and showing himself in the person of Jesus Christ.

## ABSORB

### The Bible clearly affirms the idea that Jesus is fully God!

## INTERACT

○ Which of the above passages that state that Jesus is God stand out the most to you? Why?

---

### The Meaning of "Lord"

"The New Testament word for *Lord* is the Greek word *kurios* [pronounced cure-e-os].The word was used in several ways in the ancient world. In its most common usage it functioned as a polite word for *Sir*.

"A second use of the title *Lord* in the Greek culture was as a title given to men of the aristocratic class who were slave owners. This title was used figuratively for Jesus throughout the New Testament. He was called 'Master' by his disciples. . . . Here the believer is seen as a possession of Jesus. Jesus owns His people. He is not a despot or tyrant, as we might expect in an earthly slave/master situation. . . .

"The third and most important meaning of the title *Lord* was the imperial usage. Here the title was given to one who had absolute sovereignty over a group of people. It is a usage that was usually understood politically.

"Perhaps the most striking aspect about the title *Lord* was its relationship to the Old Testament. The Greek translation of the Old Testament used the word *kurios* to translate the Hebrew word *Adonai* [pronounced Ah-doe-nigh], a title used for God Himself . . . and He [Jesus] receives the title *Adonai* that had formerly been exclusively restricted to God the Father.

"The exalted title Lord belonged to Jesus alone, and Christians paid with their lives to maintain the assertion."[a]

"To call Jesus 'Lord' was radical not only from a Roman standpoint but especially from a Jewish standpoint, for it is the title given to God Himself in the Old Testament."[b]

**R. C. Sproul**

[a]*Who Is Jesus?* (Wheaton: Tyndale, 1986), 33–36.
[b]*Essential Truths of the Christian Faith* (Wheaton: Tyndale, 1992), 104.

---

○ In light of the many passages teaching the deity of Christ, why do you think cults and others deny his deity?

## LISTEN: Jesus Is Lord

Jesus is called "Lord" in the exalted sense, which is a title reserved for God. Deuteronomy 10:17 says of God: "For the LORD your God is God of gods* and Lord of lords, the great God, mighty and awesome."

Now look carefully—Revelation 17:14 and 19:16 identify the Lamb (Jesus) as the King of kings[4] and Lord of lords: "These will make war with the Lamb, and the Lamb will overcome them, for He is Lord of lords and King of kings; and those who are with Him are called, chosen, and faithful" (Rev. 17:14). "And He has on His robe and on His thigh a name written: KING OF KINGS AND LORD OF LORDS" (Rev. 19:16).

--- ABSORB ---

**It is clear that Jesus is identified in the Scriptures as Lord in the exalted sense!**

--- INTERACT ---

○ What do you think of when you hear the title "King of kings and Lord of lords"?

## LISTEN: The Importance of It All

The reason why these passages of Scripture are so important is that Christ deserves to be worshiped as the glorious Son of God! After all, he created us: "All things were made through Him, and without Him nothing was made that was made" (John 1:3). He redeemed us and purchased us with his blood. As is recorded in a majestic scene in the book of Revelation, all of the angels

---

* 1 Cor. 8:5 states that there are "gods" only in the sense of "so-called" gods. People make "gods" of things but they are not real—though people actually worship these "gods."

in heaven with all the uncountable multitudes of worshipers cry out saying, "Worthy is the Lamb [Jesus] who was slain / To receive power and riches and wisdom, / And strength and honor and glory and blessing!" (Rev. 5:12). Christ is worthy of all honor and praise for who he is—not just a good man but the exalted Son of God!

When people criticize God for allowing suffering and pain to enter into the world, they overlook that God himself was manifested in the flesh in this sin-cursed world. In the classic words of Dorothy Sayers: "For whatever reason God chose to make people as they are—limited and suffering and subject to sorrows and death—He had the honesty and courage to take His own medicine. Whatever game He is playing with His creation, He has kept His own rules and played fair. He can exact nothing from us that He has not exacted from Himself."[5]

## ABSORB

**There are numerous passages of Scripture that reveal that Jesus is fully God. Jesus has two natures: he is fully God and fully man.**

## INTERACT

○ How can knowing that the Son of God became a human help us appreciate God all the more when we go through times of trouble?

**Reflect:** Think about how amazing it is that God the Son would actually come to this planet to die for people who were in rebellion against him. How can that motivate us to carry out the mission that Christ gave to you and me: to make disciples of Jesus Christ in the power of the Holy Spirit? How can I best pray for you until our next meeting?

## CULTIVATING SPIRITUAL HABITS

**Read:** Philippians 2 and Luke 1:26–38

**Journal:** Read through Revelation 19. Jot down in your journal anything that stands out to you about Christ.

### Memorize

*He said to them, "But who do you say that I am?" Simon Peter answered and said, "You are the Christ, the Son of the living God."*

MATTHEW 16:15–16

# Jesus's Humanity

## The Uniqueness of Christ (Part 2)

**Purpose of Session Seventeen:** This session (and the last) focuses on the nature of Christ, who is both fully God and fully man. In this session we look at Christ's human nature. (In the last session we looked at Christ's divine nature.)

## LISTEN: Two Natures

The British author H. G. Wells once wrote: "I am an historian, I am not a believer, but I must confess as a historian that this penniless preacher from Nazareth is irrevocably the very center of history. Jesus Christ is easily the most dominant figure in all history."[1] Wells was correct—Jesus is the very center of history, and the more we understand the unique person of Christ, the more we will be able to appreciate and worship him for who he really is.

The ancient church spent a considerable amount of time and energy defining the connection between the two natures of Christ, which resulted in the Creed of Chalcedon (AD 451). (The text of the creed is included in the appendix to this session.) This creed has been received as the standard orthodox definition of the person of Christ.

— ABSORB —

The ancient church realized the high value of understanding the union of the two natures of Christ. In the incarnation, the divine nature of the Son was united but not mixed with his human nature, in one divine person, Jesus Christ, who was both truly God and truly man.

---- **INTERACT** ----

○ What do you imagine it was like for Jesus to grow up being both truly God and truly man?

## LISTEN: Jesus Is Fully Man

Not only is Jesus God but he is also a man—a real human being. Theologians call this the "incarnation" of Christ. This term "incarnation" is of Latin origin, meaning "becoming-in-flesh."[2] This truth is taught in places such as John 1:14, where God the Son is referred to as the Word becoming flesh: "And the Word became flesh and dwelt among us, and we beheld His glory, the glory as of the only begotten of the Father, full of grace and truth."

As we have seen from Scripture, God the Son has always been God. There never was a time when he was not God. But the Son of God has not always been man. It was not until the incarnation, approximately two thousand years ago, that God the Son became a man—this is what Christians celebrate at Christmas. But what does the Bible mean when it describes God the Son becoming a man? It does *not* mean that he stopped being God and started being man. He remained fully God but became a real man—he was also fully man.

A question arises: Which person of the Trinity became incarnate (became flesh/human) in Jesus Christ? The biblical answer is that only the person of God the Son became incarnate. The Father did not become incarnate and neither did the Holy Spirit. This is important to realize; the *Father* sent the Son into the world: "God [the Father] so loved the world that He gave His only begotten Son. . . . For God did not send His Son into the world to condemn the

---

### Fully God, Fully Man

"The glory of the incarnation is that it presents to our adoring gaze not a humanized God or a deified man, but a true God-man—one who is all that God is and at the same time all that man is: one on whose almighty arm we can rest, and to whose human sympathy we can appeal. We cannot afford to lose either the God in the man or the man in the God. Our hearts cry out for the complete God-man whom the Scriptures offer us."

**Benjamin Warfield[a]**

[a]Fred G. Zaspel, *The Theology of B. B. Warfield: A Systematic Summary* (Wheaton: Crossway, 2010), 278.

world, but that the world through Him might be saved" (John 3:16–17). Jesus explained to his disciples that he would return "to My Father" (John 14:12).

## ABSORB

**It was God the Son who became a man. The other persons of the Trinity—the Father and the Holy Spirit—did not become incarnate.**

## INTERACT

○ C. S. Lewis wrote, "The central miracle asserted by Christmas is the Incarnation. They say that God became Man. . . . If the thing happened, it was the central event in the history of the Earth."[3] What do you think about his comment?

## LISTEN: Born of a Virgin

Now if God the Son became a human, then how did that happen? The Bible records that Jesus was supernaturally conceived by the Holy Spirit and born of a virgin (Luke 1:34: "Then Mary said to the angel, 'How can this be, since I do not know a man?'"). We should not be surprised that something profoundly special would have to occur for God the Son to become flesh! J. I. Packer eloquently says:

> The Word had become flesh: a real human baby. He had not ceased to be God; He was no less God then than before; but He had begun to be man. He was not now God minus some elements of His deity, but God plus all that He had made His own by taking manhood to Himself. . . . The mystery of the incarnation is unfathomable. We cannot explain it; we can only formulate it. Perhaps it has never been formulated better than in the words of the Athanasian Creed. "*Our Lord Jesus Christ, the Son of God, is God and man; . . . perfect God, and perfect man: . . . who although he be God and man; yet he is not two, but one Christ; one, not by conversion of the Godhead into flesh; but by taking of the manhood into God.*"[4]

If Jesus had been conceived by the ordinary process of conception between Joseph and Mary, he would have been *only* a man, with only a human nature but without a divine nature. As a consequence, he would not have been

The divine Son became a Jew; the Almighty appeared on earth as a helpless human baby, unable to do more than lie and stare and wriggle and make noises, needed to be fed and changed and taught to talk like any other child. . . . The more you think about it, the more staggering it gets.

**—J. I. Packer,**
***Knowing God***

*Immanuel* (God with us); He would have been simply *agathos anthropos* (a good man). He would be unable to rescue others from sin. Yet when you take into account the incredible life, ministry, and especially the miracles of Christ, they point not only to his human nature but also to his divinity. Think about Jesus's challenge to some skeptics of his day, who accused him of blasphemy because he called himself the "Son of God": "If I do not do the works of My Father, do not believe Me; but if I do, though you do not believe Me, believe the works, that you may know and believe that the Father is in Me, and I in Him" (John 10:37–38).

## ABSORB

**Jesus was not conceived by the ordinary process of conception between Joseph and Mary. He was supernaturally conceived by the Holy Spirit and born of a virgin.**

## INTERACT

○ A skeptic once asked a Christian this question: "If I should tell you that a child had been born in this city without a father, would you believe it?" The Christian answered, "Yes, if he should live as Jesus lived."[5] What was the point the Christian was trying to make?

## LISTEN: Jesus Lived a Real Human Life

We must be careful to recognize that although Jesus was perfect God and perfect man, he lived the real life of a human. He had to grow up and learn like other boys and girls: "And Jesus increased in wisdom and stature, and in favor with God and men" (Luke 2:52). It is important to realize that Jesus experienced real hunger and thirst (Matt. 4:2; John 19:28). The Scriptures record that Jesus could tire—he became weary from a long journey (John 4:6). He even felt deep emotional pain: "And being *in agony*, He prayed more earnestly" (Luke 22:44).

## ABSORB

### Jesus lived a real life of a human. He had a real human body. Christ's humanity was like our humanity.

The mystery of the humanity of Christ, that He sunk Himself into our flesh, is beyond all human understanding.

—**Martin Luther, Table Talk**

## INTERACT

○ How does it make you feel to know that God the Son became a real human who experienced real hunger, thirst, pain, temptation, and so on?

○ Why is it sometimes difficult to picture Jesus as being fully man?

## LISTEN: The Two Natures Remain Distinct

Theologian R. C. Sproul gives a concise summary of the historic understanding of the two natures of Christ:

> That God the Son took upon Himself a real human nature is a crucial doctrine of historic Christianity. The great ecumenical Council of Chalcedon in AD 451 affirmed that Jesus is truly man and truly God and that the two natures of Christ are so united as to be without mixture, confusion, separation, or division, each nature retaining its own attributes.
>
> The true humanity of Jesus has been assaulted chiefly in two ways. The early church had to combat the heresy* of *docetism*, which taught that Jesus did not have a real physical body or a true human nature. They argued that Jesus only "seemed" to have a body but in reality was a phantom sort of being. Over against this, John strongly declared that those who denied that Jesus came truly in the flesh are of the Antichrist.
>
> The other major heresy the church rejected was the *monophysite* heresy. This heresy argued that Jesus did not have two natures, but one. This single nature was neither truly divine nor truly human but a mixture of the two. . . . The monophysite heresy involves either a deified human nature or a humanized divine nature.[6]

---

\* "Heresy" is a teaching contrary to the truth.

Think for a moment why it would distort the truth about the person of Christ to mix his two natures[7] together and not let each nature stand on its own. If the two natures were mixed, he wouldn't have been able to have a true experience of what it means to be human!

Sproul continues,

> We must distinguish between the two natures of Jesus without separating them. When Jesus hungers, for example, we see that as a manifestation of the human nature, not the divine. What is said of the divine nature or of the human nature may be affirmed of the person. On the cross for example, Christ, the God-man, died. This, however, is not to say that God perished on the cross. Though the two natures remain united after Christ's ascension, we must still distinguish the natures regarding the mode of His presence with us. Concerning His human nature, Christ is no longer present with us. However, in His divine nature, Christ is never absent from us.
>
> Christ's humanity was like ours. He became a man "for our sakes." He entered into our situation to act as our Redeemer. . . .
>
> In redemption there is a twofold exchange. Our sins are imparted to Jesus. His righteousness is imparted to us. He receives the judgment due to our imperfect humanity, while we receive the blessing due to His perfect humanity. In His humanity Jesus had the same limitations common to all human beings, except that he was without sin. In His human nature He was not omniscient. His knowledge, though true and accurate as far as it went, was not infinite. There were things He did not know such as the day and the hour of His return to earth. Of course in His divine nature He is omniscient and His knowledge is without limit.
>
> As a human being Jesus was restricted by time and space. Like all human beings He could not be in more than one place at the same time. He sweated. He hungered. He wept. He endured pain. He was mortal, capable of suffering death. In all these respects He was like us.[8]

## ABSORB

**Jesus is truly man and truly God, and "the two natures of Christ are so united as to be without mixture, confusion, separation, or division, each nature retaining its own attributes."**

## INTERACT

○ Does it now make sense to you that when Jesus lived on this earth as a human, he experienced hunger, thirst, and pain, and even did not know when the future time of his return would be?

## LISTEN: Christ's Humiliation

Theologians refer to the Son of God leaving the glory of heaven (which he shared with the Father) as the time of his *humiliation*. The Son of God humbled himself (Phil. 2:5–8) and took on a lowly status and position of being a servant. For more than thirty years (until his resurrection and exaltation) he lived as a humble servant of God, submitting himself always to his Father's will. He voluntarily gave up the brilliant glory that he had eternally experienced with the Father. In his incarnation, he did nothing from his own initiative but always perfectly obeyed his Father—without ever sinning. He did not do tricks using his divine nature in order to make life more pleasant for himself. Any divine power he exerted from his divine nature was always at the direction of the Father: "I can of Myself do nothing. . . . I do not seek My own will but the will of the Father who sent Me" (John 5:30). This helps us to understand statements Jesus made *as a man*, such as: "If you loved Me, you would rejoice because I said, 'I am going to the Father,' for My Father is greater than I" (John 14:28). As a man, Jesus was less than the Father. As God, Jesus was equal to God. Jesus never gave up his essential divine attributes or nature as God. But he voluntarily lived *as a man* in a state of humility. As the resurrected Servant/Messiah, he is highly exalted with great glory as our conquering Savior. Paul writes, "That at the name of Jesus every knee should bow, of those in heaven, and of those on earth, and of those under the earth, and that every tongue should confess that Jesus Christ is Lord, to the glory of God the Father" (Phil. 2:10–11).

> He was poor, that he might make us rich. He was born of a virgin, that we might be born of God. He took our flesh, that he might give us His Spirit. He lay in the manger, that we may lie in paradise. He came down from heaven, that he might bring us to heaven.
>
> **—Thomas Watson,**
> ***A Body of Divinity***

### ABSORB

**The Son of God voluntarily laid aside his heavenly glory, status, and privileges to humble himself in order to live as a servant and to die for our sins.**

### INTERACT

○ Can you imagine what it was like for the Son to experience the glory of heaven with his Father from all eternity and then suddenly enter this fallen world? Why would this be considered a display of true love?

○ How does it make you feel to know that Jesus experienced fully the pain and punishment that we deserved?

## LISTEN: Two Natures but One Person

Even though Christ has two natures, he is not two people. Jesus never speaks of himself as "we," only as "I." The historical statement of orthodoxy is that *Christ is two natures united in one person forever.*

The Creed of Chalcedon carefully states that Christ is "to be acknowledged in two natures . . . concurring in one Person and one Subsistence, not parted or divided into two persons, but one and the same Son, and only begotten, God the Word, the Lord Jesus Christ."

Therefore we must realize that the biblical teaching of the two natures of Christ is a mystery that is difficult for us to fully grasp. The one constant is that Christ is one person. When Christ was said to be hungry he really was hungry, even though he had a divine nature. Or when Christ said, "before Abraham was, I AM" (John 8:58), he really did exist before Abraham existed, even though he didn't become a man until the incarnation. Most of all, when Christ died upon the cross, he really died as a human being—"Christ died for our sins" (1 Cor. 15:3). Yet there is a mystery here because the divine cannot die, but "God so loved the world that He gave His only begotten Son" (John 3:16). The Scriptures define Christ always as one person, even though he is fully God and fully man. To be able simply to live with this mystery keeps us from developing odd or even heretical teachings that distort the understanding of the person of Christ.[9]

### ABSORB

**Even though Christ has two natures, he is only one person.**

### INTERACT

○ Do you agree with J. I. Packer's statement: "The mystery of the incarnation is unfathomable"? Why?

The incarnation of Jesus Christ is God's undeniable evidence that relevance to culture is not optional.

**—Erwin McManus,**
***An Unstoppable Force***

## LISTEN: Jesus—Two Natures Forever

When Jesus arose and ascended into heaven as a man, it was in a glorified body. Philippians 3:21 says that when Christ returns he "will transform our lowly body that it may be conformed to His glorious body." Christ now has a body—a glorified one. Christ is *two natures* united in *one person* forever.

### ABSORB

**The Son of God is undiminished deity, along with glorified humanity, united in one person forever.**

### INTERACT

○ What has been the most helpful piece of information that you have learned in this session about the uniqueness of the person of Christ?

**Reflect:** The Son of God voluntarily laid aside his heavenly glory, status, and privileges to humble himself in order to live as a servant and to die for our sins. We should regularly ask ourselves: "Am I ready to lay aside glory, status, and privileges to serve others to better their lives and lead them to the kingdom of God?"

Now that you know more about the two natures of Christ, read the Creed of Chalcedon in the appendix to this session and pick out key phrases that help you understand the unique person of Christ. How can I pray for you until we meet next time?

### CULTIVATING SPIRITUAL HABITS

**Read:** John 10:1–30 and Jude 20–24

**Journal:** Read the Creed of Chalcedon again, and this time write down key phrases you have learned from the Scriptures in this session.

## Memorize

*For unto us a Child is born,*
*Unto us a Son is given;*
*And the government will be upon His shoulder.*
*And His name will be called*
*Wonderful, Counselor, Mighty God,*
*Everlasting Father, Prince of Peace.*

ISAIAH 9:6

# The Creed of Chalcedon (AD 451)

We, then, following the holy Fathers, all with one consent, teach men to confess one and the same Son, our Lord Jesus Christ, the same perfect in Godhead and also perfect in manhood; truly God and truly man, of a reasonable [rational] soul and body; of one substance with the Father as regards his Godhead, and at the same time of one substance with us as regards his manhood; like us in all respects, apart from sin; as regards his Godhead, begotten of the Father before the ages, but yet as regards his manhood begotten, for us men and for our salvation, born of the Virgin Mary, the Mother of God, according to the Manhood; one and the same Christ, Son, Lord, only begotten, to be acknowledged in two natures, inconfusedly, unchangeably, indivisibly, inseparably; the distinction of natures being by no means taken away by the union, but rather the property of each nature being preserved, and concurring in one Person and one Subsistence, not parted or divided into two persons, but one and the same Son, and only begotten, God the Word, the Lord Jesus Christ; even as the prophets from earliest times spoke of him, and our Lord Jesus Christ himself taught us, and the creed of the fathers has handed down to us.

SESSION EIGHTEEN

# Kept by God

## Preservation, Perseverance, and Assurance (Part 1)

**Purpose of Session Eighteen:** This session and the next describe how God preserves and keeps those who are his children and calls on us to persevere in the faith. We will also focus on how God wants his children to live with the joy and the blessed assurance that they truly know him and have his eternal love and salvation.

## LISTEN: Preservation and Perseverance

There is nothing more important than the condition of our souls before God. We all want to know and feel that we are right with God! Yet even though we know we are justified by faith alone in Christ and that God is in the lifelong process of sanctifying us, sometimes our sanctification feels painfully slow, and the thought enters our minds: "I hope I really am saved." Even though you may have been a Christian for a long time, you may still find yourself occasionally lashing out in unrighteous anger, or becoming impatient, or allowing lust to enter your heart, or struggling with resentment, or not loving your neighbor as yourself. Does this mean that you have lost your salvation or that you are no longer justified by God?

We must be careful to avoid extremes when we consider our status with God in light of our ongoing sin. One extreme is to live in a state of anxiety and fear, where we frequently doubt our salvation because we realize we sometimes sin through anger, lust, lack of love, and so on. Some Christians become obsessive or perfectionistic, and begin to doubt their salvation, finding it hard to comprehend that God deals with his children in the same manner as a loving earthly father deals with his children who at times need correction. The other extreme is to think that once you have confessed faith in Christ, then you have "fire insurance from hell" and your lifestyle no longer matters. This mistaken idea—that as long as you *say* you believe in Christ, you can live a morally lawless, disobedient life and still be right with God—is called "antinomianism" (from the Greek *anti*, "against," and *nomos*, "law"). This extreme is a distortion of the grace of God and could lead to a shocking discovery at the final judgment day (Matt. 7:23).

Can a person lose his or her justification status? Can a true believer *fall away* in the sense of losing one's salvation? Can a true believer live such a sinful life or live in such unbelief that he or she really falls away from the faith and actually loses his or her salvation?

In order to answer these questions, there are several Scripture passages that we must look at carefully. In these two sessions you will discover first of all that it is God who *preserves* you (not you yourself). God himself is committed to preserving you and keeping you in the faith. Second, if you are truly born again, you *will* persevere in the Christian faith. It doesn't mean that those who are genuinely saved will never fall into sin or unbelief, but such a person will not, in the ultimate sense, "fall away" if he or she has truly been born again. If a person does not continue in the faith, then that is an indication that there was no genuine faith in the first place. This teaching has historically been called the perseverance of the saints.

## ABSORB

"The perseverance of the saints [believers] means that all those
who are truly born again will be kept by God's power and will
persevere as Christians until the end of their lives, and that only those
who persevere until the end have been truly born again."[1]

## INTERACT

○ Why do you think some Christians are tempted to give up the Christian life and simply live their lives any way they want?

God is the decisive keeper of my soul.

—**John Piper,**
**"Learning to Pray**
**in the Spirit and**
**the Word, Part 1"**

○ What are some of the ways that you sense that God has not given up on you and is still working in your life and preserving you?

## LISTEN: *God* Keeps Us from Falling

One of the most encouraging discoveries in the Bible is that God does not leave us on our own when he saves us. He is the "author and finisher of our faith" (Heb. 12:2). It is true that *we* as believers have the responsibility before God to persevere in the faith, but the wonderful news is that "it is God who works in you both to will and to do for His good pleasure" (Phil. 2:13). God is at work in us so that we want to do his good pleasure and so that we also actually live it out. There are several passages from the Bible that give us great hope that it is *God* who keeps us so that we will never perish in hell. One of the greatest things in the world is to be kept by God:

> "Now to Him who is able to keep you from stumbling [falling, KJV], / And to present you faultless / Before the presence of His glory with exceeding joy, / To God our Savior, / Who alone is wise, / Be glory and majesty, / Dominion and power, / Both now and forever. / Amen." (Jude 24–25)

Notice that Jude states that it is *God* who is able to keep you from falling. He is the one who will "present you faultless before the presence of His glory." That should give us great hope and comfort.

There is another encouraging Scripture passage in which Christ promises to give eternal life to his own and to keep them so that they will never perish. He reinforces this truth by adding that *no one* is able to snatch them out of his hand or his Father's hand: "My sheep hear My voice, and I know them, and they follow Me. And I give them eternal life, and *they shall never perish*; neither shall anyone snatch them out of My hand. My Father, who has given them to Me, is greater than all; and no one is able to snatch them out of My Father's hand. I and My Father are one" (John 10:27–30).

This powerful New Testament passage makes it clear that when God promises eternal life to his children, it is assured. He keeps them forever!

— ABSORB —

**God is the keeper of our souls. He keeps us by working *in* us so that we want to do his good pleasure, so that we do not turn from him and fall away. When God gives eternal life, he protects us so that we will never perish and no one will be able to snatch us from his hand.**

## INTERACT

○ Jude states that it is *God* who is able to keep you from falling. Which would you prefer—that ultimately *you* are the one who keeps yourself saved or that God is the one who keeps you saved? Why?

○ When it says in verse 28 that "they shall never perish," how do you feel personally about this promise to you? What does that mean to you?

### Glory, Majesty, Dominion, and Authority Keep Us Safe for Everlasting Joy

"When I think about finishing these laps in my race, I am simply amazed that I have lasted—lasted as a Christian, lasted as a pastor, lasted as a husband and father. . . . If my faith in Jesus, and my eagerness to know him and his word, and my thrill at preaching, and my love for the church, and my fitness for ministry and for heaven, . . . depended decisively on me, I would have ceased to be a Christian long ago. I would have ceased to care about the word of God. . . . I would have given up on the church and ceased to be fit for ministry or heaven. I would have given myself to sexual indulgence and ceased to be married. . . . If the decisive cause of my faithfulness to Christ in any of those expressions must come from me, it will not come, because it is not there. Therefore, I am amazed that I am still a Christian and love the ministry. And I feel some sense of the wonder that Jude seems to feel:

"'Now to him who has been mighty to keep *me* from stumbling [falling] and to present *me* blameless before the presence of his glory with great joy, to the only God, *my* Savior, through Jesus Christ *my* Lord, be glory, majesty, dominion, and authority, before all time and now and forever. Amen.'

"That's what it took to keep me from falling—and what it will take to get me home before the presence of his glory, blameless and full of unbridled joy. And that's what it will take to keep you believing, and ministering, and holy to the end of your days, and then get you home."

**John Piper[a]**

[a]Speaking at a Together for the Gospel Conference, Louisville , KY, April 12, 2012. (Piper was a pastor for 32 years and has been a believer for 60 years, a husband for 44 years, and a father for 40 years.)

## LISTEN: None Will Be Lost—All Are Saved

There is an important passage in the Gospel of John in which Jesus says that all the people that the Father gives to him will come to him and *none of them* will be lost, and he promises to resurrect them: "All that the Father gives Me will come to Me, and the one who comes to Me I will by no means cast out. . . . This is the will of the Father who sent Me, that of all He has given Me *I should lose nothing, but should raise it up at the last day*" (John 6:37, 39).

While we, as followers of Jesus, do have a responsibility to persevere in the faith, if God abandoned us to our own efforts, we would be sunk. (Later in this session, we will look at our responsibility to persevere.) We must respond to God in faith, but our great hope is in knowing that *God* is the keeper of our souls. The Lord even goes so far as to seal his own with the Holy Spirit in order to keep them. This seal, which is the Holy Spirit himself, is the guarantee of all the further blessings of eternal life: "In Him you also trusted, after you heard the word of truth, the gospel of your salvation; in whom also, having believed, you were *sealed with the Holy Spirit of promise*, who is the *guarantee* of our inheritance until the redemption of the purchased possession, to the praise of His glory" (Eph. 1:13–14).

The word "guarantee" in this verse is a legal and commercial term that means "deposit, down payment, or pledge" and represents "a payment which obligates the contracting party to make further payments."[2] All true believers are sealed with the Holy Spirit, who is God's special guarantee that we will experience our full future inheritance in heaven.

The grace that God gives us is not only for coming to faith in Christ but also for confirming us (or sustaining us) to the end. Listen to the promise given in 1 Corinthians: "I thank my God always concerning you for the grace of God which was given to you by Christ Jesus, . . . who will also *confirm you* [sustain or keep you strong] *to the end*, that you may be blameless in the day of our Lord Jesus Christ" (1 Cor. 1:4, 8).

### ABSORB

Jesus promises that all the people whom the Father gives to him will come to him and none will be lost. They will for certain be resurrected at the last day. The Lord goes so far as to seal us with his Holy Spirit, who is the guarantee of our heavenly inheritance.

--- INTERACT ---

○ How can it get better than this—that God himself promises to keep us by sealing us with his Spirit? What do you picture in your mind as to what happens when you are sealed by the Holy Spirit?

## LISTEN: The Call to Persevere—To Continue

Because God keeps us, we remain saved. This is God's divine work! But God also uses his appointed means of grace to keep us. The *means* is the way or instrument by which something happens. For example, we are saved by the grace of God through the means of faith. God's grace enables us to believe, but it is through the instrument of faith that we are saved. Ephesians 2:8 says, "For by grace you have been saved through faith, and that not of yourselves; it is the gift of God." If you do not exercise faith in Christ, then you are not saved. In the same way, it is God's grace and power that keeps us, but God uses *means* to do that.

God keeps us by his power *through our faith*: "[We] are kept by the power of God *through faith* for salvation ready to be revealed in the last time" (1 Pet. 1:5). We are dependent on God's work to enable us to continue following Christ, but *we* must continue in the faith. If we do not continue in the faith, then we were never really born again. There are several passages that highlight this truth: Colossians 1:21–23 points out that Christ has reconciled us in order to present us holy and blameless in the sight of God *if we continue in the faith*: "He has reconciled [you] . . . to present you holy, and blameless, and above reproach in His sight—if indeed you continue in the faith, grounded and steadfast, and are not moved away from the hope of the gospel which you heard." The sign that we have been truly reconciled to God is that we continue (persevere) in the faith.

Hebrews 3:14 explains that the evidence that we have become real partakers of Christ and his salvation is if we maintain our confidence (our faith in Christ) to the end: "For we have become partakers of Christ if we hold the beginning of our confidence steadfast to the end." John Piper comments on this verse:

Notice the wording carefully. It does *not* say: "We will become partakers of Christ in the future if we hold fast to our assurance." It says, "We have become partakers [in the past] if we hold fast our assurance." In other words, the holding fast to our assurance verifies that something real and lasting has happened to us, namely, we became partakers of Christ. We were truly born again. We were truly converted. We were truly made part of Christ's house.

What then would be the conclusion if we do *not* hold fast to our assurance? The answer is not that you stop being a partaker of Christ, but that you had

Though Christians be not kept altogether from falling, yet they are kept from falling altogether.

**—William Secker, Puritan pastor**

never become a partaker of Christ. Read it carefully: "We have become partakers of Christ *if* we hold fast to our assurance." And so, "If we do *not* hold fast to our confession, then we *have not* become partakers of Christ."[3]

Paul explains in 1 Corinthians 15:1–2 that you are saved *if* you hold fast to the word, which is the gospel message he preached: "Moreover, brethren, I declare to you the gospel which I preached to you, which also you received and in which you stand, by which also you are saved, if you hold fast that word which I preached to you." If you don't hold fast to the word, if you turn from the gospel, then that is evidence that you have not been saved.

Theologian Louis Berkhof makes an important observation concerning this balance between God keeping us and our responsibility to take hold of the "means" of grace to follow Christ: "Although the Bible tells us that we are kept by the grace of God, it does not encourage the idea that God keeps us without constant watchfulness, diligence, and prayer on our part."[4]

## ABSORB

**"All who are truly born again will persevere to the end."[5]**

## INTERACT

○ Why would it be reckless and spiritually dangerous to think that you could persevere in the faith yet neglect the very things that God has told us are so crucial, such as the Word, prayer, service, and

---

### On the Perseverance of the Saints

"Those whom God has accepted in his Beloved, effectually called, and sanctified by his Spirit, can neither totally nor finally fall away from the state of grace, but shall certainly persevere in it to the end and be eternally saved. . . .

"Nevertheless, they may—through the temptations of Satan and of the world, the pervasiveness of the corruption remaining in them, and the neglect of the means by which they are to be preserved—fall into grievous sins and for a time continue in them. In so doing they incur God's displeasure and grieve his Holy Spirit; some measure of God's graces and comforts is taken from them; they have their hearts hardened and their consciences wounded; they harm others and give them occasion to sin, and bring temporal judgments upon themselves."

**Westminster Confession of Faith[a]**

[a](Committee for Christian Education and Publications, Presbyterian Church in America, 1990), chap. 17, secs. 1 and 3.

the gathering together with the church for fellowship, communion, instruction, and worship?

## LISTEN: Reasons Genuine Believers Will Persevere

Why will those who are genuine believers persevere in the faith? First, God promises in his Word that those who are his will never completely fall or perish. At the beginning of this session, we listed several passages that promise God will keep his own and that they will never perish.

Second, when God chose us, he did so *before* the world was created: "just as He chose us in Him [Christ] *before* the foundation of the world" (Eph. 1:4). This means that God is not limited by time. He has full knowledge of the future before it happens. When God chose you before the world was created, he set in motion a process that he is committed to finishing. This process, or unbreakable chain of events, is listed in Romans 8:29–30: "For whom *He foreknew*, He also *predestined* to be conformed to the image of His Son, that He might be the firstborn among many brethren. Moreover whom He predestined, these He also *called*; whom He called, these He also *justified*; and whom He justified, these He also *glorified*."

So God chose us and planned out our destiny. It is unthinkable that before the foundation of the world God chose someone but then needed to look ahead *a second time* and "un-choose" them. It is clear from God's initial choosing that their future is certain in God's eyes, and God will make sure that his children will persevere: "Whom He foreknew, He also predestined . . . these He also called . . . these He also justified . . . and . . . these He also glorified." The apostle Paul points out the security that belongs to those who belong to Christ: "Nevertheless the solid foundation of God stands, having this seal: 'The Lord knows those who are His'" (2 Tim. 2:19). Those who are the Lord's are kept by the Lord and will therefore persevere to the end.

If I did not believe the doctrine of the final perseverance of the saints, I think I should be of all men the most miserable, because I should lack any ground for comfort.

**—Charles Spurgeon,** ***Autobiography***

— ABSORB —

**Those who are truly born again will persevere because God promises to keep them. Also, God chose us to be his own before the creation of the world. Before time, God set in motion a chain of events that would ensure that we would persevere to the end.**

## INTERACT

○ We can only see the future as "yet to be," but God sees the future as if it is "now." How does it make you feel to know that God chose you before the world began? Is that hard to comprehend?

**Reflect:** Ask yourself, especially when you are feeling spiritually apathetic, "Am I being reckless and neglecting things such as the Word, prayer, service, and the gathering together with the church for fellowship, communion, instruction, and worship?"

Think about how God has been the keeper of your soul. How can I pray for you until we meet next time?

### CULTIVATING SPIRITUAL HABITS

**Read:** Matthew 7:21–23; 1 Corinthians 6:9–11; Jeremiah 31:31–34; 32:38–40; Hebrews 8:7–13

**Journal:** Think back to a couple of different times when God has shown you great mercy in keeping you from falling. Jot down those times and reflect on the kindness and grace of God that have kept you safe in Christ.

#### Memorize

*Now to Him who is able to keep you from stumbling [falling],*
*And to present you faultless*
*Before the presence of His glory with exceeding joy,*
*To God our Savior,*
*Who alone is wise,*
*Be glory and majesty,*
*Dominion and power,*
*Both now and forever.*
*Amen.*

JUDE 24–25

# Living by God's Power

## Preservation, Perseverance, and Assurance (Part 2)

**Purpose of Session Nineteen:** In this session, a continuation of the last session, we focus on how God preserves and keeps us, how we are to persevere in the faith, and how we have the assurance of God's eternal love and salvation.

## LISTEN: God Works on Our "Want To"

The apostle John made this exclamation: "Behold what manner of love the Father has bestowed on us, that we should be called children of God!" (1 John 3:1). God as our Father is a key component to understanding the way he protects and preserves his children. What is amazing about God's love and grace for his children is that he works in our minds and hearts so that those who are born again will *want* to continue in the faith. In the Letter to the Philippians, Paul commands us who are believers to work out our own salvation. This means that *we* have the responsibility to follow Christ by faith and to do what he wants us to do. But the Scriptures also tell us that it is God who actually is at work in us so that we *want* to do his will and carry it out! "Therefore, my beloved, as you have always obeyed, not as in my presence only, but now much more in my absence, work out your own salvation with fear and trembling; *for it is God who works in you both to will and to do* for His good pleasure" (Phil. 2:12–13). Therefore, those who are truly born again will persevere because God is powerfully at work in them.

Believers are also given a godly fear of the Lord, so that they will not depart from him. A significant passage in Jeremiah (chaps. 31 and 32) describes the new covenant—the same covenant that Jesus initiated at the Last Supper. The book of Hebrews speaks plainly about Christ being the mediator of a better covenant—the new covenant that was predicted in Jeremiah—and a covenant that applies to all believers in Christ, even gentiles. Galatians 3:7–9 reveals that we are beneficiaries of God's promises to Abraham if we have the faith of Abraham and belong to Jesus Christ:[1] "So then those who are of faith are blessed with believing Abraham" (Gal. 3:9). Part of the promise of the new covenant is that God actually puts his fear in our hearts so that we will not depart from the Lord and will persevere in the faith:[2] "And I will make an everlasting covenant with them, that I will not turn away from doing them good; but *I will put My fear in their hearts so that they will not depart from Me*" (Jer. 32:40).

Sin and the child of God are incompatible. They may occasionally meet; they cannot live together in harmony.

**—John R. W. Stott**

---

### ABSORB

**God is at work in our minds and hearts to persevere in the faith. The new covenant promises that the Lord is keeping and sustaining us by putting his fear in our hearts so that we will not depart from him.**

---

### INTERACT

○ How can it give us more hope and confidence to live for Christ, knowing that God is keeping and sustaining us by putting his fear in our hearts so that we will not depart from him?

## LISTEN: Warnings from God

The warnings of God are often the means by which God keeps his children from departing from the faith. Many times the apostles wrote to the churches and gave warnings. For example, the writer of Hebrews gives a very strong warning against departing from the living God: "Beware, brethren, lest there be in any of you an evil heart of unbelief in departing from the living God; but exhort one another daily, while it is called 'Today,' lest any of you be hardened through the deceitfulness of sin. For we have become partakers of Christ if we hold the beginning of our confidence steadfast to the end" (Heb. 3:12–14). And Hebrews 12:14 warns that without holiness no one will see the Lord: "Pursue . . . holiness, without which no one will see the Lord."

A question naturally arises: If God's own children are truly kept by God, and they cannot be lost, then why are there warnings given to the churches to beware of falling away (or departing) from the living God? The answer is that God's warnings are the very means of grace by which he keeps his children from turning away and departing from him. Because God has implanted a godly fear in their hearts (Jer. 32:40), his children will take to heart the warnings and disciplining measures of God so as not to fall away. Theologian Louis Berkhof writes: "These warnings regard the whole matter [of departing from the faith] from the side of man and are seriously meant. They prompt self-examination, and are instrumental in keeping believers in the way of perseverance. They do not prove that any of those addressed will apostatize, but simply that the use of means is necessary to prevent them from committing this sin."[3]

Berkhof describes how God can promise that our status is safe, definite, and sure but at the same time use warnings as the very means to maintain our status (that is, to carry out his promised protection). Berkhof points to Acts 27 where the apostle Paul is a prisoner aboard a ship in the midst of a severe storm. The people on the ship believe they are going to die. Paul tells them that God promises he will save everyone on board. Yet, along with this promise from God, Paul warns that unless the men stay in the ship, they cannot be saved:

> And now I [Paul] urge you to take heart, for there will be no loss of life among you, but only of the ship. For there stood by me this night an angel of the God to whom I belong and whom I serve, saying, "Do not be afraid, Paul; you must be brought before Caesar; and indeed *God has granted you all those* [all the lives of those] *who sail with you.*" Therefore take heart, men, for I believe God that it will be just as it was told me. However, we must run aground on a certain island. (Acts 27:22–26)

In other words, God sent an angel to tell them that Paul, along with everyone else on the ship, would be safe. This was a definite and sure promise of protection from God. But that night when the ship was anchored close to land, some of the sailors attempted to sneak off the ship in a small boat. So Paul spoke to the Roman officer in charge and warned them: "Unless these men stay in the ship, you cannot be saved" (Acts 27:31). The result? The soldiers cut the ropes to the boat so that the sailors couldn't escape, and everyone stayed in the ship; thus, everyone was protected! Think about this: their safety and protection had *already* been certain and sure, but the warning was the means that God used to keep them from departing from the ship.

That is why theologians such as Millard Erickson (following G. C. Berkouwer) write concerning the warnings of departing from the living God: "There is a logical possibility of apostasy, but it will not come to pass in the case of believers. . . . God does this, not by making it impossible for believers to fall away, but by making it certain that they will not!"[4]

————— **ABSORB** —————

### God's *warnings* are often the very means of grace by which he keeps his children from turning away and departing from him.

————— **INTERACT** —————

○ Can you think of any warnings that God has already used in your life to keep you in the faith?

## LISTEN: Discipline from God

Perhaps another illustration can serve to shed light on how our heavenly Father protects and keeps us: A father who deeply loves his four-year-old son takes him to the front of the house and says, "I am going to let you ride your tricycle in the driveway, but you must not go out into the street because if you do you might get hit by a car. So whatever you do, do not go into the street because you could die!" The father's warning is real, and the consequences are deadly. It is a legitimate warning; if a car traveling fifty miles per hour hits his child on a tricycle, the child could die. But the dad is actually more concerned than the child regarding the son's safety and protection. The son is allowed the freedom each day to ride his tricycle in the driveway but always under the watchful, caring, protective eye of the loving father. If his son edges toward the busy street, then the father makes sure to use the means of warnings, reprimands, correction, and even firm discipline—whatever means necessary—to prevent his son from choosing to go too far. In the end, the father's warnings and discipline are the means that awaken a healthy fear in the son, so that his son chooses (on his own) not to go into the street. The warning of getting hit by a car was a genuine warning; there was a real and present danger. But the warnings were the very means the father used to prevent his son from getting hurt. The boy was kept from death by his father's warnings. At the same time, let us not miss the precommitment of the protecting and sustaining love of the father for the son—the father loved his son so much that he would have never let his son venture into the street.

The same is true for the warnings of God to his children. The warnings of God prompt self-examination and are instrumental in keeping true believers (those truly born into God's family) in the way of perseverance. The warnings are often the very means of grace to keep his own from departing from the faith. As the warnings prompt self-examination, the true child of God will think something to the effect: "I must check myself to see if I really am a true follower of Christ." As 2 Corinthians 13:5 states: "Examine yourselves as to whether you are in the faith." Those truly born again will do that.

### ABSORB

**Our Father's words of warning and acts of discipline are the very means to ensure that we will not depart from the faith. The warnings of God prompt self-examination and are instrumental in keeping believers (those truly born into God's family) in the way of perseverance.**

### INTERACT

○ Hebrews 12:6–7 states: "For whom the LORD loves He chastens [disciplines] / . . . God deals with you as with sons." Have you ever been disciplined by the Lord? What do we normally learn from being disciplined?

## LISTEN: Warnings of Serious Self-Deception

Jesus said that at the judgment day there would be many who claim that they had believed in Christ and had even called him "Lord," but their lifestyle, the way they lived their lives, will demonstrate that they had not been regenerated. These are Christ's words: "Not everyone who says to Me, 'Lord, Lord,' shall enter the kingdom of heaven, but he who does the will of My Father in heaven. Many will say to Me in that day, 'Lord, Lord, have we not prophesied in Your name, cast out demons in Your name, and done many wonders in Your name?' And then I will declare to them, 'I never knew you; depart from Me, you *who practice lawlessness*!'" (Matt. 7:21–23).

Notice that these people had prophesied in Christ's name—they had spoken on behalf of Christ. They no doubt seemed spiritual in the eyes of others. They also had ministered in the name of Christ. Yet their fatal flaw of self-deception is that they had never really repented of their sins. Jesus describes their lifestyle as "lawless"—they did not seek to live according to the teachings of Christ. They were not truly following Christ in pursuing a life of obedience. It is important to note that Jesus does not say, "I knew you at one time but then you lost your salvation." He says, "I *never* knew you!" They had never really been born again, even though they had confessed the name of Christ.

The apostle Paul also warns that we must beware of being deceived into thinking we are right with God if we have never repented of our old sinful lifestyles:

> Do you not know that the unrighteous will not inherit the kingdom of God? Do not be deceived. Neither fornicators, nor idolaters, nor adulterers, nor homosexuals, nor sodomites, nor thieves, nor covetous, nor drunkards, nor revilers, nor extortioners will inherit the kingdom of God. And such were some of you. But you were washed, but you were sanctified, but you were justified in the name of the Lord Jesus and by the Spirit of our God. (1 Cor. 6:9–11)

Notice that the Scriptures state: "And such *were* some of you." When you come to authentic faith in Christ, you become a new creation. If you *were* a fornicator, then you have turned from fornication. If you *were* a thief, you have stopped stealing, or if you *were* a drunkard, then you have stopped abusing alcohol. This doesn't mean that you will never again struggle with such sins, but it means that you have decisively turned away from such a pattern of living. If you do not turn from your sins, then you are inviting self-deception. Again, this does not mean that you will never again cave into the temptation to sin—but it does mean that you do not live a life described by Christ as "practicing [moral] lawlessness."

### ABSORB

**There are some who claim to be Christians whose actions, choices, and lifestyles may reveal that they have never been born again.**

The perseverance of the saints has not so much to do with *sinless perfection* as it does with *sinless direction.*

### INTERACT

○ Why do you think Jesus puts so much importance on not merely "saying" the right things but also actually doing the will of the Father?

○ What is the difference between our daily struggle with the flesh and living a lifestyle of unrepentant sin as described in 1 Corinthians 6:9–11?

## LISTEN: Continuing with Christ—The Proof of Reality

One of the key indicators that your faith in Christ is real is that you remain (continue) with Christ. There will be some people, like Judas, who may appear to be a close follower of Christ but later depart. Judas is a classic biblical example of someone "falling away" or "departing" from the faith. Judas was part of the inner core of disciples, and from all outward appearances he seemed to be a committed follower of Christ. If you had lived then and observed Judas, you probably would have concluded that he was a genuine Christian. Yet the Scriptures give us a different description of Judas's heart. Jesus uncovers the real character and heart of Judas when he says, "Did I not choose you, the twelve, and *one of you is a devil*?" (John 6:70). Jesus knew Judas's heart was not that of a child of God but a child of the devil. In fact, Jesus knew *from the very beginning* that Judas was among the group who did not truly believe and that Judas would go so far as to betray him: "'But there are some of you who do not believe.' For Jesus knew from the beginning who they were who did not believe, and who would betray Him" (John 6:64).

Judas departed from the faith; he fell away; he departed from the living God; and he did not continue with Christ. Judas was an apostate—he departed from Christ. The reality is that he appeared to be a close follower of Christ, but he had never really been regenerated—born again. When people depart from the faith, it reveals that they were really never of the faith. The apostle John describes it like this: "They went out from us, but they were not of us; for if they had been of us, they would have continued with us; but they went out that they might be made manifest, that none of them were of us" (1 John 2:19).

Because these people did not continue with the Christian faith, with Christ's church, and with the teachings of the apostles, then it eventually became clear that they never really belonged to the true Christian faith.

### ABSORB

We are not always good judges of others. Some Christians *appear* to be real followers of Christ, and then it seems that they fall away in the sense that they lose their salvation. But the reality is that they were never saved in the first place. Only Jesus knows a person's heart from the beginning. "They went out from us, but they were not of us; for if they had been of us, they would have continued with us" (1 John 2:19).

───── **INTERACT** ─────

◯ If you lived in Jesus's day and saw Judas hanging out for three years with Jesus and his disciples, would you have thought he had become a real believer?

◯ Why do you think that Judas could be described as having lived one of the most tragic lives ever?

## LISTEN: God's Promises, the Spirit's Witness, and Our Assurance

Well over a century ago the gifted hymn-writer and poet Fanny Crosby composed these words (part of the classic hymn "Blessed Assurance"): "Blessed assurance, Jesus is mine! / O, what a foretaste of glory divine! / Heir of salvation, purchase of God, / Born of His Spirit, washed in His blood." Every true follower of Christ desires to have the assurance that "*Jesus is mine*"; we want to know that we really know him and most of all that he knows us and keeps us. God offers every child assurance of his or her salvation. We are designed by God to live in this blessed assurance.

We can have this assurance because God has promised that we can know him and that he will preserve those who know him. God expects us to believe his promises! Not only does the apostle Paul pray that Christ would preserve

## Who Shall Separate Us from the Love of Christ? (Romans 8:35)

"The answer to that question is, Nothing! Which means that all those who belong to Christ will persevere. They must, and they will. It is certain. Why? Because God is already now in Christ 100% for us. Perseverance is not the means by which we get God to be for us; it is the effect of the fact that God is already for us. You cannot ever make God be for you by your good works because true Christian good works are the fruit of God's already being for you. 'By the grace of God I am what I am, and his grace toward me was not in vain. On the contrary, I worked harder than any of them, though it was not I, but the grace of God that is with me' (1 Cor. 15:10). My hard work is not the cause but the result of blood-bought grace."

**John Piper[a]**

[a]"Getting Older to the Glory of God," in *Stand: A Call for the Endurance of the Saints*, ed. John Piper and Justin Taylor (Wheaton: Crossway, 2008), 42.

us until he returns, but Paul also states that Christ will do it: "Now may the God of peace Himself sanctify you completely; and may your whole spirit, soul, and body be preserved blameless at the coming of our Lord Jesus Christ. He who calls you is faithful, *who also will do it*" (1 Thess. 5:23–24). If God says he will do it, then we would be negligent not to believe him.

Also, the Bible tells us that we can *know* that we have eternal life: "These things I have written to you who believe in the name of the Son of God, that you may know that you have eternal life, and that you may continue to believe in the name of the Son of God" (1 John 5:13).

These specific promises (plus *all* of the promises about God keeping us and never allowing us to perish) can give us tremendous assurance. Faith is taking God at his word.

The New Testament also reveals that there is a real, experiential gift that God gives through his Spirit where we can sense that we are children of God: "The Spirit Himself bears witness with our spirit that we are children of God" (Rom. 8:16). We know that we are his because we have an internal verification or witness by the Holy Spirit that we are actually God's children, a witness that is always in concert with the truth of the gospel of Jesus Christ.

## ABSORB

**Because God's promises are to be believed, we can have the assurance that he will keep us. Also, God gives us the Holy Spirit's internal witness that we are the children of God.**

## INTERACT

○ Have you ever sensed the Spirit of God bearing witness with your spirit that you are a child of God?

## LISTEN: Making Our Calling and Election Sure

The apostle Peter writes that God's divine power has given us everything we need for life and godliness. He instructs us to live a life of faith, virtue, knowledge, self-control, endurance, godliness, brotherly kindness, and most of all, love. Then he describes how we gain assurance: "Therefore, brethren, be even more diligent to make your call and election sure, *for if you do these*

## Four Essentials for Finishing Well

"Over the last few years [Bridges is now in his eighties] I have given a lot of thought to how one finishes well. Although a number of things could be said, I have come to the conclusion that there are four fundamental actions we can take to help us finish well. There may be other issues that are important, but I believe these four are fundamental. They are:

- daily time of focused personal communion with God
- daily appropriation of the gospel
- daily commitment to God as a living sacrifice
- firm belief in the sovereignty and love of God."

**Jerry Bridges[a]**

[a]"Four Essentials for Finishing Well," in *Stand: A Call for the Endurance of the Saints*, ed. John Piper and Justin Taylor (Wheaton: Crossway, 2008), 18.

*things you will never stumble* [*fall*]; for so an entrance will be supplied to you abundantly into the everlasting kingdom of our Lord and Savior Jesus Christ" (2 Pet. 1:10–11).

When you trust in the redemption of Christ alone to save you, there is an outflow where we as Christians seek the Lord by pursuing a life of faith and obedience. Peter describes it as living a life of faith, love, brotherly kindness, and so on. Then Peter clearly declares: "If you do these things you will never fall."

### ABSORB

**The confirmation that you have been called and elected is that you can see the power of God bringing progress in your sanctification. There is a real assurance that accompanies a life of faith in Christ and seeking the will of God.**

### INTERACT

○ Which of the above three things (God's promises, the Spirit's witness, or living a virtuous life) has helped you the most to experience God's assurance of your salvation?

**Reflect:** Motivation is key to our lives. Train yourself to see the warnings and discipline of God as good things for your life. They are some of the very means that he uses to keep our souls.

Underlying the whole subject of preservation, perseverance, and assurance is the reality that behind all of our efforts to be faithful is the Father's love to preserve us and his persevering commitment! How can I best pray for you until the next session?

## CULTIVATING SPIRITUAL HABITS

**Read:** Isaiah 40

**Journal:** With your journal in hand, read through the verses that have been listed in this session. Write down any verses that stand out to you and explain why they are meaningful.

### Memorize

*And I will make an everlasting covenant with them, that I will not turn away from doing them good; but I will put My fear in their hearts so that they will not depart from Me.*

JEREMIAH 32:40

# God's Unique Character

## The Attributes of God (Part 1)

**Purpose of Session Twenty:** These final five sessions focus on the many attributes of God—those qualities and characteristics that constitute who and what he is. Our goal is to better know, understand, love, and glorify our awesome God. In this session, we cover the attributes of God that are unique to himself: self-existence, immutability, eternity, omnipresence, and unity.

## LISTEN: Defining the Attributes of God

When we talk about the attributes of God we are referring to various aspects of God's character and nature. These are permanent qualities; they are intrinsic to who God is. Some theologians call them the *perfections* of God. Learning about the character of God helps us to actually know God better. Church historian John Hannah describes the importance of the balance of having an accurate knowledge of God and living out that knowledge in real life. Hannah writes: "No one can walk with a person he or she does not know; neither can we say we walk with God if we do not have an accurate knowledge of Him. Theology is not about an admiration of a series of gathered insights, however wonderful these insights may be; it is about responding appropriately and regularly to God. The church has at times swung between an arid faith full of knowledge but with little vitality and an experience-centered faith with little intellectual content. An overemphasis in either direction has proven destructive to Christian experience."[1]

J. I. Packer, in his classic work *Knowing God*, describes those who really know God:

1. Those who know God have great energy for God.
2. Those who know God have great thoughts of God.
3. Those who know God show great boldness for God.
4. Those who know God have great contentment in God.[2]

## ABSORB

The attributes of God are those qualities, traits, and characteristics of God that constitute who and what he is. These attributes refer to the various aspects of God's character, nature, or perfections. Learning about the character of God helps us to actually know God better.

## INTERACT

○ What would you think are some of the benefits of knowing what God is really like?

---

### "Don't give me theology—just give me Jesus."

Can you have Jesus without theology? Not really, because theology is *the study of God*. The real issue facing us is whether our study of God truly reflects what Jesus is like. Church historian John Hannah writes:

> The quest for the knowledge of God is not an idle pastime. . . . Spiritual vitality in any era is found in people who know their God, and . . . the greatest danger for the church is ignorance of God. Fears and adversaries come and go on the pages of history, but only those who know God can change the course of human events, bring permanence from impermanence, and speak a word of peace in a world that knows only the struggle for self-advancement and self-fulfillment. . . . While theology is not to be confused with the Bible, there is an inseparable linkage between the two. As the Spirit of God and the Word of God are never severed (that is, God most assuredly speaks through His Word to our conscience), so the Word and theology are inseparable. Theology is the fruit of the study of the Word.[a]

[a] John D. Hannah, *Our Legacy: History of Christian Doctrine* (Colorado Springs: NavPress, 2001), 10–11.

## LISTEN: Communicable and Incommunicable Attributes

In attempting to better understand God, various methods of classifying God's attributes have been used. One method commonly used by Reformed theologians classifies God's attributes into two categories—the *communicable* and the *incommunicable*. The communicable attributes are those that God "communicates" to us—he shares or imparts these attributes of his to us to some degree. The communicable attributes are those most analogous to human nature. An example of a communicable attribute is *love*. Even though God is perfect love, he imparts that attribute to us so that we to some degree love too.

God's incommunicable attributes are those attributes that are unique to God; he does not share or communicate them to us. The incommunicable attributes are those attributes that are least analogous to human nature. An example of an incommunicable attribute is *self-existence*. Only God is self-existent; all other creatures derive their existence from him. Humans are not self-existent, omnipresent, and so on, but we have the capacity to be loving, gracious, merciful, and just. It is obvious that there are limitations in trying to precisely categorize the character and nature of God, but there has been a long history of sound biblical theologians who have found this method helpful. What matters most is not the categorization but the attributes themselves, which reveal to us who God is and what he is really like.

In this session we will first discuss five incommunicable attributes of God: self-existence, immutability (unchangeableness), eternal nature, omnipresence, and unity. In the next two sessions we will discuss God's communicable attributes.

### ABSORB

**God's communicable attributes are those attributes that humans possess to a degree. God's incommunicable attributes are those attributes that only God has.**

### INTERACT

○ What does it mean to share an attribute of God? Why can't we share all of God's attributes?

## LISTEN: The Self-Existence of God

The *self-existence* of God is sometimes written as the *aseity* of God. The word comes from the Latin *a*, meaning "from," and *se*, meaning "oneself" (thus, "from oneself"). The idea is that God is underived, necessary, nondependent in his existence. His self-existence is also called the independence of God.[3] When Moses met God in the burning bush, he asked, "'Indeed, when I come to the children of Israel and say to them, "The God of your fathers has sent me to you," and they say to me, "What is His name?" what shall I say to them?' And God said to Moses, 'I AM WHO I AM.' And He said, 'Thus you shall say to the children of Israel, "I AM has sent me to you"'" (Exod. 3:13–14).

The Hebrew phrase "I AM" suggests that he simply exists! Nobody, no power brought him into existence. No one made God; he has unexplainably always existed! He had no beginning nor does he have an end. There is no reality outside of God that did not come from God. He is the source of all being. Anything that has "the power of being" in and of itself and is not dependent on something else for its existence is transcendent. He is completely absolute in his existence. "God is not dependent upon anything outside of Himself, but He is self-sufficient in His whole being, in His decrees, and in all His works."[4] There was never a time when God was not.

Wayne Grudem makes an important observation concerning God's self-existence/independence:

> People have sometimes thought that God created human beings because He was lonely and needed fellowship with other persons. If this were true, it would certainly mean that God is not completely independent of creation. It would mean that God would *need* to create persons in order to be completely happy or completely fulfilled in His personal existence.
>
> . . . Among the persons of the Trinity there has been perfect love and fellowship and communication from all eternity. The fact that God is three persons yet one God means that there was no loneliness or lack of personal fellowship on God's part before creation. . . .
>
> It is not just that God *does not* need the creation for anything; God *could not* need the creation for anything. . . .
>
> The balancing consideration with respect to this doctrine is the fact that *we and the rest of creation can glorify God and bring him joy*. This must be stated in order to guard against any idea that God's independence makes us meaningless. . . . We are in fact very meaningful because God has created us and he has determined that we would be *meaningful to him*. That is the final definition of genuine significance.[5]

--- ABSORB ---

God's self-existence means God is completely absolute in his existence; he is independent in himself. God is the great uncaused Cause: he causes everything to depend on him.

--- INTERACT ---

○ What thoughts about God arise when you consider that he has always existed?

○ Some of the reasons why it is important to know about the self-existence of God are (1) it moves us to have a greater wonder and awe of God; (2) we can know that God is dependent on no one, therefore we can know that God will never manipulate or use us; (3) it moves us to gratefulness; and (4) it leads us to a greater appreciation for the person of Christ. Which of these reasons resonates with you the most?

## LISTEN: The Immutability of God

The *immutability* of God is sometimes called the *unchangeableness* of God. The Lord says in Malachi, "For I am the LORD, I do not change" (Mal. 3:6). God is always the same in who he is—all his perfections, all his purposes, and all his promises never change. Psalm 33:11 states: "The counsel of the LORD stands forever, / The plans of His heart to all generations." Psalm 102:25–27 accentuates the truth that even though the universe changes, God remains the same: "Of old You laid the foundation of the earth, / And the heavens are the work of Your hands. / They will perish, but You will endure; / Yes, they will all grow old like a garment; / Like a cloak You will change them, / And they will be changed. / But You are the same, / And Your years will have no end." James, in the New Testament, also highlights that with God's character and being, there is absolutely no changing: "Every good gift and every perfect gift is from above, and comes down from the Father of lights, with whom there is no variation or shadow of turning" (James 1:17). God is completely independent, yet the Bible describes God in terms of having

## God Is Bigger Than You Think

"It has been said by some one that 'the proper study of mankind is man.' I will not oppose the idea, but I believe it is equally true that the proper study of God's elect is God; the proper study of a Christian is the Godhead. The highest science, the loftiest speculation, the mightiest philosophy, which can ever engage the attention of a child of God, is the name, the nature, the person, the work, the doings, and the existence of the great God whom he calls his Father. There is something exceedingly improving to the mind in a contemplation of the Divinity. It is a subject so vast, that all our thoughts are lost in its immensity; so deep, that our pride is drowned in its infinity."

Charles Spurgeon[a]

[a]"The Immutability of God," sermon delivered on January 7, 1855, http://www.spurgeon.org/sermons/0001.htm.

an emotional life—he rejoices, he is grieved, he is angry, he is moved to pity, and he empathizes with human pain and grief. However, God is *never* a victim. People and angels cannot inflict suffering on God so that in some sense God becomes a victim of his creatures' sins. Packer adds light when he writes: "God's experiences do not come upon Him as ours come upon us. His are foreknown, willed, and chosen by Himself, and are not involuntary surprises forced on Him from outside, apart from His own decision, in the way that ours regularly are. . . . If, therefore, we can learn to think of the *chosenness* of God's grief and pain as the essence of His impassibility, we will do well."[6]

### ABSORB

**God's immutability means that God is forever the same in his divine being, perfections, purposes, and promises.**[7]

### INTERACT

○ People often change in their attitudes, intentions, purposes, and promises, but God never changes. Why should it give us great comfort and security knowing that through eternity, God will always be the same in his divine being, perfections, purposes, and promises?

## LISTEN: The Eternity of God

The *eternity* of God is sometimes called the *infinity* of God. The Scriptures describe God as "the eternal God" (Deut. 33:27) and "the King eternal" (1 Tim. 1:17). And Psalm 90 describes God's infinity with respect to time: "Before the mountains were brought forth, / Or ever You had formed the earth and the world, / Even from everlasting to everlasting, You are God" (Ps. 90:2). God is titled "Alpha and Omega," and He "inhabits eternity" (Isa. 57:15). Because he is eternal he is not locked into time—he created time. Notice that God stands above time and is able to see both the past and future as present. "Remember the former things of old, / For I am God, and there is no other; / I am God, and there is none like Me, / *Declaring the end from the beginning*, / And from ancient times things that are not yet done, / Saying, 'My counsel shall stand, / And I will do all My pleasure'" (Isa. 46:9–10).

God has always existed. From all eternity God has had infinite joy and is gloriously happy. God always does what he pleases and has never been bored! Eternity would be a scary thought if we could not experience that kind of eternal joy.

Even though God is eternal, God sees and acts in time. We make this observation from passages such as Galatians 4:4–5, which states that at just the right time in history God sent his Son into this world: "But when the fullness of the time had come, God sent forth His Son, born of a woman, born under the law, to redeem those who were under the law." God is the Lord over time and uses time for his own purposes and glory!

---

### Eternity

"The subject is one of which the wisest man can only take in a little. We have no eyes to see it fully, no line to fathom it, no mind to grasp it; and yet we must not refuse to consider it. There is a depth of stars in the heavens above us, which the most powerful telescope cannot pierce; yet it is well worth it to look into them and learn something, even if we cannot learn everything. There are heights and depths about the subject of eternity which mortal man can never comprehend; but God has spoken of it, and we have no right to turn away from it completely."

**J. C. Ryle**[a]

[a]*Practical Religion* (Lafayette, IN: Sovereign Grace, 2001), 255.

--- **ABSORB** ---

God's eternity means that "God has no beginning, end, or succession of moments in His own being, and He sees all time equally vividly; yet God sees events in time and acts in time."[8]

--- **INTERACT** ---

○ What is your conception of heaven and eternity? How important do you think joy and happiness are to eternity?

## LISTEN: The Omnipresence of God

The *omnipresence* of God is sometimes called the *immensity* of God. When we say that God is *omnipresent* we mean that God is everywhere. There is no place within or outside the universe where God is not. This is not to say that God's form is spread out so that parts of him exist in every place and location. As will be seen later in the next session, God is spirit and does not occupy space in the sense that physical objects occupy space. Theologian R. C. Sproul makes this important observation:

> He [God] has no physical qualities that can occupy space. The key to understanding this paradox is to think in terms of another dimension. . . . God is not only present in all places but God is fully present in every place. This is called His immensity. Believers living in New York enjoy the fullness of the presence of God while believers in Moscow enjoy that same presence. His immensity, then, does not refer to His size, but to His ability to be fully present everywhere.[9]

Psalm 139:7–10 explains that there is no place in the universe where one can flee from God's presence: "Where can I go from Your Spirit? / Where can I flee from Your presence? / If ascend into heaven, You are there; / If I make my bed in hell, behold, You are there. / If I take the wings of the morning, / And dwell in the uttermost parts of the sea, / Even there Your hand shall lead me, / And Your right hand shall hold me."

God cannot be contained by any amount of space. First Kings 8:27 records, "Behold, heaven and the heaven of heavens cannot contain You. How much less this temple which I have built!"

Stephen Charnock, in his seventeenth-century classic *The Existence and the Attributes of God*, explains: "Nor will it follow, that because God is essentially everywhere, that everything is God. God is not everywhere by any conjunction, composition or mixture with anything on earth. When light is in every part of a crystal globe, and encircles it close on every side, do they become one? No; the crystal remains what it is, and the light retains its own nature."[10]

Therefore we conclude that he must be everywhere in an extraordinarily unique way. Yet there are verses that speak of being in the actual presence of God: "In Your presence is fullness of joy" (Ps. 16:11). This infers that although God's presence in one sense is everywhere, in another sense he makes known his presence in exceptional ways. What should be our response to all of this as we contemplate the great mysterious being of God?

Charnock thoughtfully suggests:

> How should we never think of God without a holy admiration of His greatness, and a deep sense of our own littleness! . . . We should be swallowed up in admiration of the immensity of God, as men are at the first sight of the sea, when they behold a mass of waters, without beholding the bounds and immense depth of it. Since God fills heaven and earth with His presence, we should fill heaven and earth with His glory.[11]

## ABSORB

**God's omnipresence means that God is present in all places. God is not limited by time or space. He is able to be present in his fullness at all times and in all places.[12]**

## INTERACT

○ Reflect on Charles Spurgeon's words: "There is something exceedingly improving to the mind in contemplation of the Divinity. It is a subject so vast, that all our thoughts are lost in its immensity; so deep, that our pride is drowned in its infinity." Do you think Spurgeon was correct? Why?

## LISTEN: The Unity of God

The *unity* of God is sometimes called the *simplicity* of God. We have seen in an earlier session that God reveals himself as *one God* who eternally exists as three distinct persons—Father, Son, and Holy Spirit. God is one in essence and three in person. It is clearly taught both in the Old and New Testaments that there is but one God: "To you it was shown, that you might know that the LORD Himself is God; there is none other besides Him. Therefore know this day, and consider it in your heart, that the LORD Himself is God in heaven above and on the earth beneath; there is no other" (Deut. 4:35, 39); "Jesus answered him, 'The first of all the commandments is: "Hear, O Israel, the LORD our God, the LORD is one"'" (Mark 12:29).

God has many attributes, and the Bible never identifies one of his attributes as more important than all the rest. As theologians point out:

> God's attributes cannot be separated from His Being. God and His perfections are one. We may not think of love and righteousness as incidental aspects of God's character; on the contrary, God is with His whole Being love and righteousness, grace and holiness. Because this is so, one attribute cannot be limited by another. We may not say, for example, that God is not infinitely righteous because He is love. Though the attributes are many, God is one. While we distinguish the attributes for purposes of study, we can never separate them.[13]

> The attributes all equally qualify the entirety of the divine being and each other. . . . Preserving the divine simplicity or indivisibility, God's love is always holy love, and God's holiness is always loving holiness. Hence it is futile to argue for the superiority of one divine attribute over another. Every attribute is essential; one cannot be more essential than another.[14]

Louis Berkhof points out that the attributes of God are inseparable from his being or essence—the simplicity of God means that God's attributes are not "superadded to His essence. Since the two are one, the Bible can speak of God as light and life, as righteousness and love, thus identifying Him with His perfections."[15]

When theologians describe the "simplicity" of God, they use the term to describe the condition of being free from being divided into parts. God is not made up of parts and is not susceptible to division in any sense of the word. Even though God is not susceptible to division, nor is one of his attributes more important than the others, we do see different attributes emphasized at different times in the Scriptures. Ultimately we love and worship God for who he is completely in his whole being—the one true living God.

---

### ABSORB

**God's unity means that there is only one God who is not made up of parts and not susceptible to division.**

### INTERACT

○ Sometimes people say things like, "I think of God as the God of love, mercy, and grace. I don't like to think of him as a God of justice and wrath." What is wrong with that type of thinking?

**Reflect:** Our spiritual vitality is inseparably linked to knowing God. Think about ways that knowing God better can help you to have energy and boldness for God. Am I planning anything that will further the mission that Christ gave to the church (making disciples)? What can I be praying for you until our next session?

## CULTIVATING SPIRITUAL HABITS

**Read:** Isaiah 48:9–11; Romans 11:33–36; Psalm 119:89–90; Exodus 34:1–17

**Journal:** Read through the definitions of the first five attributes of God and write down praises to God for who he is.

### Memorize

*Now to the King eternal, immortal, invisible, to God who alone is wise, be honor and glory forever and ever. Amen.*

1 TIMOTHY 1:17

# God's Shared Character

## The Attributes of God (Part 2)

---

**Purpose of Session Twenty-One:** In this session we continue our five-part series on the attributes of God—those qualities and characteristics of God that constitute who and what he is. In this session we will begin to cover those attributes of God that are shared or imparted to people: spirituality, omniscience, wisdom, truthfulness, omnipotence, goodness, and love.

---

## LISTEN: Enjoying God

It is amazing that we, as followers of Christ, have the incredible hope of spending eternity with the almighty, glorious God.

Jonathan Edwards explained it this way: "The enjoyment of [God] is the only happiness with which our souls can be satisfied. To go to heaven, fully to enjoy God, is infinitely better than the most pleasant accommodations here. Fathers and mothers, husbands, wives, or children, or the company of earthly friends, are but shadows; but God is the substance. These are but scattered beams, but God is the sun. These are but streams. But God is the ocean."[1]

The greatest part of our future eternity will be to enjoy God!

But God has also designed us to enjoy him *now*! And we glorify him by enjoying him. The Westminster Shorter Catechism asks, "What is the chief end of man?" It answers, "Man's chief end is to glorify God, and to enjoy him forever." John Piper proposes this modification: "The chief end of man is to glorify God BY enjoying him forever. God *is most glorified in us when we are most satisfied in Him*."[2]

> Man's chief end is to glorify God, and to enjoy him forever.
>
> **—Westminster Shorter Catechism, 1647**

---

## ABSORB

### The enjoyment of God is our ultimate happiness.

---

## INTERACT

○ There are a lot of things that people enjoy in life: eating good food, spending time with friends, looking at beautiful places, playing or watching sports, listening to music, reading interesting books, playing with children, watching great films, and going on vacations. How does a person enjoy God?

○ What do you think this means: "God is most glorified in us when we are most satisfied in him"?

## LISTEN: The Spirituality of God

We will now look at attributes of God that are communicable, meaning attributes that God communicates (imparts) to us to some degree. The first one we'll look at is *spirituality*. The Bible does not merely say that God is *a spirit* but that *God is Spirit*. The "essence" (or "the essential nature" or "substance" or "the being of God") describes that which makes God, God. It is that which underlies all outward manifestations of God—the reality itself. The Bible says that the essence of God is spirit. God does not have a physical, material body, nor is his essence (what he is made of) any kind of matter like much of the rest of creation.[3] The New Testament says that God is invisible: "Now to the King eternal, immortal, *invisible*, to God who alone is wise, be honor and glory forever and ever. Amen" (1 Tim. 1:17). Also, the New Testament reveals that no person has seen or can see God. "He who is the blessed and only Potentate [Absolute Sovereign], the King of kings and Lord of lords, who alone has immortality, dwelling in unapproachable light, *whom no man has seen or can see*, to whom be honor and everlasting power. Amen" (1 Tim. 6:15–16).

Jesus himself also emphasized that no one has ever seen God except for Jesus: "Not that anyone has seen the Father, except He who is from God; He has seen the Father" (John 6:46). God also spoke directly to Moses and said: "For no man shall see Me, and live" (Exod. 33:20).

Immediately a question arises: Didn't God appear to Moses in the burning bush and on Mount Sinai, and didn't God in some way appear to Abraham and Jacob, as well as to the people of Israel as a pillar of cloud by day and fire by night? Theologians call such an appearance a "*theophany*" (thee-off-uh-nee), which means an appearance of God in visible form. This type of appearance is temporary and is a gracious condescension of God to relate to his human creation. Sometimes theologians call the appearance of the Son of God (before he came to earth in the flesh) a "Christophany" (Chris-toff-uh-nee)—a pre-incarnate appearance of Christ in human form (at times referred to as the "Angel of the Lord").

So, the answer to our question is yes, God has appeared in some visible manifestations of himself, but no one has ever seen God in his *total essence*—in his pure, invisible, unapproachable light. Yet Jesus gives us this amazing promise: "Blessed are the pure in heart, / For they shall see God" (Matt. 5:8). Ancient church leaders referred to this as the "beatific vision" of God. It is incredible to think that one day this promise will come true for us. What that will fully entail is yet to be revealed at that future day, but we know it will be like nothing else we have experienced in life.

— **ABSORB** —

**God's spirituality means that the essence of God is spirit and is distinct from this physical world and universe. The essence of God is immaterial, invisible, and without parts or dimensions, and is "more excellent than any other kind of existence."[4]**

— **INTERACT** —

○ Why do you think no one is able to see God (in his total essence) and live?

○ Consider that in the Ten Commandments God forbids us to carve or create an image of him in any form. Do you think any representation of God would actually enhance the understanding of who he is? Could a representation ever do him justice? In what ways is Jesus a true and accurate representation of God?

## LISTEN: The Omniscience of God

The word "omniscience" means "knowing everything," "to have all (*omni*) knowledge (*science*)." God is the only one who possesses infinite, limitless knowledge. Psalm 147:5 declares, "Great is our Lord, and mighty in power; / His understanding is infinite." God's knowledge complements his omnipotence; not only does God know the future, but he actually brings the future to pass: "I am God, and there is no other; / I am God, and there is none like Me, / Declaring the end from the beginning, / And from ancient times things that are not yet done, / Saying, 'My counsel shall stand, / And I will do all My pleasure'" (Isa. 46:9–11).

The Scriptures tell us that every action and event is known to God: "There is no creature hidden from His sight, but all things are naked and open to the eyes of Him to whom we must give account" (Heb. 4:13). God knows people's thoughts and hearts (Ps. 139:1–4). God knows minute things—"the very hairs of your head are all numbered" (Matt. 10:30). He knew that Tyre and Sidon would have repented had they seen the miracles that Christ performed in the first century (Matt. 11:21). God fully knows himself (1 Cor. 2:10–11). Stephen Charnock in his classic volumes on God's attributes writes, "God knows Himself, and He only knows Himself. This is the first and original knowledge, wherein He excels all creatures. No man doth exactly know himself . . . much less still the nature and perfection of God."[5]

Theologian J. I. Packer points out that there can be something very encouraging in applying the omniscience of God personally to our own lives. Each individual believer can reason that God fully knew ahead of time all of my worst sins and failures. Because God can see into the future, his love toward me is completely realistic—he knew everything about my life but still sent Christ to die for me. I may become very disillusioned about myself, yet for some unfathomable reason he actually wants me as his friend (John 15:15)! His omniscience helps me to appreciate the depth of his love.[6]

---

### The Deepest Law of Acceptance and the Omniscience of God

"The fact is that in the cross God demonstrates the deepest law of acceptance. For to be convinced that I have been accepted, I must be convinced that I have been accepted at my worst. This is the greatest gift an intimate relationship can offer—to know that we have been accepted and forgiven *in the full knowledge of who we are*, an even greater knowledge than we have about ourselves. This is what the cross offers."

**Rebecca Pippert**[a]

[a]*Hope Has Its Reasons* (New York: Harper and Row, 1989), 105; emphasis added.

## ABSORB

God's omniscience means God has all knowledge. He, "in an entirely unique manner, knows Himself and all things possible and actual," whether they be past, present, or future.[7] His knowledge of all past, present, and future events is exhaustive, and his knowledge is perfect from all eternity.

## INTERACT

○ Other than God, who knows you best? Have they seen you in both good times and not-so-good times?

○ How can knowing about God's omniscience be helpful when we struggle with sin and temptation?

## LISTEN: The Wisdom of God

Three times the New Testament announces that God *alone* is wise. First Timothy 1:17 says, "Now to the King eternal, immortal, invisible, to God who *alone* is wise, be honor and glory forever and ever. Amen." Jude 25 likewise declares, "To God our Savior, / Who *alone* is wise, / Be glory and majesty, / Dominion and power, / Both now and forever. / Amen." And in Romans 16:27, Paul writes, "To God, *alone* wise, be glory through Jesus Christ forever."

God does not want us to forget that in the final analysis, all wisdom is derived from him—if any wisdom is experienced by creatures, it is because God shares some of his wisdom! Packer makes this observation about God's wisdom:

What does the Bible mean when it calls God *wise*? In Scripture wisdom is a moral as well as an intellectual quality, more than mere intelligence or knowledge, just as it is more than mere cleverness or cunning. To be truly wise, in the Bible sense, one's intelligence and cleverness must be harnessed to a right end. Wisdom is the power to see, and the inclination to choose, the best and highest goal, together with the surest means of attaining it.[8]

The wisdom of God is seen in his plans and designs for this world and for you and me. The apostle Paul burst out in praise thinking about God's great wisdom: "Oh, the depth of the riches both of the wisdom and knowledge of God! How unsearchable are His judgments and His ways past finding out! '*For who has known the mind of the* Lord? / *Or who has become His counselor?*' / '*Or who has first given to Him* / *And it shall be repaid to him?*'" (Rom. 11:33–34).

Try to imagine the immense wisdom it would take to create from nothing the human brain and body, or the ecosystem of earth, or the makeup of the stars and galaxies and the universe itself.

The wisdom of God devised a way for the love of God to deliver sinners from the wrath of God while not compromising the righteousness of God.

**—John Piper,**
**Desiring God**

---

### ABSORB

**God's wisdom is that perfection whereby God applies his knowledge to always see, choose, and implement the best and highest goals for his glory.[9]**

---

### INTERACT

○ How do you picture the mind of God being able to design the universe and the world and all the intricate things on this planet? Talk for a moment about the makeup of something complex that God has made.

## LISTEN: The Truthfulness of God

The *truthfulness* of God is sometimes called the *faithfulness* of God. The Lord is the true God, as opposed to the idols and false gods of this world. He knows things as they really are, and he is always committed to perfectly keeping his word: "But the Lord is the true God; / He is the living God and the everlasting King" (Jer. 10:10); "The entirety of Your word is *truth*, / And every one of Your righteous judgments endures forever" (Ps. 119:160). God will never lie, break a promise, or fail to fulfill his covenant—"God is not a man, that He should lie, / Nor a son of man, that He should repent. / Has He said, and will He not do? / Or has He spoken, and will He not make it good?" (Num. 23:19).

Jesus the Son of God is the embodiment of truth; he says of himself, "I am the way, *the truth*, and the life" (John 14:6). In the book of Revelation, Christ returns in victory and is described as that one who is called "Faithful and True" (Rev. 19:11). "Forever, O Lord, / Your word is settled in heaven. / Your *faithfulness* endures to all generations" (Ps. 119:89–90).

---

### ABSORB

**God's truthfulness means the Lord is the only true God who will always do what he says and fulfill what he has promised. His words and revelation of reality are perfectly reliable. "His words are both true and the final standard of truth."[10]**

---

### INTERACT

○ Why is it that even though God will always perfectly keep his promises, we sometimes struggle with taking him at his word—such as when we worry or fear? Why don't we instead claim such promises of God as found in Psalm 50:15: "Call upon Me in the day of trouble; / I will deliver you, and you shall glorify Me"?

## LISTEN: The Omnipotence of God

The term *omnipotence* comes from two Latin words, *omni* (all) and *potens* (powerful), meaning *all-powerful*. God has all power! Jesus prayed to his Father, "Abba, Father, all things are possible for You" (Mark 14:36). Jesus also taught his disciples, "With men this is impossible, but with God all things are possible" (Matt. 19:26). Try to picture the kind of power it would take to set galaxies into existence. These galaxies weigh multiple trillions of tons. Jeremiah 32:17 says, "Ah, Lord God! Behold, You have made the heavens and the earth by Your great power and outstretched arm. There is nothing too hard for You." There is nothing (or no thing) that can restrict God's power. Yet his power is in harmony with what and who he is. God cannot lie (Heb. 6:18) because God is the God of truth. He cannot be tempted with evil (James 1:13) because God is perfectly pure. Theologian R. C. Sproul writes:

> Every theologian is sooner or later asked a question by a student that is posed as an impossible nut to crack. The old query is this: Can God make a rock so big that He cannot move it? . . .
> What omnipotence does mean is that God holds all power over His creation. No part of creation stands outside the scope of His sovereign control. . . . The nut can be cracked. The answer is no. God cannot build a rock so big that He

could not move it. Why? If God ever built such a rock He would be creating something over which He had no power. He would be destroying His own omnipotence. God cannot stop being God; He cannot not be omnipotent.[11]

With the goodness of God to desire our highest welfare, the wisdom of God to plan it, and the power of God to achieve it, what do we lack? Surely we are the most favored of all creatures.

—A. W. Tozer, *The Knowledge of the Holy*

---

### ABSORB

**God's omnipotence means God has absolute power over his creation. He has all power to do whatever he wills to do that is in harmony with his nature and perfections.**

---

### INTERACT

○ We are sometimes faced with impossible rivers to cross. Why would meditating on the omnipotence of God give you hope or strength during such times?

## LISTEN: The Goodness of God

If you were to ask people in our society, "Do you consider yourself to be a good person?" most would respond in the affirmative. Yet Jesus the Son of God explains that "no one is good but One, that is, God" (Matt. 19:17). Many people find this hard to comprehend because when they speak about themselves being "good," they normally mean that they are decent and considerate. But in God's understanding of good, he means absolute moral perfection! When Moses encountered the Lord, God said, "I will cause all My goodness to pass in front of you" (Exod. 33:19 NIV). In some way God was showing Moses the sum total of his revealed excellencies. When the Bible speaks about the goodness of the Lord, it often focuses on the generous grace, mercy, patience, and kindness that flow from his being. This is seen in Jeremiah 33:11, "The LORD is good, / For His mercy endures forever." Also this can be seen in Exodus 34:6–7: "The LORD, the LORD God, merciful and gracious, longsuffering, and *abounding in goodness* and truth, keeping mercy for thousands, forgiving iniquity and transgression and sin, by no means clearing the guilty." And Psalm 86:5 highlights the mercy and grace of God, which are expressions of His goodness: "For You, Lord, are good, and ready to forgive, / And abundant in mercy to all those who call upon You."

The goodness of God prompts him to deal generously in mercy, grace, patience, and kindness:

Mercy describes God's goodness toward those in misery and distress. Jesus's parable of the unforgiving servant describes how the servant failed to show mercy by failing to forgive. *To forgive* is an expression of mercy. To help or assist someone in their time of need is to show mercy, like the Good Samaritan (Luke 10:37).

Grace is unmerited favor. Grace describes God's goodness in showing favor toward those who deserve only judgment.[12]

Patience (or longsuffering) describes God's goodness in being slow to anger.

Kindness is something that appeals to every one of us. When someone is kind toward us they display a concern and pleasant disposition toward us. Romans 2:4 also tells us that it is the kindness of God that leads us to repentance.

All these things—mercy, grace, patience, and kindness—flow from the goodness of God. Charles Spurgeon remarks on what our response to God's goodness should be: "To us needy creatures the goodness of God is the first attribute which excites praise, and that praise takes the form of gratitude. We praise the Lord truly when we give Him thanks for what we have received from His goodness. Let us never be slow to return unto the Lord our praise, to thank Him is the least we can do—let us not neglect it."[13]

### ABSORB

**God's goodness means God's absolute moral perfection. "All that God is and does is worthy of approval."[14] This perfection prompts him to deal generously in mercy, grace, patience, and kindness.**

### INTERACT

○ What expressions of God's goodness do you appreciate most (mercy, grace, patience, or kindness)?

Your worst days are never so bad that you are beyond the reach of God's grace. And your best days are never so good that you are beyond the need of God's grace.

—**Jerry Bridges,** *The Discipline of Grace*

## LISTEN: The Love of God

The love of God is, in a certain sense, an exercise of his goodness. But it is also unique in and of itself because love's basic meaning comes back to God—1 John 4:8 says: "*God is love!*" Love cannot exist without God. There has existed an immeasurable love between the members of the Trinity from all eternity. As Jesus was praying to his Father, he spoke of the eternal love that existed between them before the world was ever created: "You loved Me before the foundation of the world" (John 17:24). Also John 3:35 records, "The Father loves the Son, and has given all things into His hand."

Love is about giving. It is self-giving for the benefit of others. The Father, Son, and Holy Spirit have given the fellowship of each other to each other from all eternity. The ultimate gift, the ultimate good a person could ever receive, is God! Therefore, the love of God is the sharing and giving of himself to others.

The love we receive from God is undeserved and is initiated by God himself: "In this is love, not that we loved God, but that He loved us and sent His Son to be the propitiation for our sins" (1 John 4:10). God loves his own glory and is committed to His glory above everything. He actually created us for his glory: "Bring My sons from afar, / And My daughters from the ends of the earth— / Everyone who is called by My name, / *Whom I have created for My glory*" (Isa. 43:6–7).

God created the world with the end in view that he would be glorified. And the most loving thing God could give us is the opportunity to forever enjoy his glory. Jonathan Edwards's classic work *The End for Which God Created the World* demonstrates that the chief and ultimate purpose for which God created this world and us was to display his own glory in the highest happiness of his creatures. He wrote: "The enjoyment of [God] is the only happiness with which our souls can be satisfied."[15]

There is nothing more mentally stabilizing, nothing more peace-inducing, nothing more worry-suppressing than contemplating the love of God. The giving and offering of himself to us is the essence of pure love.

The irony is that while God doesn't need us but still wants us, we desperately need God but don't really want Him most of the time. He treasures us and anticipates our departure from this earth to be with Him—and we wonder, indifferently, how much we have to do for Him to get by.

—**Francis Chan,**
***Crazy Love***

— ABSORB —

**God's love is the sharing and giving of himself to others. From all eternity there has existed an immeasurable love, a self-giving between the members of the Trinity. Love is self-giving for the benefit of others. It seeks the highest good for the other. The highest good is the will of God.**

INTERACT

○ What stands out in your mind as you read the following verses? "Behold what manner of love the Father has bestowed on us, that we should be called children of God!" (1 John 3:1); and, "For I am persuaded that neither death nor life, nor angels nor principalities nor powers, nor things present nor things to come, nor height nor depth, nor any other created thing, shall be able to separate us from the love of God which is in Christ Jesus our Lord" (Rom. 8:38–39).

○ Through the centuries, books, music, poetry, and art have all tried to define and explain love. What is it about love that is so appealing to us as humans?

**Reflect:** Think about and meditate on how the attributes of God should affect how you live everyday life in this world. Also revisit the truth of what it means to really know God. It's one thing to know about God, it's another thing to experience the outworking of his attributes in your walk with him.

How can I best be praying for you until we meet for the next session?

## CULTIVATING SPIRITUAL HABITS

**Read:** Isaiah 6; Revelation 4; John 12:37–40

**Journal:** Review this session and write down each attribute and your understanding of it. As you are doing so, thank God for each attribute.

### Memorize

*Ah, Lord GOD! Behold, You have made the heavens and the earth by Your great power and outstretched arm. There is nothing too hard for You.*

JEREMIAH 32:17

# More of God's Shared Character

## The Attributes of God (Part 3)

---

**Purpose of Session Twenty-Two:** This session is the third of five sessions focusing on the attributes of God. The attributes of God are those qualities and characteristics of God that constitute who and what he is. In this session we continue to cover those attributes of God that are shared or imparted to humans: God's jealousy, holiness, justice, and wrath.

---

## LISTEN: We Are Made to Know God

In his classic work *Knowing God*, J. I. Packer writes:

> What were we made for? To know God. What aim should we set ourselves in life? To know God. What is the "eternal life" that Jesus gives? Knowledge of God. "This is life eternal, that they might know Thee, the only true God, and Jesus Christ, whom Thou hast sent" (John 17:3). What is the best thing in life, bringing more joy, delight, and contentment, than anything else? Knowledge of God. "Thus saith the LORD, Let not the wise man glory in his wisdom, neither let the mighty man glory in his might, let not the rich man glory in his riches; but let him that glories glory in this, that he *understands* and *knows* Me" (Jer. 9:23f.).[1]

Studying the attributes of God isn't something that should be seen as merely an intellectual pursuit. Learning about God's character helps us to know what he is really like so that we may grow to understand and know God in a more experiential, personal way!

---

### ABSORB

## The great pursuit of life is to understand and know God.

---

### INTERACT

○ Out of all the attributes listed so far, which one has given you a greater understanding of who God is and what he is really like? (The attributes we have considered are self-existence, immutability, eternity, omnipresence, unity, spirituality, omniscience, wisdom, truthfulness, omnipotence, goodness, and love.)

## LISTEN: The Jealousy of God

The Ten Commandments include these words concerning worshiping other gods: "You shall not bow down to them nor serve them. For I, the LORD your God, am a jealous God, visiting the iniquity of the fathers upon the children to the third and fourth generations of those who hate Me" (Exod. 20:5).

At first glance it might seem inappropriate for God to be "jealous." But even among humans, there are two kinds of jealousy—bad and good. The bad springs from covetousness and an infantile resentment that someone may surpass us in some manner. This vice is fed by pride. The good kind of jealousy seeks to protect a love or marriage relationship, which is only good and right. Scholar R. V. G. Tasker captures the understanding of jealousy when he writes, "Married persons who felt no jealousy at the intrusion of a lover or an adulterer into their home would surely be lacking in moral perception; for the exclusiveness of marriage is the essence of marriage."[2]

God is jealous in the latter sense. God is the only one who can ultimately satisfy our souls; when some "god" seeks to replace the true and living God, it is a dishonor to the reality that *only God* deserves first place in our lives. All other so-called "gods" are only counterfeits—they eventually bring only pain and disappointment. Anything less than giving the Lord full loyalty would be an attempt to deface the glory of God. God must be jealous because he, himself, is the greatest good and the greatest gift to his creatures. He will defend his honor and glory. Not to do so would be for God to be both unrighteous and unloving!

What comes into our minds when we think about God is the most important thing about us! . . . It is impossible to keep our moral practices sound and our inward attitudes right while our idea of God is erroneous or inadequate. If we would bring back spiritual power to our lives, we must begin to think of God more nearly as He is!

—**A. W. Tozer,** *The Knowledge of the Holy*

The Christian life
is a process of God
breaking our idols
one by one.
**—Elisabeth Elliot**

— **ABSORB** —

### God's jealousy is that perfection that seeks to protect and honor the glory of God because not to do so would be for him to be both unrighteous and unloving!

— **INTERACT** —

○ What is the point of this quote: "Married persons who felt no jealousy at the intrusion of a lover or an adulterer into their home would surely be lacking in moral perception; for the exclusiveness of marriage is the essence of marriage"? Does understanding the healthy jealousy of married persons help you understand God's holy jealousy?

## LISTEN: The Holiness of God

The basic idea behind the Hebrew word for "holy" is that of *separateness* or *apartness*.[3] When this Hebrew term is used of God, the idea is that God is separate and distinct from all his creatures because he is exalted above them in infinite majesty. The majesty of God's holiness is described like this: "Who is like You, O LORD, among the gods? / Who is like You, glorious in holiness, / Fearful in praises, doing wonders?" (Exod. 15:11); and "No one is holy like the LORD, / For there is none besides You, / Nor is there any rock like our God" (1 Sam. 2:2).

The holiness of God awakens in us a sense of "absolute nothingness, a creature-consciousness or creature-feeling, leading to absolute self-abasement."[4] The holiness of God in this sense reveals that God is absolutely distinct from all his creatures—exalted above them in infinite majesty. Some theologians call this the *majestic holiness* of God. R. C. Sproul describes two aspects of God's holiness:

> The biblical word *holy* has two distinct meanings. The primary meaning is "apartness" or "otherness." When we say that God is holy, we call attention to the profound difference between Him and all creatures. It refers to God's transcendent majesty. He is "other" or different from us in His glory. . . . The secondary meaning of holy refers to God's pure and righteous actions. God does what is right. He never does what is wrong. God always acts in a righteous manner because His nature is holy.[5]

The prophet Isaiah saw the Lord in an exalted display of his holiness as the seraphim of heaven were calling out, "Holy, Holy, Holy is the Lord of Hosts." Isaiah was so overcome by the holiness of God that he reacted with feelings of impurity: "Woe is me, for I am undone! / Because I am a man of unclean lips, / And I dwell in the midst of a people of unclean lips; / For my eyes have seen the King" (Isa. 6:5). Theologians sometimes refer to this secondary meaning as God's *ethical holiness*, which means God is pure, has no communion with sin, and is absolutely morally excellent. God is separate from moral evil and sin. His ethical holiness is moral excellence or ethical perfection. Theologian Louis Berkhof writes: "If man reacts to God's majestic-holiness with a feeling of utter insignificance and awe, his reaction to the ethical holiness reveals itself in a sense of impurity, a consciousness of sin. . . . This ethical holiness of God may be defined as *that perfection of God, in virtue of which He eternally wills and maintains His own moral excellence, abhors sin, and demands purity in His moral creatures.*"[6]

The holiness of God is something that is fully integrated with all the other attributes of God—God's love is a *holy love*, his wisdom is a *holy wisdom*, his justice is a *holy justice*, his wrath is a *holy wrath*, and so on.

## ABSORB

**God's holiness means that God is separate and distinct from all his creatures in his glory; he eternally maintains the glory of his own moral excellence, abhors sin, and demands purity in his moral creatures.**

## Culture and Holiness

"The level of our obedience is most often determined by the behavior standard of other Christians around us. . . . Many Christians have what we might call a 'cultural holiness.' They adapt to the character and behavior pattern of Christians around them. As the Christian culture around them is more or less holy, so these Christians are more or less holy. But God has not called us to be like those around us. He has called us to be like himself. Holiness is nothing less than conformity to the character of God."

**Jerry Bridges[a]**

[a]*The Pursuit of Holiness* (Colorado Springs: NavPress, 1996), 22.

○ What do you think the apostle Peter meant when he wrote, "As He who called you is holy, you also be holy in all your conduct, because it is written, 'Be holy, for I am holy'" (1 Pet. 1:15–16)?

## LISTEN: The Justice of God

The *justice* of God is sometimes listed as the *righteousness* of God. Most of us are extremely sensitive to the issue of justice when it comes to our own lives. Think about the justice statements that people make in everyday life: "You smashed into my car, you should pay." "You took my parking place after I waited for the car to pull out, you shouldn't have done that." "I did more than half the work, I should get paid more than you." "You injured my child, you should have to pay punitive damages." "There is an error on this bill; we only ordered two pizzas." In Deuteronomy 32:4 Moses relays an inspired song to the people of Israel: "For all His ways are justice, / A God of truth and without injustice; / Righteous and upright is He." Abraham in Genesis 18:25 exclaims that the judge of all the earth (God) will without question do right: "Shall not the Judge of all the earth do right?" The basic idea of righteousness (or justice) is that moral creatures must adhere to the law of what is right. But God does not adhere to any law because there is no law above God. God's very moral nature and character are the final standard of what is right.

Theologian Sam Storms provides a good overview of the justice of God:

Punishment is justice
for the unjust.

—**Augustine**

> When we speak about the justice of God, we have in mind the idea that God always acts in perfect conformity and harmony with his own character. Some suggest that justice is thus a synonym for righteousness. Whatever God is, says, or does, by virtue of the fact that it is God, makes it righteous. Right and wrong are simply, and respectively, what God either commands or forbids. In other words, God doesn't do or command something because it is right. It is right because it is done or commanded by God. Righteousness or rectitude or good do not exist independently of God as a law or rule or standard to which God adheres or conforms. Rather, righteousness or rectitude or good are simply God acting and speaking.
>
> Justice, therefore, is God acting and speaking in conformity with who he is. To say that God is just is to say that he acts and speaks consistently with whatever his righteous nature requires. To be unjust is to act and speak inconsistently with whatever his righteous nature requires. That, of course, is a contradiction. That would be to assert that the righteous God acts unrighteously. By definition, that is impossible.[7]

John Piper describes God's righteousness as "His unswerving commitment to uphold and display the infinite worth of His glory in all that He does."[8] And when we as humans fall short of the glory of God, that requires punishment: "For the wages of sin is death" (Rom. 6:23).

God expresses to us what is right in his moral law. Even if someone has never heard of the Ten Commandments, the *work of the law* is still written on his or her heart according to Romans 2:15: "who show the work of the law written in their hearts, their conscience also bearing witness." God has instituted a moral code in this world and has imposed just laws on all creatures. When people break the laws of God, it is necessary that he treats them according to what they deserve; this is justice. Because the judge of all the earth does what is right, we are to do justice to each other. Proverbs 21:3 states: "To do righteousness and justice / Is more acceptable to the LORD than sacrifice."

— ABSORB —

### God's justice means that "God always acts in accordance with what is right and is himself the final standard of what is right."[9]

— INTERACT —

○ Why do you think that justice is so important to us?

○ What would the world be like if God was not just? Would there be any hope for the future?

## LISTEN: The Wrath of God

J. I. Packer helps us to understand our culture's attitude toward God's wrath:

> "Wrath" is an old English word defined in my dictionary as "deep, intense anger and indignation." "Anger" is defined as "stirring of resentful displeasure and strong antagonism, by a sense of injury or insult"; "indignation" as "righteous anger aroused by injustice and baseness." Such is wrath. And wrath, the Bible tells us, is an attribute of God. . . . The modern habit throughout the Christian church is to play this subject down. Those who still believe in the wrath of God

## Is It Wrong for God to Seek His Own Glory?

John Piper explains how God's righteousness is connected to valuing what should be valued most—namely, God! Unrighteousness would be to not value what should be valued most.

> It is crucial to say that God is the most valuable being in the universe. We are quite secondary. And since God is the ultimate value in the universe it is only right and fitting that He be honest about that; that He tell us so, and that for our own good He seek our love and admiration. Sometimes people ask, why is it right for God to seek His glory, but wrong for us to seek our glory? Why would we be vain and God be righteous? The answer is that God's righteousness and our righteousness are exactly the same—God is righteous to esteem most highly what is most valuable in the universe, namely, God. And we are righteous to esteem most highly what is most valuable in the universe, namely, God. There is no inconsistency here. Righteousness means having a right response to what is infinitely glorious and perfect. And that is God. For us to be righteous, we must love God with all our heart and soul and mind and strength. For God to be righteous, He too must love HIMSELF with all his heart and soul and mind and strength. Otherwise he would be an idolater. He would be giving supreme devotion to something that does not have supreme value.[a]
>
> God's righteousness is His unwavering commitment to uphold and display the infinite worth of His glory in all that He does, which would seem to require punishment for all who have "fallen short of the glory of God" (Rom. 3:23). "The righteousness of God" must be His unswerving commitment always to preserve the honor of His name and to display His glory. But since God's righteousness and His mercy are not ultimately at odds, He made a way to "be both just and the justifier of him who has faith in Jesus" (Rom. 3:26).[b]

Piper's clarification helps us to understand why God does everything for his own glory. It is absolutely right for God to seek his glory but wrong for us to seek our glory because he *must* esteem most highly what is most valuable in the universe, namely, himself. But we would be wrong to seek our own glory because we, too, are to esteem most highly what is most valuable in the universe, which is God alone!

[a] John Piper, "The Joyful Duty of Man," Desiring God Ministries, January 22, 1989, http://www.desiringgod.org/ResourceLibrary/Sermon/.
[b] John Piper, *God's Passion for His Glory* (Wheaton: Crossway, 1988), 33, 141.

Hell is the backdrop that reveals the profound and unbelievable grace of the cross. It brings to light the enormity of our sin and therefore portrays the undeserved favor of God in full color.

**—Francis Chan and Preston Sprinkle,** *Erasing Hell*

say little about it; perhaps they do not think much about it. To an age which has unashamedly sold itself to the gods of greed, pride, sex, and self-will, the Church mumbles on about God's kindness, but says virtually nothing about His judgment. . . . The fact is that the subject of divine wrath has become taboo in modern society, and Christians by and large have accepted the taboo and conditioned themselves never to raise the matter."[10]

Sin always hurts, defaces, and harms people and dishonors God. There is nothing inherently good about sin. God's grace is greater than our sin, and God's wisdom and power conquer sin; but moral evil is always a detestable thing, worthy of being hated. If God did not hate sin, then the universe would slip into moral chaos. Therefore, if God did not manifest his hatred of sin by displays of his wrath, we as fallen creatures would never grasp the serious and repugnant nature of sin. The Bible reveals a common pattern: people persistently rebel against the goodness of God after repeated warnings; then, after much longsuffering, the sin finally reaches the level where God's wrath is poured out against the rebellion.

We can see clearly the wrath of God displayed both in the Old and New Testaments.

Old Testament: "Who can stand before His indignation? / And who can endure the fierceness of His anger? / His fury is poured out like fire" (Nah. 1:6). This is just one of the many Old Testament passages that highlight the wrath of God.

New Testament: Jesus brought judgment on those who misused the temple of God: "And He found in the temple those who sold oxen and sheep and doves, and the money changers doing business. When He had made a whip of cords, He drove them all out of the temple, with the sheep and the oxen, and poured out the changers' money and overturned the tables. And He said to those who sold doves, 'Take these things away! Do not make My Father's house a house of merchandise'" (John 2:14–16).

It is noteworthy that the book of Revelation pictures the return of Christ in great victory and judgment, pouring out wrath on the nations: "Now out of His [Jesus's] mouth goes a sharp sword, that with it He should strike the nations. And He Himself will rule them with a rod of iron. He Himself [Jesus Himself!] treads the winepress of the fierceness and wrath of Almighty God" (Rev. 19:15).

— **ABSORB** —

**God's wrath is his intense displeasure and hatred toward sin and moral evil.**

## Grappling with the Reality of Wrath and Hell

"There are times when you have no right to think or speak or feel moderately. You shall not give a moderate warning to a neighbor that his house is on fire nor moderately seek to rescue your child from drowning nor moderately snatch your wife from the hands of ruffians. You shall be as harsh as truth and as uncompromising as justice. You shall not equivocate. You shall not excuse. You shall not draw back. You shall be heard."

**Donald Grey Barnhouse[a]**

[a]*Romans: Expositions of Bible Doctrines*, vol. 1 (Grand Rapids: Eerdmans, 1959), 160.

## INTERACT

○ Why do you think it is much easier to discuss God's kindness with people rather than God's judgment and wrath? Why would it be important at some point to bring up the subject?

○ How do you picture the expression on Jesus's face when he took the whip and forced these people out of the temple? Is it difficult for you to picture Christ's anger? Why or why not?

## LISTEN: Further Descriptions of God

There are other descriptions of God that theologians generally do not list when classifying the attributes of God. Yet these descriptions reveal aspects about God that are attractive and praiseworthy. Three noteworthy descriptions of God found in the Bible are that he is perfect, beautiful, and blessed (*his perfection*, *his beauty*, *his blessedness*).

Jesus said that our Heavenly Father is "perfect" (Matt. 5:48). The term "perfect" means "complete, lacking nothing." God does not lack anything desirable. There is nothing desirable that could be added to God!

There is a sense that all of God's attributes shine forth in a way that is described in terms of aesthetics—namely *the beauty* of the Lord. David sings out in Psalm 27:4: "One thing I have desired of the LORD, / That will I seek: / That I may dwell in the house of the LORD / All the days of my life, / To behold the *beauty* of the LORD." God is the sum of all desirable qualities that reflect an everlasting aesthetic attraction.

---

### Wrath and Hell

"God's wrath in the Bible is something which men choose for themselves. Before hell is an experience inflicted by God, it is a state for which man himself opts, by retreating from the light which God shines in his heart to lead him to Himself.... In the last analysis, all that God does subsequently in judicial action towards the unbeliever, whether in this life or beyond it, is to show him, and lead him into, the full implications of the choice he has made."

**J. I. Packer[a]**

[a]*Knowing God* (Downers Grove, IL: InterVarsity, 1973), 134.

---

The Bible describes God as being *blessed*. First Timothy 1:11 describes "the glorious gospel of the *blessed* God." When you probe what it means to say that God is "blessed" (the Greek word is *makarios*, which is often translated "blessed" or "fortunate" or "happy"), you discover that blessedness is linked to the idea of being in a desired state of reality—happiness! God enjoys the state of absolute, eternal happiness. [11] This is part of the glorious gospel, the glorious good news about God. John Piper, in his work *The Pleasures of God*, writes about this blessedness of God:

> And this is the gospel: "The gospel of the glory of the happy God." It is good news that God is gloriously happy. No one would want to spend eternity with an unhappy God. If God is unhappy then the goal of the gospel is not a happy goal, and that means it would be no gospel at all. But in fact Jesus invites us to spend eternity with a happy God when he says, "Enter into the joy of your master" (Matt. 25:23). Jesus lived and died that His joy—God's joy—might be in us and our joy might be full (John 14:11; 17:13). Therefore the gospel is "the gospel of the glory of the happy God." [12]

## ABSORB

**God's perfection means he possesses all excellent qualities and doesn't lack anything desirable. God's beauty means he is the sum of all desirable qualities. God's blessedness means that he exists in the state of absolute, eternal happiness.**

## INTERACT

○ All the fullness of joy is in God—he is perfectly happy. How does it make you feel to know that throughout all eternity you will share in the kind of joy and happiness that God experiences?

**Reflect:** Reflect on how God's justice can move you to be more of a person of justice in our culture. Also, a penetrating question to ask our souls is: "Am I really loving my neighbor as myself if I am not looking for ways to share the gospel with him or her?"

Missions is not the ultimate goal of the church. Worship is. Missions exists because worship doesn't. Worship is ultimate, not missions, because God is ultimate, not man. When this age is over, and the countless millions of the redeemed fall on their faces before the throne of God, missions will be no more. It is a temporary necessity. But worship abides forever.

**—John Piper, *Let the Nations Be Glad***

The holiness, the justice, and wrath of God should lead us to deeply appreciate the blessed gift of Christ's righteousness. Are there any loved ones or friends for whom we can pray that God would bring to salvation?

## CULTIVATING SPIRITUAL HABITS

**Read:** Genesis 37, 39–45, 50

**Journal:** Pick out one particular attribute and write about what stands out to you about that attribute. As you are doing so, thank God for that particular attribute.

### Memorize

*Holy, holy, holy is the* L*ORD of hosts;*
*The whole earth is full of His glory!*

ISAIAH 6:3

# The Sovereign God

## The Attributes of God (Part 4)

**Purpose of Session Twenty-Three:** This is the fourth session of five focusing on the attributes of God. The attributes of God are those qualities and characteristics of God that constitute who and what he is. In these final two sessions we focus on the sovereignty of God.

## LISTEN: God's Sovereignty and Man's Responsibility

The *sovereign will* of God is inseparably connected with his *omnipotence* (some theologians even label God's omnipotence as his *sovereign power*). Whatever God wills or purposes to happen will indeed come to pass; his omnipotence makes certain that his sovereign will is perfectly carried out. As we approach this subject, we should remember the humility of the apostle Paul as he reflected on the incredible decisions, plans, purposes, ways, and will of God: "Oh, the depth of the riches both of the wisdom and knowledge of God! How unsearchable are His judgments and His ways past finding out! 'For who has known the mind of the LORD? / Or who has become His counselor?' / 'Or who has first given to Him / And it shall be repaid to him?' / For of Him and through Him and to Him are all things, to whom be glory forever. Amen" (Rom. 11:33–36).

The purpose of this session is to give you a deep and greater appreciation of the biblical presentation of the sovereignty of God.

There have been volumes written on the subject of God's sovereignty and man's responsibility. Sometimes Christians enter into hot debates in which they wind up either nullifying God's sovereignty or diminishing man's responsibility.

These two sessions seek to help you appreciate the sovereignty of God and draw strength, hope, and courage from it, and at the same time acknowledge that the choices we make are real and have eternal consequences.

The sovereignty-responsibility tension is not a problem to be solved; rather it is a framework to be explored.

—**D. A. Carson,**
***Divine Sovereignty and Human Responsibility***

## ABSORB

**The Word of God presents a strong, unwavering view of God's sovereignty and at the same time a vivid reality of the responsibility of man. In order to remain biblical, we are committed to holding on to both truths.**

## INTERACT

○ The apostle Paul states that God's wisdom, knowledge, decisions, and ways are so magnificent that we cannot grasp the depth and brilliance of the divine mind that put this all together: "*Oh, the depth of the riches both of the wisdom and knowledge of God!*" What is something you can see with your eyes that God has done that you find astonishing?

## LISTEN: A Biblical Case Study of the Sovereignty of God

The famous account of Joseph in the Old Testament gives us great insight into how the will of God and the will of humans intersect. Joseph was a teenager with the blessing of God on his life. He loved his father, Jacob, and his father deeply loved him—so much so that Jacob gave Joseph a special coat of distinction (traditionally translated as the "coat of many colors"). His ten brothers became insanely jealous, decided to kill him, and threw him into a pit. At the last moment, instead of murdering Joseph, they sold him to slave traders who were traveling to Egypt. In the ancient world to be sold into slavery in Egypt was in essence to be forever separated from one's family. The brothers took Joseph's coat and dipped it in goat's blood to make it appear to Joseph's father that he had been killed by a wild animal. Joseph became a slave in Egypt, but every step of the way the Lord's hand of favor was upon him. Eventually, through some of the most providential circumstances, including Joseph interpreting Pharaoh's dreams, Joseph became the prime minister over all of Egypt. For seven years Joseph led Egypt in a grain storage program. At the end of the seven years, as God had formerly revealed to Joseph, there came a fierce famine in the land of the Middle East. Joseph's brothers were eventually forced to travel to Egypt to buy grain in order to survive the drought. In Egypt they never dreamed that they would see their brother Joseph, but they eventually came face-to-face with him. They were in total shock. Listen carefully to what Joseph said to his brothers who had sold him into slavery over twenty years before:

> And Joseph said to his brothers, "Please come near to me." So they came near. Then he said: "I am Joseph your brother, whom you sold into Egypt. But now, do not therefore be grieved or angry with yourselves because *you sold me* here; for *God sent me* before you to preserve life. . . . And *God sent me* before you to preserve a posterity for you in the earth, and to save your lives by a great deliverance. So now *it was not you who sent me here, but God*." (Gen. 45:4–8)

> "But as for you, *you meant evil against me*; *but God meant it for good*, in order to bring it about as it is this day, to save many people alive." (Gen. 50:20)

Joseph's words give us insight into the sovereignty of God. Remember, God's sovereignty means that God rules as King (in the most absolute sense of the word) and that *nothing* happens within this universe (or outside this universe) without his direction or permission. Joseph's brothers meant evil against Joseph, and they committed a serious sin against their brother. They took away his freedom for many years. They were absolutely wrong, sinful, and guilty in their choice. But God had a much larger, overriding plan: he himself sent Joseph to Egypt so that Joseph's whole family could be spared from dying in the famine and so that he could form them into a nation in Egypt. Recall Joseph's words: "It was not you who sent me here, but God." God had a plan, and he was carrying out that plan. But at the same time he used the wicked acts of Joseph's brothers to accomplish his will. The Bible says that God works all things after the counsel of his will: "In Him also we have obtained an inheritance, being predestined according to the purpose of Him who *works all things according to the counsel of His will*" (Eph. 1:11).

## ABSORB

**Joseph's brothers were totally responsible for the evil they committed against Joseph—*they meant it for evil*. Yet *God meant it for good*. Recall Joseph's words: "It was not you who sent me here, but God." God all along had an infinitely larger, sovereign plan: he himself sent Joseph to Egypt so that Joseph's whole family could be spared from dying in the famine and so that God could form them into a nation in Egypt.**

## INTERACT

○ Try to explain how Joseph's brothers intended evil and harm against Joseph, while God at the same time had a sovereign plan for Joseph that was intended for Joseph's good.

○ If you were Joseph and were sold to slave traders and taken away from your family and homeland, would it have been hard for you to see the hand of God in it? How easy would it be for you to forgive your brothers?

○ Why do you think Joseph said to his brothers, "It was not you who sent me here, but God"?

## LISTEN: The Sovereignty of God

The sovereignty of God means that all things are under his rule and control and that nothing happens in this universe without his direction or permission. God works not just some things but all things after the counsel of his own will. God's purpose is all-inclusive and is never thwarted. Isaiah 46:9–10 gives a clear picture of the extent of God's absolute authority and control: "For I am God, and there is no other; / I am God, and there is none like Me, / Declaring the end from the beginning, / And from ancient times things that are not yet done, / Saying 'My counsel shall stand, and I will do all My pleasure.'"

John Piper has defined sovereignty this way: "It is not merely that God has the power and right to govern all things but that He does so always and without exception."[1] In other words, God is sovereign not only in principle but also in practice. God is clothed with absolute authority and power over all his creatures and creation, and works all things after the counsel of his own will. "All things are dependent on him and subservient to him."[2] Nothing in the entire universe can dictate to God what he should do or keep him from accomplishing what pleases him. God has absolute freedom! When we speak about the sovereignty of God, in short we are simply saying God is in control!

## Cosmic Treason against the Perfectly Pure Sovereign

"Sin is cosmic treason. Sin is treason against a perfectly pure Sovereign. It is an act of supreme ingratitude toward the One to whom we owe everything, to the One who has given us life itself. Have you ever considered the deeper implications of the slightest sin, of the most minute peccadillo? What are we saying to our Creator when we disobey Him at the slightest point? We are saying no to the righteousness of God. We are saying, 'God, Your law is not good. My judgment is better than Yours. Your authority does not apply to me. I am above and beyond Your jurisdiction. I have the right to do what I want to do, not what You command me to do.'"

**R. C. Sproul**[a]

[a]*The Holiness of God* (Wheaton: Tyndale, 1985), 115–16.

## ABSORB

God's sovereignty means that *all* things are under his rule and control and that nothing happens in this universe without his direction or permission. He works *all* things after the counsel of his own will.[3] To put it simply, God is in control!

## INTERACT

○ Think about what it means that God is in total, absolute control of everything! He does everything he pleases (of course it never pleases him to go against his holy nature). What must it be like to be God?

## LISTEN: Concurrence—People Act, God Acts

R. C. Sproul gives further insight in explaining how God has a divine plan and is ruling over all things in the universe but at the same time allowing people to make real choices. This theological truth is called *concurrence* and refers to the coterminous actions of God and humans. This means that at the same time human agents are acting, God is acting in and through them.[4] We are creatures with a will of our own. We make choices. Yet the causal power we exert is secondary. God's sovereign providence stands over and above our actions. He works out his will through the actions of human wills, without violating the freedom of the human will. "The clearest example of concurrence that we find in Scripture is in the case of Joseph and his brothers. Though Joseph's brothers incurred true guilt through their treachery against him, the providence of God was working even through their sin."[5]

The Westminster Confession says that the Scriptures teach that God is the primary cause of all things but at the same time uses *secondary causes* (real choices made by people) to accomplish his will. But God does it in such a way that he is not the author of sin (sin and evil are not morally chargeable to him), nor does he invalidate the reality of personal decisions that people make. "God from all eternity did, by the most wise and holy counsel of His own will, freely and unchangeably ordain whatsoever comes to pass; yet so, as thereby *neither is God the author of sin*, nor is violence offered to the will of the creatures, nor is the liberty or contingency of second causes taken away, but rather established."[6]

This is an incredible mystery. God works everything out according to the counsel of his will but does it so that sin and evil are not morally chargeable to him but are always chargeable to the ones who actually commit the sins. "Second causes" refers to actions or events attributable to agents other than God. "Liberty" is another word for freedom, and "contingency" implies that an action was not compelled.[7] God did not coerce the brothers of Joseph to commit their sin of treachery, yet God foreordained that these events occur through the free choices of men. In other words, God can be in control without taking away our free choices. Nor do the free choices of people determine the course of the future—God determines the future. People are free and God is free. But when our freedom clashes with God's freedom, God is more free! That is because only God is sovereign, not humans! It is no wonder when theologians try to grasp the infinite wisdom and plans and ways of God, they concede: *finitum non capax infinitum*[8] ("the finite cannot grasp the infinite").

Paul describes an astonishing promise from God: "And we know that all things work together for good to those who love God, to those who are the called according to His purpose" (Rom. 8:28).

## ABSORB

**Concurrence means that at the same time human agents are acting, God is acting in and through them. God works everything out according to the counsel of his will but does it so that sin and evil are not morally chargeable to him but are always chargeable to the ones who actually commit the sins.**

**INTERACT**

○ Discuss how Joseph's brothers could make a real, sinful choice of selling their brother to slave traders but at the same time God had already determined in his divine will and plan to send Joseph to Egypt.

○ How can knowing that God is sovereign help you face difficulties and trials? How would you feel if God was not sovereign over such things?

## LISTEN: Sovereign Will and Prescriptive Will

Now if God "works all things according to the counsel of His will" (Eph. 1:11), then does that mean that Joseph's brothers were doing "the will of God" when they sold him into slavery? The Scriptures teach that in one sense there is an eternal, *sovereign will* of God, which is his all-inclusive plan in which he works *all things* according to his will (including the evil disobedient acts of his creatures). Some theologians also call this sovereign will God's *will of decree* because it is immutable and fixed. But in another sense there is the *prescriptive will* of God (also called by theologians God's *moral will* or *will of command* or *will of desire*), which is what God commands of us. This prescriptive moral will also includes his disposition or attitude toward good and evil. God's prescriptive will is like a doctor's prescription that, if taken, has beneficial effects but also can be refused. God's prescriptive will is often refused; it is often not obeyed. When Jesus taught us to pray "Thy will be done on earth as it is in Heaven," Christ was assuming that God's will (his *prescriptive will*) is not always obeyed here on earth. So, biblically speaking, there are two ways in which God "wills." To answer the question, were Joseph's brothers doing the will of God?, yes, it was in God's ultimate, *sovereign will* that Joseph be sent to Egypt, but at the same time Joseph's brothers committed the sins of jealous hatred and lying, and so were *not* obeying God's will because lying and jealousy are against the prescriptive will of God. Understanding that there are two different meanings for the term "will of God" in the Bible will help you to understand how God is sovereign over all things and yet disapproves of many sinful acts, though those very acts accomplish his purpose. The classic example is the crucifixion and sacrifice of Christ. In one sense it was God's *sovereign will* that Christ would come to this earth to give his life as a sacrifice for our sins. But at the same time the act of torturing and murdering the Son of God was wicked and against the *prescriptive will* of God. Notice in the New Testament passage below that the crucifixion happened because, as Peter says, it was the "determined *purpose* [*boule*] *of God*" (the Greek term *boule* is also translated "will" or "plan"). However, the hands that put Christ to death are described as "lawless" (disobedient), meaning this was a highly sinful act against the *prescriptive will* of God. Peter said:

> Men of Israel, hear these words: Jesus of Nazareth, a Man attested by God to you by miracles, wonders, and signs which God did through Him in your midst, as you yourselves also know—Him, being delivered by the *determined purpose* and foreknowledge of God, you have taken by *lawless* hands, have crucified, and put to death; whom God raised up, having loosed the pains of death, because it was not possible that He should be held by it. (Acts 2:22–24)

Herod, Pontius Pilate, the gentiles, and the people of Israel were all guilty of plotting against the Holy Son of God to kill him. To crucify the Son of God was the most horrific crime of history—so there is no question that they were committing a wicked crime against the *prescriptive will* of God. Yet at the same time this all unfolded according to the *sovereign will* of God. "For truly against Your holy Servant Jesus, whom You anointed, both Herod and Pontius Pilate, with the Gentiles and the people of Israel, were gathered together to do whatever Your hand and Your *purpose* [*boule*] determined before to be done" (Acts 4:27–28).

## ABSORB

**The *sovereign will* of God is his all-inclusive plan in which he works all things according to the counsel of his will. Nothing happens without his direction or active permission. God's *sovereign will* is what he ordains to come to pass. It always rules and overrules where the *prescriptive will* has been disobeyed. God is in control!**

## INTERACT

○ Why do you think it is important to know the difference between the sovereign will of God and the prescriptive will of God?

## All of God's Sovereignty Mediated through Christ

"Everything that is coming to us from God comes through Christ Jesus. Christ Jesus has won our pardon; he has reconciled us to God; he has canceled our sin; he has secured the gift of the Spirit for us; he has granted eternal life to us and promises us the life of the consummation; he has made us children of the new covenant; his righteousness has been accounted as ours; he has risen from the dead, and all of God's sovereignty is mediated through him and directed to our good and to God's glory."

**D. A. Carson**[a]

[a]*A Call to Spiritual Reformation* (Grand Rapids: Baker, 1992), 189.

○ Is it hard for you to conceive how God could have a predetermined plan (his sovereign will) to send Christ into the world as a sacrifice for our sins but at the same time hold people accountable for making their own choices to disobey God's prescriptive will by killing his Son?

## LISTEN: God's Happiness

John Piper, in his book *Desiring God*, describes how God can say, "I will do *all* My pleasure" (which refers to his sovereign will) and at the same time allow people to disobey his prescriptive will (moral will), which doesn't give him pleasure but grieves and angers him:

> How can we affirm the happiness of God on the basis of His sovereignty when much of what God permits in the world is contrary to His own commands in Scripture? How can we say God is happy when there is so much sin and misery in the world? . . . The infinite complexity of the divine mind is such that God has the capacity to look at the world through two lenses. . . .
>
> When God looks at a painful or wicked event through His narrow lens, He sees the tragedy or the sin for what it is in itself and He is angered and grieved. "I have no pleasure in the death of anyone, says the LORD God" (Ezek. 18:32). But when God looks at a painful or wicked event through His wide angle lens, He sees the tragedy or the sin in relation to everything leading up to it and everything flowing out from it. He sees it in all the connections and effects that form a pattern or mosaic stretching into eternity. This mosaic in all its parts—good and evil—brings Him delight.[9]

The appeal to God's sovereignty is not to foster hope that we will be spared all difficulty, but to foster confidence that when those difficulties come we are not abandoned. Things have not fallen out of hand. We can still rely on the God who has permitted us to face these things to supply us with the grace and help we need to be faithful under such circumstances.

**—D. A. Carson,**
***Jesus' Sermon on the Mount***

## ABSORB

Within the infinite complexity of God's mind he has the capacity to see the world through two lenses. Through the narrow lens he sees the tragedy or sinful event and is angered or grieved by it. But at the same time, through the wide angle lens he sees the big picture, the beautiful mosaic of his sovereign will that brings him great, superseding, eternal delight!

## INTERACT

○ Can you think of parallels of humans using both narrow and wide angle perspectives? For example: a parent is grieved by a child having to undergo a painful surgery to save the child's life but still joyfully chooses the operation for the child.

**Reflect:** If you are facing a problem, difficulty, disappointment, or even a dead end, think about how the sovereignty of God can give you clear perspective. It is the greatest comfort for the believer to know that God is in control! No matter what confronts us in life, God's sovereign will is working all things together for our good.

How can I best pray for you until the next session?

## CULTIVATING SPIRITUAL HABITS

**Read:** Romans 8 and 9

**Journal:** Reread the beginning of this session about Joseph, then write in your journal about how God meant it for good for Joseph even though his brothers meant evil against him.

### Memorize

*But as for you, you meant evil against me; but God meant it for good, in order to bring it about as it is this day, to save many people alive.*

GENESIS 50:20

# The Mystery of Sovereignty

## The Attributes of God (Part 5)

---

**Purpose of Session Twenty-Four:** This is the fifth and final session focusing on the many attributes of God. This session is a continuation of the last session, which focuses on the sovereignty of God.

---

## LISTEN: Living with Mystery

God's sovereignty means that *all* things are under his rule and control, and that nothing happens in this universe without his direction or permission. He works *all* things after the counsel of his own will. To put it simply, God is in control! However, we must live with mystery and not knowing; the apostle Paul states that there are things in the mind of God that are so brilliant and complex that they are past finding out: "How unsearchable are His judgments and His ways past finding out! 'For who has known the mind of the LORD?'" (Rom. 11:33–34). John Flavel, a seventeenth-century pastor from Oxford, wrote in the introduction of his work *The Mystery of Providence*: "The greatness of God is a glorious and unsearchable mystery: 'For the Lord most high is terrible [awesome]; He is a great King over all the earth' (Ps. 47:2)."[1]

The unsearchable mystery is that God is much greater than we can imagine! For millenia scholars and pastors have asked the same deep theological questions concerning evil, pain, suffering, human freedom/responsibility, and God's sovereignty. Today we are still faced with mystery. John Piper writes:

The most profound thing we can say about suffering and evil is that, in Jesus Christ, God entered into it and turned it for good. The origin of evil is shrouded in mystery. "Free will" is just a name for the mystery. It doesn't explain why a perfect creature chose to sin. Another name for the mystery is "the sovereignty

---

## Don't Dispel Mystery

"We like to tie up everything into neat intellectual parcels, with all appearance of mystery dispelled and no loose ends hanging out. Hence we are tempted . . . to suppress, or jettison, one truth in the supposed interests of the other, and for the sake of a tidier theology. . . . The temptation is to undercut and maim the one truth by the way in which we stress the other: to assert man's responsibility in a way that excludes God from being sovereign, or to affirm God's sovereignty in a way that destroys the responsibility of man. Both mistakes need to be guarded against."

**J. I. Packer**[a]

[a]*Evangelism and the Sovereignty of God* (Downers Grove, IL: InterVarsity, 1961), 25.

---

of God." As true and biblical as it is, this too leaves questions unanswered. The Bible does not take us as far as we might like to go. Rather it says, "The secret things belong to . . . God" (Deuteronomy 29:29).[2]

### ABSORB

**When we are prepared to affirm what the apostle Paul declared— "How unsearchable are His judgments and His ways past finding out"—then we will be positioned to let what the Scriptures teach about *God's sovereignty* and *man's responsibility* stand. If we let Scripture speak, we will learn to live with the mystery!**

### INTERACT

○ Why do you think humans insist that we should be given full and complete answers to every question that we have about God (especially since the Word has already stated things such as, "The secret things belong to God" and "It is the glory of God to conceal a matter")?

○ Do you think we would become bored with God if we could completely figure him out?

## LISTEN: What Is Providence?

The providence of God is "the invisible hand of God"[3] at work carrying out every detail of his sovereign will and plan.

The Westminster Confession gives an excellent definition of the providence of God: "God, the great Creator of all things, doth uphold, direct, dispose and govern all creatures, actions, and things, from the greatest even to the least, by His most wise and holy providence, according to His infallible foreknowledge, and the free and immutable counsel of His own will, to the praise of the glory of His wisdom, power, justice, goodness, and mercy."[4]

In other words, the providence of God is the carrying out of every detail of God's sovereign will and plan. Sometimes the "invisible hand of God" becomes so apparent that his hand almost seems visible—some things are obviously more than mere coincidence! Nothing can happen apart from the providence of God. Jesus said: "Are not two sparrows sold for a copper coin? And not one of them falls to the ground *apart from your Father's will*" (Matt. 10:29). Nothing can happen apart from the Father's will! Even when God *permits* people to commit evil acts of sin, he still *chooses* to permit them. He could stop them, and sometimes he does. For example, God kept Abimelech[5] from sinning concerning Abraham's wife (Gen. 20:6). Yet at other times he permits people to commit unspeakable sins. Also, due to the fall of humans there are staggering consequences of sin that affect our entire world, some of them bringing deep suffering and pain to humankind. God could stop any consequence at any time, but often he chooses to permit them to run their course. In some sense God ordains what happens or it could not happen. Augustine was right when he argued that God, *in some sense*, ordains everything that comes to pass. By using the phrase "in some sense," he was attempting to preserve the mystery of the relationship between divine sovereignty and human responsibility.[6]

---

## What God Permits, He *Chooses* to Permit

"If I choose to sin this afternoon, God has the *power* to prevent me from sinning if He so chooses. He also has the *right* to prevent me from sinning since He is sovereign. If he 'permits' my sin, this does not mean He sanctions it or gives His permission in the sense that He deems it lawful. He may let it occur without intervening to stop it. . . . But what God permits to happen He still *chooses* to permit. That is, since He could stop it and decides not to stop it, He exercises His permission according to His good pleasure. In some sense He ordains that it happens or else it could not happen."

**R. C. Sproul**[a]

[a]*The Invisible Hand: Do All Things Really Work for Good?* (Dallas: Word, 1996), 82–83; emphasis in original.

---

**ABSORB**

## Providence is the invisible hand of God at work carrying out every detail of his sovereign will and plan.

---

**INTERACT**

○ Recall the details of your coming to faith in Christ. How do you see the hand of God in it?

## LISTEN: The Profound Comfort of God's Sovereignty

One day when I was a young man in seminary, I was talking with my friend Dwayne and another friend about an assignment in which we had to write a title and outline for a sermon we were required to preach. The title and passage I chose was "The Sovereignty of God in the Christmas Events (Matt. 1 and 2)." One friend remarked that a sermon on the sovereignty of God was not very practical. Suddenly Dwayne, who had seemed a bit despondent, sat up and spoke with tears welling up in his eyes, "What do you mean the sovereignty of God is not practical? It's the only thing that has kept me going these past months!" Shortly after that, we discovered his young wife had left him. It was a very difficult time in Dwayne's life. Being convinced of the sovereignty of God helped him keep his sanity and gave him hope for the future.

As followers of Christ, holding on to the truth of the sovereignty of God is what keeps us going during the most difficult times of life. Knowing that you have a special place in God's heart and that he is working all things together for good gives you strength to face the worst of life's trials. God describes his people with a deeply affectionate term—*the elect*. Colossians 3:12 says, "Therefore, as the elect of God, holy and beloved, put on tender mercies, kindness, humility. . . ." The word "elect" (Greek: *eklektos*[7]) means "chosen" or "select." This means that God in his great mercy and grace *chose you*, selected you, to be a part of his family. The New Testament reveals that God chose us before the world was even created, and God predestined us to be adopted as sons into his family. God did this so that we will praise him for the glory of his great grace: "Blessed be the God and Father of our Lord Jesus Christ . . . just as He *chose us* in Him [Christ] *before* the foundation of the world, that we should be holy and without blame before Him in love, having *predestined*

us to *adoption as sons* by Jesus Christ to Himself, according to the good pleasure of His will, to the praise of the glory of His grace" (Eph. 1:3–6).

---

### — ABSORB —

**God has designed his sovereignty to give us deep and profound comfort and encouragement. We are the elect of God! God actually chose us in Christ before the creation of the world!**

---

### INTERACT

○ God in his great sovereign plan decided to create you and to redeem you in Christ and adopt you into his own family. How does it make you feel to know that he chose you before the world was created?

○ How does it make you feel to know that you are called the "elect of God"?

○ Why do you think being convinced of the sovereignty of God helps us to go through deep trials and recover from broken dreams?

> There is no attribute more comforting to His children than that of God's sovereignty. Under the most adverse circumstances, in the most severe trials, they believe that sovereignty has ordained their afflictions, that sovereignty overrules them, and that sovereignty will sanctify them all.
>
> **—Charles Spurgeon, "Divine Sovereignty"**

## LISTEN: God Chose Us—The Unbroken Chain of Events

The Scriptures spell out an unbroken chain of events that occurs for every Christian: "For whom He foreknew, He also predestined to be conformed to the image of His Son, that He might be the firstborn among many brethren. Moreover whom He predestined, these He also called; whom He called, these He also justified; and whom He justified, these He also glorified" (Rom. 8:29–30).

foreknew → predestined → called → justified → glorified

As you read the chain of events in Romans 8:29, you observe that it begins by God *foreknowing* certain individuals. Before God can predestine anyone for anything, he must have them in mind as objects of his choice or selection.[8] And whom God *foreknew* (had in mind as objects of choice, of selection), these individuals are the ones he predestined to be like Christ; and those whom he predestined he also called, and whom he called he justified, and then glorified. ("Glorified" is in past tense because in God's eyes it is so certain that it is as good as done.) This is an unbroken chain of events set in motion by God himself. Some people have attempted to interpret this verse to mean that God foreknew who would believe in Christ and who would not, and predestined those who would believe to be saved. They come to this conclusion in an attempt to solve the mystery as to why God would choose certain people and not others. But here is where we must allow mystery to remain mystery: God selects or chooses based on his own sovereign reasons—God chooses for reasons known only to himself. It is hard for humans to let mystery remain mystery! Notice carefully that this verse does not say *what* God foreknew about certain individuals, but *whom* God foreknew. It simply says that those whom he foreknew (whom he had in mind as objects of his choice and selection) he predestined, called, justified, and finally glorified. The shade of meaning for the word "foreknow" is found a couple of chapters later in Romans 11:2, where Paul states that it would be absurd to think that God would cast away the Israelites "whom He foreknew" (selected beforehand). There is a Jewish (Hebraic) use of the word *to know*. For example, God said to Jeremiah that he had *known* (selected) Jeremiah before he was ever born: "Before I formed you in the womb I *knew* you" (Jer. 1:5). This meaning here of "knew" means that God had selected, or chosen, Jeremiah before he was ever created.

In Amos 3:2 the Lord says to Israel: "You only *have I known* of all the families of the earth." It is obvious that God has knowledge of every family on earth. Therefore, the term "know" must mean that God knows Israel in a special way, in the sense of relationship—only Israel has he selected. Thus, in Romans 8:29 when the apostle Paul says, "For whom He foreknew," it means for whom he beforehand selected. Again, we are not told in this verse why God selected beforehand certain individuals and not others. But in the very next chapter (Rom. 9) the apostle is clear that God chose Jacob over Esau before either was born or before they had committed either good or evil. Romans 9:11 says that God's choice is based on God's election and not the actions of Jacob and Esau (although it is noteworthy that both were sinners and neither were deserving of God to choose them): "For the children [Jacob and Esau] not yet being born, nor having done any good or evil, that the purpose of God *according to election* might stand, not of works but of Him who calls."

Then Paul clarifies even further that when God made his choice it was not something found in humans. Romans 9:16 says, "So then it is not of him *who wills*; nor of him *who runs*, but of God who shows mercy." Notice the wording: God's choice was not based on the willing choice of humans (the volitional choice to believe) nor was it based on any positive exertion (running), but it was simply based on the mercy of God. You see this clearly when Paul defends God's choice of choosing Jacob over Esau by reminding us of what God said to Moses, "I will have mercy on whomever I will have mercy, and I will have compassion on whomever I will have compassion" (Rom. 9:15).

This means that God has the divine sovereign right to show mercy as He wills! None of us deserves the mercy of God. Neither Jacob nor Esau deserved for God to show them mercy. God was not unrighteous or unjust for choosing Jacob and passing over Esau. God was not unjust to choose Israel to be his chosen nation and to not choose other nations of the earth. R. C. Sproul writes, "The principle is that of the sovereignty of God's mercy and grace. By definition grace is not something God is required to have. It is His sovereign prerogative to grant or withhold it. God does not owe grace to anyone. Grace that is owed is not grace. Justice imposes obligation, but grace, in its essence, is voluntary and free."[9]

God owed neither Jacob nor Esau any measure of mercy or grace. If God had chosen neither, he would not have been unjust—because both Jacob and Esau were sinners. Because God chose Jacob over Esau does not mean that Esau was a victim of cruelty or injustice. Sproul explains, "Among the mass of fallen humanity, all are guilty of sin before God and exposed to His justice, no one has any claim or entitlement to God's mercy."[10]

— ABSORB —

**There remains a true mystery when trying to discover why God chose us who are followers of Christ. God selected, predestined, called, justified, and glorified us. Why he so mercifully and graciously chose you or me can be found in reasons known only to God. Our response to this mystery is that we will praise the glory of his grace forever!**

— INTERACT —

○ When you stand back and think of God's astonishing grace and mercy he has poured upon your life, how does that make you feel?

○ Since we know we don't deserve God's mercy, how should this affect how we treat others?

## LISTEN: God Has Good Reasons

As we probe the Scriptures about how we came to know Christ, it becomes increasingly clear that it was because of God's sovereign grace that drew us to him when we were in rebellion. He opened our hearts to the gospel and saved us by his grace through faith in Christ. The apostle Paul put it in profoundly simple terms when he said that it is because "of Him [of God] you are in Christ Jesus" (1 Cor. 1:30). God chose you—elected you from the foundation of the world and "predestined you unto adoption as sons"—for reasons known only to himself—"according to the good pleasure of His will." If you think this might seem random or whimsical or arbitrary of God, then listen to Sproul's explanation:

> That God chooses according to the good pleasure of His will does not mean that His choices are capricious or arbitrary. An arbitrary choice is one made for no reason at all. Though . . . God's election is based on nothing foreseen in the individuals' lives, this does not mean that He makes the choice for no reason at all. It simply means that the reason is not something God finds in us. In His inscrutable, mysterious will, God chooses for reasons known only to Himself. He chooses according to His own pleasure, which is His divine right. His pleasure is described as His good pleasure. If something pleases God, it must be good. There is no evil pleasure in God.[11]

### ABSORB

**It is because of his sovereign will, which is absolutely good and perfect, that he has chosen you and me.**

### INTERACT

○ When Paul says it is because of him (God) that you are in Christ Jesus, what do you think he means?

○ Think about what God has done in your own life. What would your life be like today if God had not drawn you to himself and opened your heart to the gospel?

## Who's at Fault?

"Everywhere in Scripture, it is a leading principle that man can lose his own soul, that if he is lost at last it will be his own fault, and his blood will be on his own head. The same inspired Bible which reveals this doctrine of election is the Bible which contains the words, 'Why will ye die, O house of Israel?'—'This is the condemnation, that light is come into the world, and men loved darkness rather than light, because their deeds were evil.' The Bible never says that sinners miss heaven because they are not elect, but because they 'neglect the great salvation,' and because they will not repent and believe. . . . God gives men what they choose, not the opposite of what they choose. Those who choose death, therefore, have only themselves to thank that God does not give them life. The doctrine of divine sovereignty does not affect the situation in any way."

**J. I. Packer[a]**

[a]*Evangelism and the Sovereignty of God* (Downers Grove, IL: InterVarsity, 1961),105–6.

## LISTEN: God's Love Is Real for Those Who Reject Him

As stated at the beginning of this session in our discussion of mystery, our aim is to let Scripture stand—to let it teach us what God has said about his choosing us and also about his love for all people.

Let us not forget that God shows astonishing love and kindness to *all* humans (Matt. 5:43–48). At the final judgment, if any person is condemned to hell he or she cannot claim that God has not extended kindness, love, and the offer of salvation. There are clear offers of the gospel to anyone who would choose to come to God: "The Spirit and the bride say, 'Come!' . . . And let him who thirsts come. *Whoever desires*, let him take the water of life freely" (Rev. 22:17).

Even though there is mystery, if we let the Scriptures speak and if we live with the mystery, then we will be truly biblical in our theology. That God chose *you* to be his own does not mean that he has no real love for those who end up perishing. Theologian and pastor John Piper points out how God's love is very real for those who reject the gospel:

I do not deny that Jesus wept over Jerusalem. I do not deny that He felt genuine compassion for perishing people. I do not deny that God loves the world of lost men—elect and non-elect. On the contrary, all I want to do is try to give an account for how both of these biblical teachings can be so—the plain teaching of the Bible on election *and* the plain teaching that God has sincere compassion for the non-elect which He expresses in various ways in the Bible. I do not allow some alien logic to force me to choose between these two teachings of Scripture. . . . In other words, God has a real and deep compassion for perishing sinners. His expression of pity and His entreaties have heart in them. There is a genuine inclination in God's heart to spare those who have committed treason against His kingdom. . . . In His great and mysterious heart there are kinds of longings and desires that are real.[12]

## ABSORB

**Jesus has genuine compassion for perishing people. God loves the world of lost people. There is a real feeling of pity toward those who are heading toward hell. If some are lost, it is because they refuse the salvation that God freely offers.**

## INTERACT

○ What do you think this verse means: "Say to them: 'As I live,' says the Lord God, 'I have no pleasure in the death of the wicked, but that the wicked turn from his way and live'" (Ezek. 33:11)?

**Reflect:** We will close out this final session with some thoughtful words from the nineteenth-century prince of preachers, Charles Spurgeon. He was willing to live with the mystery of God choosing us based on his own sovereign reasons while at the same time those who perish cannot lay the blame at God's door.

> If any of you want to know what I preach every day, and any stranger should say, "Give me a summary of his doctrine," say this, "He preaches salvation all of grace, and damnation all of sin. He gives God all the glory for every soul that is saved, but he won't have it that God is to blame for any man that is damned." That teaching I cannot understand. My soul revolts at the idea of a doctrine that lays the blood of man's soul at God's door. . . . Every man who loses everlasting life rejects it himself. God denies it not to him—he will not come that he may have life. . . . He [God] saves man by grace, and if men perish they perish justly by their own fault. "How," says someone, "do you reconcile these two doctrines?" My dear brethren, I never reconcile two friends, never. These two doctrines are friends with one another; for they are both in God's Word, and I shall not attempt to reconcile them. If you show me that they are enemies, then I will reconcile them.

"But," says one, "there is a great deal of difficulty about them." Will you tell me what truth there is that has not difficulty about it? "But," he says, "I do not see it." Well, I do not ask you to see it; I ask you to believe it. There are many things in God's Word that are difficult, and that I cannot see, but they are there, and I believe them. I cannot see how God can be omnipotent and man be free; but it is so, and I believe it.[13]

Preaching a few months ago in the midst of a large congregation of Methodists, the brethren were all alive, giving all kinds of answers to my sermon, nodding their heads and crying, "Amen!" "Hallelujah!" "Glory be to God!" and the like. They completely woke me up. My spirit was stirred, and I preached away with an unusual force and vigor; and the more I preached the more they cried, "Amen!" "Hallelujah!" "Glory be to God!" At last, a part of the text led me to what is styled high doctrine. So I said, this brings me to the doctrine of Election. There was a deep drawing of breath. "Now, my friends, you believe it"; they seemed to say "No, we don't." But you do, and I will make you sing "Hallelujah!" over it. I will so preach it to you that you will acknowledge it and believe it. So I put it thus: Is there no difference between you and other men? [in other words—you once were spiritually lost like others but now you are saved—Is that not true?] "Yes, yes; glory be to God, glory!" There is a difference between what you were and what you are now? "Oh, yes! oh, yes!" There is sitting by your side a man who has been to the same chapel as you have, heard the same gospel, he is unconverted, and you are converted. Who has made the difference, yourself or God? "The Lord!" said they, "the Lord! glory! hallelujah!" Yes, cried I, and that is the doctrine of Election; that is all I contend for, that if there be a difference the Lord made the difference. Some good man came up to me and said, "Thou'rt right, lad! thou'rt right. I believe *thy* doctrine of Election; I do not believe it as it is preached by some people, but I believe that we must give the glory to God, we must put the crown on the right head."

After all, there is an instinct in every Christian heart, that makes him receive the substance of this doctrine, even if he will not receive it in the peculiar form in which *we* put it. That is enough for me. I do not care about the words or the phraseology, or the form of creed in which I may be in the habit of stating the doctrine. I do not want you to subscribe to my creed, but I do want you to subscribe to a creed that gives God the glory of His salvation.[14]

Spurgeon lived with the mystery; we should too. To God be the glory, great things he has done!

## CULTIVATING SPIRITUAL HABITS

**Read:** Read again Romans 8 and 9

**Journal:** Go back and scan the titles of each session. Jot down in your journal why this study guide has been beneficial to you. Be praying and ask God if he wants to use you to disciple someone else. Think of the impact this could have on someone else's life!

### Memorize

*And we know that all things work together for good to those who love God, to those who are the called according to His purpose.*

ROMANS 8:28

# Notes

## How This Guide Works

1. J. I. Packer and Gary A. Parrett, *Grounded in the Gospel: Building Believers the Old-Fashioned Way* (Grand Rapids, Baker Books, 2010), 184.

## Session One  Declared Not Guilty: *Understanding Justification (Part 1)*

1. For example, Eph. 2:8–9 clearly states that we are saved by the grace of God, not by works: "For by grace you have been saved through faith, and that not of yourselves; it is the gift of God, *not of works*, lest anyone should boast."

2. The Hebrew word for "vain" (*shav*) in Exod. 20:7 is the same term used in Ps. 127:1, "Unless the Lord builds the house, / They labor *in vain* who build it." Here the Hebrew term means that those who labor do so with the end result that it is "useless" or "with no good purpose." So to use the name of the Lord "in vain" is to use it in a useless way—a way in which there is no good purpose.

3. C. S. Lewis, *The Last Battle*, The Chronicles of Narnia (New York: HarperCollins, 1994), 127.

4. Leon Morris, *The Apostolic Preaching of the Cross* (Grand Rapids: Eerdmans, 1955), 224–74. Morris in this extensive work clearly demonstrates that the apostle Paul is using the term "to justify" in a legal (forensic) sense. He writes in his chapter on justification, "This last passage [Rom. 3:4, which states, "That You (God) may be justified in Your words"] refers to God being justified, which is enough to show that the meaning of the word must be something like 'declare righteous', for it is impossible to think that the apostle (or, for that matter, the psalmist Paul is quoting) meant that God was to be 'made righteous'. He is affirming that in the process of judgment God's words would show that He is righteous. We have another reference to God's being justified in Luke 7:29, and on to Christ in 1 Timothy 3:16. This little group of passages is very important, for it shows, at the very least, that the New Testament writers could understand *dikaioo* [δικαιοω, pronounced dick-i-ah-o] as signifying 'to declare righteous' or 'to show as righteous'" (p. 259).

5. John Stott, *The Cross of Christ* (Downers Grove, IL: InterVarsity, 1986), 190.

6. John Stott, *The Message of Galatians* (Chicago: InterVarsity, 1968), 60.

## Session Two  God Pays the Price: *Understanding Justification (Part 2)*

1. C. S. Lewis, *Mere Christianity* (San Francisco: HarperCollins, 2001), 3.

2. Leon Morris, *The Apostolic Preaching of the Cross* (Grand Rapids: Eerdmans, 1955), 22, 58.

3. Adolph Deissmann, *Light from the Ancient East: The New Testament Illustrated by Recently Discovered Texts of the Graeco-Roman World*, trans. Lionel R. M. Strachan (Grand Rapids: Baker, 1965), 327–28.

4. John Piper, *The Passion of Jesus Christ* (Wheaton: Crossway, 2004), 21. This definition of propitiation is substantiated by Morris, *Apostolic Preaching of the Cross*, 161–85.

5. John Stott, *The Cross of Christ* (Downers Grove, IL: InterVarsity, 1986), 174.

6. Augustine, quoted by John Calvin, *Institutes* II:16:4.

7. Jerry Bridges and Bob Bevington, *The Great Exchange: My Sin for His Righteousness* (Wheaton: Crossway, 2007), cover page. The title of their book is a clear picture of what imputation is.

8. Charles Hodge, *An Exposition of the First and Second Corinthians* (Wilmington, DE: Sovereign Grace Publishers, 1972), 286. John Piper, in his excellent work *Counted Righteous in Christ: Should We Abandon the Imputation of Christ's Righteousness?* (Wheaton: Crossway, 2002), writes, "I don't know a better summary of the implications of 2 Corinthians 5:21 ["He made Him who knew no sin to be sin on our behalf, so that we might become the righteousness of God in Him] than the words of Charles Hodge: 'There is probably no passage in the Scriptures in which the doctrine of justification is more concisely or clearly stated than in [2 Cor. 5:21]. Our sins were imputed to Christ, and His righteousness is imputed to us. He bore our sins; we are clothed in His righteousness. . . . Christ bearing our sins did not make Him morally a sinner . . . nor does Christ's righteousness become subjectively ours, it is not the moral quality of our souls. . . . Our sins were the judicial ground of the sufferings of Christ, so that they were a satisfaction of justice; and His righteousness is the judicial ground of our acceptance with God, so that our pardon is an act of justice. . . . It is not mere pardon, but justification alone, that gives us peace with God'" (pp. 82–83).

## Session Three  Incredible Spiritual Benefits: *Calling, Regeneration, Conversion, Salvation, Adoption*

1. Louis Berkhof, *Systematic Theology* (Grand Rapids: Eerdmans, 1972), 454–79.

2. David C. Needham, *Birthright: Christian, "Do You Know Who You Are?"* (Portland: Multnomah, 1982), 239–58. Needham draws from John Murray's and D. Martyn Lloyd-Jones's clarifications of the old man / new man and flesh. Lloyd-Jones (*The New Man: An Exposition of Romans 6* [Edinburgh: Banner of Truth, 1972], 78–84) writes: "The Heidelberg Catechism rightly draws a distinction between 'the old man' and 'the flesh.' 'The old man is crucified and buried with Him, so that the corrupt inclinations of the flesh may no more reign in us.'" The "flesh" no longer reigns in us and thus has lost its controlling power but is now an opposing force that seeks to tempt us.

3. Berkhof, *Systematic Theology*, 487.

4. Wayne Grudem, *Bible Doctrine: Essential Teachings of the Christian Faith* (Grand Rapids: Zondervan, 1999), 307.

5. J. I. Packer, *Concise Theology: A Guide to Historic Christian Beliefs* (Wheaton: Tyndale, 1993), 147.

6. R. C. Sproul, *Essential Truths of the Christian Faith* (Wheaton: Tyndale, 1992), 159.

7. Packer, *Concise Theology*, 147.

8. J. I. Packer, *Knowing God* (Downers Grove, IL: InterVarsity, 1973), 181–82.

9. Wayne Grudem, *Christian Beliefs* (Grand Rapids: Zondervan, 2005), 97–98.

## Session Four  Temptations of the Flesh: *Overcoming Temptation (Part 1)*

1. John Piper, "The War Within: Flesh vs. Spirit, Galatians 5:16–18," Desiring God Ministries, June 19, 1983, http://www.desiringgod.org/ResourceLibrary/Sermons/ByDate/1983/398_The_War_Within_Flesh_vs_Spirit/.

2. Desiring God staff, "What is the Biblical Evidence for Original Sin?," January 23, 2006, http://www.desiringgod.org/ResourceLibrary/AskPastorJohn/ByTopic/50/1452_What_is_the_biblical_evidence_for_original_sin/.

3. John Owen, *The Works of John Owen* (Carlisle, UK: The Banner of Truth Trust, 1967), 6:167. When J. I. Packer wrote the endorsement of Owen's treatment of sin in an introduction to the 1983 Multnomah Press edition of *Sin and Temptation*, he wrote about the impact that Owen's writings had on his life and highlighted the importance of having a correct biblical understanding of how the flesh affects our lives: "He [Owen] told me how to understand myself as a Christian and live before God in a morally and spiritually honest way, without pretending either to be what I am not or not to be what I am. It is not too much at all to say that God used him to save my sanity."

4. Piper, "The War Within."

5. Ibid.

6. J. I. Packer, *Keep in Step with the Spirit* (Grand Rapids: Revell, 1984), 127–28, 161. Packer discusses the line of reasoning in Rom. 7 where Paul develops an argument exonerating the law, saying that the law is good and the problem does not lie in the law. Packer makes a strong case for the Augustinian view of this passage. The Augustinian view understands Rom. 7:14–25 to be speaking of a regenerate person (a Christian). The experience of this passage "is one which even the most sanctified of believers may expect to encounter until the resurrection of the body. This view has been embraced by Augustine, Martin Luther, John Calvin, John Owen, W. G. T. Shedd, Charles Hodge, John Murray, G. C. Berkouwer, C. E. B. Cranfield, James Dunn, Anders Nygren, C. K. Barrett, J. I. Packer, and John Stott, just to mention a few." See Sam Storm's excellent summary: Sam Storms, "Romans 7," April 13, 2007, Enjoying God Ministries, http://www.enjoyinggodministries.com/article/romans-7/. See also Packer's appendix in *Keep in Step with the Spirit*, 263–70.

7. Xenos Christian Fellowship, "Our New Identity in Christ," Christian Principles Unit 2, Revised July 23, 2003, http://www.xenos.org/classes/principles/cpu2w3.htm; emphasis in original.

8. Thomas Watson, *The Christian Soldier; or Heaven Taken by Storm: Shewing the Holy Violence a Christian is to Put Forth in the Pursuit after Glory* (New York: Robert Moore, 1810), 17.

## Session Five  Temptations of the Devil and the World: *Overcoming Temptation (Part 2)*

1. Martin Luther, *Faith Alone: A Daily Devotional*, ed. James Galvin (Grand Rapids: Zondervan, 1998), 67. The selections are taken from Luther's sermons, commentaries, and other devotional studies, which were written between 1513 and 1546. They have been freshly translated into English.

2. To understand the meaning of temptation, we look at the Greek word *peirazo* (the New Testament was originally written in Greek; it is pronounced pay-rah-zo). This word is used in both a negative and a positive way. When *peirazo* is used in a negative way it means "to try or test with a bad, sinister motive in order to produce failure." In those contexts it means "to tempt, or to entice to sin." The devil will tempt us with the motive and goal of causing us to sin. When *peirazo* is used in a positive way it means "to test or try with a good motive and goal." God will test us with the motive and goal to help us grow, to make us depend on him more, and to become more like Christ. So when this word (*peirazo*) is used of the devil, it is normally translated "to tempt." When *peirazo* is used of God, it is normally translated "to test." Temptation is a tool of the devil to lure us into sin and destruction, while testings (or trials) are a tool of God to lead us into spiritual maturity. (The English word "covet" is somewhat analogous, in that it can have either positive or negative connotations.)

3. Grownups, and even children, eventually get around to asking the question, "If God knew ahead of time before he created humans that they would choose to disobey him and bring pain and misery into this world, why would he still create humans?" Think of all the consequences of disobeying God: broken relationships, hatred, cruelty, sorrow, sickness, oppression, and so on. Why couldn't God have created humans who could not make bad choices? Could not God have programmed us so that we could only make good and loving choices, and then there would be no injustices and evil in the world? C. S. Lewis takes on this question in his classic book *Mere Christianity*. He points out that if we, as created beings, had no real freedom to choose to obey or disobey God and could choose only good, then could we be

really free? Lewis argues that a creature who can only choose good has no choice at all but resembles a robot more than a human with a free will. He points out that it is our freedom to choose that makes it possible for us to really love. For us to love, must we not have the choice to love God or turn from him? Ultimately, as Rom. 9:22–23 suggests, God thought it worthwhile to create creatures who would go wrong in order to bring about the greatest display of his glory. God's glory would be manifested in a far more glorious way by creating creatures who could go wrong than by not doing so. We his children would never understand the mercy of God and the riches of his grace had he not created a plan that allows evil to enter into human and angelic history. See *Mere Christianity*, esp. bk. 2, chap. 3, "The Shocking Alternative."

4. Westminster Confession of Faith (Committee for Christian Education and Publications, Presbyterian Church in America, 1990), chap. 3, sec. 1; emphasis added.

5. C. S. Lewis, *The Screwtape Letters* (New York: Macmillan, 1974), 3.

6. John Piper, *Future Grace* (Portland: Multnomah; Downers Grove, IL: InterVarsity, 1995), 9–10, 327, 336.

7. Catherine Marshall, *A Man Called Peter and the Prayers of Peter Marshall: A Spiritual Life* (New York: Sterling, 1996), 329.

## Session Six  Becoming More and More Like Christ: *Sanctification*

1. Walter A. Elwell, ed., *Evangelical Dictionary of Theology* (Grand Rapids: Baker, 1984), 969.

2. J. I. Packer, *Concise Theology: A Guide to Historic Christian Beliefs* (Wheaton: Tyndale, 1993), 169.

3. Emphasis added. The Westminster Shorter Catechism is also known simply as the Shorter Catechism. It was written in the 1640s by English and Scottish pastors/leaders. Its simple question-and-answer format is meant to give lay people a decent grasp of biblical doctrines and beliefs.

4. Packer, *Concise Theology*, 169.

5. John Murray, "Sanctification," in *Basic Christian Doctrines*, ed. Carl F. H. Henry (Grand Rapids: Baker, 1971), 228–29. Murray points out: "When Christ died, He died to sin once for all. And the believer, called into union with Christ, dies with Christ to sin. 'We died to sin' is the answer to all licentious abuse of the doctrine of grace. If we died with Christ, we must also live with Him, 'that like as Christ was raised from the dead through the glory of the Father, even so should we walk in newness of life.' . . . The breach with sin and the newness of life are as definitive as were the death and resurrection of Christ."

6. Packer, *Concise Theology*, 169.

7. R. C. Sproul, *Essential Truths of the Christian Faith* (Wheaton: Tyndale, 1992), 123–24; emphasis added.

8. In 1643 an assembly of more than one hundred committed theologians and pastors met to develop materials to help disciple the Christians of England. During this five-year process (1643–49) they composed what has been labeled The Westminster Confession of Faith, which contains an excellent clarification of justification by faith (when a person is truly justified then he or she will also have the fruit of salvation that flows from the justification): "Those whom God effectually calls He also freely justifies; not by infusing righteousness into

them, but by pardoning their sins, and by accounting and accepting their persons as righteous: not for anything wrought in them, or done by them, but for Christ's sake alone: not by imputing faith itself, the act of believing, or any other evangelical obedience, to them as their righteousness; but by imputing the obedience and satisfaction of Christ unto them, they receiving and resting on Him and His righteousness, by faith: which faith they have not of themselves; it is the gift of God" (11.1); and "Faith, thus receiving and resting on Christ and His righteousness, is the alone instrument of justification; yet is it not alone in the person justified, but is ever accompanied with all other saving graces, and is no dead faith, but works by love" (11.2).

9. John Piper, "Jesus Christ is an Advocate for Sinners," Desiring God Ministries, 1985, http://www.desiringgod.org/ResourceLibrary/Sermons/ByDate/1985/477_Jesus_Christ_Is_an_Advocate_for_Sinners/

10. Westminster Confession, chap. 11, sec. 5.

11. Thomas Watson, quoted in John Piper, *A Godward Life: Book Two* (Portland: Multnomah, 1999), 105.

12. John R. W. Stott, *Basic Christianity* (Downers Grove, IL: InterVarsity, 1958), 135.

## Session Seven  The Power and Value of the Word: *The Importance of Scripture*

1. Richard E. Byrd, *Alone* (Washington, DC: Island Press, 2003), 114.

2. Ibid., 117.

3. Ibid., 118.

4. Leon Morris, *The Gospel According to John* (Grand Rapids: Eerdmans, 1971), 527.

5. The term "law and the prophets" was the Hebraic way of referring to the whole Old Testament. Also, the phrase "the law" was a comprehensive term for the total divine revelation of the Old Testament. See John R. W. Stott, *Christian Counter-Culture: The Message of the Sermon on the Mount* (Downers Grove, IL: InterVarsity, 1978), 73.

6. William Hendriksen, *Exposition of the Gospel According to Matthew* (Grand Rapids: Baker, 1973), 291.

7. Jesus's view of the Old Testament apparently did not include the Apocrypha but was the same as our Protestant Old Testament with 39 books. This is clear from Jesus's own reference to the Old Testament. Norman Anderson (*God's Word For God's World* [London: Hodder & Stoughton, 1981], 112) writes: "That the books He [Jesus] had in mind spanned the whole Hebrew Bible is, I think, clear from two New Testament references: first, from His allusion, in Luke 24:44, to 'the Law of Moses, the Prophets and the Psalms,' since this was tantamount to referring to the threefold structure of the Jewish Scriptures as the 'Law,' the 'Prophets,' and the 'Writings' (in which the Psalms held pride of place) and, secondly, from His allusion to 'all the righteous blood that has been shed on earth, from the blood of righteous Abel to the blood of Zechariah son of Berachiah,' since the blood of Abel is mentioned early in Genesis (4:8), the first book in the Hebrew Bible, and that of Zechariah towards the end of 2 Chronicles (24:21), the last book in the Jewish Scriptures."

8. Regarding the New Testament canon, Norman L. Geisler and William E. Nix (*A General Introduction to the Bible* [Chicago: Moody Press, 1968]) write: "It is important

to note that the church did not create the canon; it did not determine which books would be called Scripture, the inspired Word of God. Instead, the church recognized, or discovered, which books had been inspired from their inception. Stated another way, a book is not the Word of God because it is accepted by the people of God. Rather, it was accepted by the people of God because it is the Word of God. That is, God gives the book its divine authority, not the people of God. They merely recognize the divine authority which God gives to it" (p. 210). And, "The basic factor for recognizing a book's canonicity for the New Testament was divine inspiration, and the chief test for this was apostolicity. In New Testament terminology, 'the church was built upon the foundation of the apostles and prophets' (Eph. 2:20) whom Christ had promised to guide into 'all the truth' (John 16:13) by the Holy Spirit. The church at Jerusalem was said to have continued in the 'apostles teaching' (Acts 2:42). The term 'apostolic' as used for the test of canonicity does not necessarily mean 'apostolic authorship,' or 'that which was prepared under the direction of the apostles. . . . It seems much better to agree with Louis Gaussen, B. B. Warfield, Charles Hodge, J. N. D. Kelly, and most Protestants that it is apostolic authority, or apostolic approval, that was the primary test for canonicity, and not merely apostolic authorship'" (p. 283). And John Murray ("The Attestation of Scripture," in *The Infallible Word* [Philadelphia: P&R, 1946], 18) writes: "N. B. Stonehouse notes that the apostolic authority 'which speaks forth in the New Testament is never detached from the authority of the Lord. In the Epistles there is consistent recognition that in the church there is only one absolute authority, the authority of the Lord Himself. Wherever the apostles speak with authority, they do so as exercising the Lord's authority.'. . . The only one who speaks in the New Testament with an authority that is un-derived and self-authenticating is the Lord."

9. Colin Brown, ed., *The New International Dictionary of New Testament Theology* (Grand Rapids: Zondervan, 1979), 3:689, 708.

10. Blaise Pascal, *Pascal's Pensees*, trans. W. F. Trotter (New York: E. P. Dutton, 1958), 113 (fragment 425).

11. John Piper, *When I Don't Desire God: How to Fight for Joy* (Wheaton: Crossway, 2004), 123.

### Session Eight Yesterday's Prophecies and Manuscript Evidence: *Evidence for the Inspiration of the Bible (Part 1)*

1. Quoted in Doug Pollock, "Help for the Reluctant Witness," March/April, 2006, 78, DiscipleshipJournal.com, http://www.godsgps.com/storage/Reluctant%20Witness%20 Article.pdf.

2. C. S. Lewis, *Mere Christianity* (San Francisco: HarperCollins, 2001), 140.

3. Isaiah names Cyrus as the one who would come on the scene 150 years in the future, but some have doubted that predictive prophecy with such specificity is possible. So the theory of a dual authorship arose—that Isaiah wrote chapters 1–39 but chapters 40–66 are supposedly written by an unknown author or authors living at the end of the Babylonian captivity (after 540 BC). And chapters 40–66 are

called Deutero-Isaiah. Alec Motyer, in his work *The Prophecy of Isaiah* ([Downers Grove, IL: InterVarsity, 1993], 25), points out, "O.T. Allis is correct when he observes that the fragmentation of the Isaianic literature among multiple authors and along an extended time-line is historically the product of the nineteenth-century rationalism which refused to countenance predictive prophecy. Sadly, in addition to this, the prevailing spirit of scholarship was disposed to fragmentation rather than to holism, and in the case of Isaiah this meant that a literature bursting with internal evidence of its unity was rather made to burst into disparate pieces. The subsequent course of study has concentrated on the fragments until it is now widely assumed that the case for multiple authorship need no longer be argued but can be assumed. This is by no means so. The evidences of unity . . . require explanation and we must now explore the simplest explanation—that the whole literature is the product of Isaiah of Jerusalem."

The objections raised against the unity of Isaiah revolve around structure and theme, language and style, background and setting. Although it is not within the scope of this discipleship guide to give a defense of the unity of authorship of Isaiah, I would like to point to some important works that give a robust reasoned defense of the traditional understanding of Isaiah that was accepted for some twenty-five centuries: John N. Oswalt, *The Book of Isaiah, Chapters 1–39*, New International Commentary on the Old Testament, R. K. Harrison and Robert L. Hubbard, gen. eds. (Grand Rapids: Eerdmans, 1986), see "Unity of Composition," esp. 17–24; Motyer, *Prophecy of Isaiah*, 25–30; Gleason Archer Jr., *A Survey of Old Testament Introduction*, rev. ed. (Chicago: Moody, 1994), 365–90; R. K. Harrison, *Introduction to the Old Testament* (Grand Rapids: Eerdmans, 1969), 765–800.

Also, it is noteworthy that the unity of Isaiah is the witness of the New Testament. John 12:38–40 contains quotes from both sections of Isaiah (Isa. 53:1 and Isa. 6:9) and attributes them both to Isaiah the prophet. Plus there are other quotes from both sections of Isaiah showing that the writers of the New Testament understood they were both written by Isaiah.

4. Francis Brown, S. R. Driver, and Charles A. Briggs, *A Hebrew and English Lexicon of the Old Testament* (Oxford: Clarendon Press, 1974), 319. See also David Baron, *The Servant of Jehovah: An Exposition of Isaiah 53* (Minneapolis: James Family Publishers, Limited Collectors Editions, 1978), 89.

5. Also noteworthy is that the word "Servant" cannot refer to "Israel" because verse 8 states, "For He was cut off from the land of the living; / For the transgressions of *My People* He was stricken." The Servant is different from the people of Israel. One of the key interpretations of this passage by ancient rabbis was that Isa. 53 referred to the Messiah. The Babylonian Talmud records the opinions of the rabbis: "The Messiah—what is his name? . . . The Rabbis say, The leprous one; those of the house of Rabbi say, the sick one, as it is said, 'Surely he hath borne our sicknesses'" (Sanhedrin 98b). It is noteworthy as well that the description of Isa. 53 does not fit the prophet Isaiah. In fact God states that even Noah, Daniel, and Job would not be able to deliver others, only themselves: "'Even if these three men, Noah, Daniel, and Job, were in it [the land], they would deliver only themselves by their righteousness,' says the Lord GOD" (Ezek. 14:14).

Also in Jer. 24:5 the Scriptures record that the "good figs" (those taken in exile) are actually spared the severe judgment that God carried out upon the "bad figs" (the idolatrous Israelites). So the "righteous remnant" did not suffer for the sins of Israel; they were spared and kept by God. As the scholar C. H. H. Wright wrote: "[This great prophecy of Isaiah 53 was] . . . an enigma which could not be fully understood in the days before Christ, but which has been solved by the sufferings, death, resurrection, and exaltation of Him who was both Son of Man and Son of God" (quoted in Baron, *Servant of Jehovah*, 10).

6. For an excellent discussion on the chronology and meaning of the 70 weeks in Daniel, see Harold W. Hoehner, *Chronological Aspects of the Life of Christ* (Grand Rapids: Zondervan, 1977), chap. 6. This chapter builds on Hoehner's ThD dissertation, "Chronology of the Apostolic Age." The Hebrew word for "week" (*shabua*) is "a unit or period of seven." "In this passage [Dan. 9:24–27] the term [weeks] refers to units of seven years and thus Daniel is speaking of seventy of these units of seven years or a total of 490 years" (p. 117).

7. Justin Taylor, "An Interview with Daniel B. Wallace on the New Testament Manuscripts," The Gospel Coalition, March 21, 2012, http://thegospelcoalition.org/blogs /justintaylor/2012/03/21/an-interview-with-daniel-b-wallace -on-the-new-testament-manuscripts/.

8. John A. T. Robinson, *Can We Trust the New Testament?* (Grand Rapids: Eerdmans, 1977), 33–38.

9. Josh McDowell, *Evidence for Christianity* (Nashville: Thomas Nelson, 2006), 61. McDowell has taken his statistics from scholars such as Michael Welte, Kurt Aland, and Bruce Metzger (see McDowell for a fuller list of sources).

10. Josh McDowell, *The New Evidence That Demands a Verdict* (Nashville: Thomas Nelson, 1999), 43.

11. Bruce Metzger and Bart Ehrman, *The Text of the New Testament: Its Transmission, Corruption, and Restoration* (New York: Oxford, 2006), 86; emphasis added.

12. Gary R. Habermas, "Why I Believe the New Testament Is Historically Reliable," in *Why I Am a Christian: Leading Thinkers Explain Why They Believe*, ed. Normal L. Geisler and Paul K. Hoffman (Grand Rapids: Baker Books, 2006), 162–63.

13. Ravi Zacharias, *Can Man Live Without God?* (Dallas: Word, 1994), 162.

14. Arthur G. Patzia, *The Making of the New Testament* (Downers Grove, IL: InterVarsity, 1995), 138.

15. D. A. Carson, *The King James Version Debate* (Grand Rapids: Baker, 1979), 56. Also, Timothy Paul Jones, *Why Trust the Bible?* (Torrance, CA: Rose Publishing, 2007), 7. Here Jones summarizes Metzger and Ehrman, *Text of the New Testament* (pp. 288–90): "With more than 5,700 manuscripts and fragments of the New Testament available to us, it would be impossible for anyone to have modified major portions of the New Testament without their changes being quite easily noticed. In the few cases when changes were attempted, the original text can—in all but the tiniest handful of instances—be easily restored by examining the most ancient New Testament manuscripts."

Timothy Jones also has written *Misquoting Truth: A Guide to the Fallacies of Bart Ehrman's 'Misquoting Jesus'* (Downers Grove, IL: InterVarsity, 2007). This book gives the reader who has little knowledge about textual criticism

a good introduction to the subject in order to be able to see all the sides of the discussion about textual criticism. It is further noteworthy that even the prominent nineteenth-century textual scholars Westcott and Hort asserted, "If comparative trivialities such as changes of order, the insertion or omission of the article with proper names, and the like are set aside, the works in our opinion still subject to doubt can hardly amount to more than a thousandth part of the whole New Testament" (B. F. Westcott and F. J. A. Hort, eds., *New Testament in Original Greek* [New York: Harper & Brothers, 1881], 2:2). Such statements infer that we can have great confidence in trusting the Bible as being a reliable reproduction of the original manuscripts.

## Session Nine Christ's View of Scripture and Archaeological Findings: *Evidence for the Inspiration of the Bible (Part 2)*

1. Martin Abegg Jr., Peter Flint, and Eugene Ulrich, *The Dead Sea Scrolls Bible: The Oldest Known Bible Translated for the First Time into English* (San Francisco: Harper, 1999), x, xi.

2. Quoted in Josh McDowell, *The New Evidence That Demands a Verdict* (Nashville: Thomas Nelson, 1999), 75.

3. Ibid., xiv.

4. Gleason L. Archer Jr., *Old Testament Introduction* (Chicago: Moody Press, 1964), 34. William Sanford LaSor, in his work *The Dead Sea Scrolls and the Christian Faith* (Chicago: Moody Press, 1972), surveys the dates of the materials of the Dead Sea Scrolls and concludes: "In the light of all the evidence, most scholars are convinced that the Qumran materials are to be dated in the period between 175 BC and AD 68" (64).

5. Abegg, Flint, and Ulrich, *Dead Sea Scrolls Bible*, xiv.

6. Archer, *Old Testament Introduction*, 19.

7. Ibid., 58.

8. Flavius Josephus, *Against Apion* 1:42–43.

9. Will Durant, *The Story of Civilization: Caesar and Christ*, Vol. 3 (New York: Simon and Schuster, 1972), 557.

10. Lee Strobel, *The Case For Christ* (Grand Rapids: Zondervan, 1998), 333–34.

11. F. F. Bruce, *The New Testament Documents: Are They Reliable?*, rev. ed. (Grand Rapids: Eerdmans, 2007), 77.

12. Strobel, *Case For Christ*, 128.

13. William F. Albright, *The Biblical Period from Abraham to Ezra* (New York: Harper & Row, 1963), 1–2.

14. William F. Albright, *The Archaeology of Palestine* (Gretna, ST: Pelican Publishing, 1960), 127–28.

15. John Wilford, "Archaeologists Say Evidence of House of David Found," *Dallas Morning News*, August 6, 1993, 1A.

## Session Ten Jesus's Model Prayer: *The Great Value of Prayer (Part 1)*

1. You can see from the contexts of different passages in the Bible how the term "to hallow" (treat as holy) includes: believing him, trusting him, fearing him, and taking his word to heart: "Then the LORD spoke to Moses and Aaron, 'Because you did not *believe* Me, *to hallow* Me in the eyes of the children of Israel, therefore you shall not bring this assembly

into the land which I have given them'" (Num. 20:12); "He who believes in the Son of God has the witness in himself; he who does not *believe* God has made Him a liar [disrespected Him], because he has not believed the testimony that God has given of His Son" (1 John 5:10); "The LORD of hosts, Him you shall *hallow*; / Let Him be your *fear*, / And let Him be your *dread*" (Isa. 8:13); "Therefore you shall *keep My commandments*, and perform them: I am the LORD. You shall not profane My holy name, but I will be *hallowed* among the children of Israel. I am the LORD who sanctifies you" (Lev. 22:31–32).

2. John R. W. Stott, *Through the Bible, Through the Year* (Grand Rapids: Baker Books, 2006), 203.

3. Some translations say, "Deliver us from *evil*." The reason for this is that the Greek word is in both the masculine and neuter gender. So the Greek word can be translated as "the Evil One" (masculine) or simply "evil" (neuter). But even if you recognize it as "evil," still the "Evil One" (Satan) is almost always involved in temptation; therefore the practical outworking of this prayer would be essentially the same.

4. John R. W. Stott, *Christian Counter-Culture: The Message of the Sermon on the Mount* (Downers Grove, IL: InterVarsity, 1978), 150. This is Stott's paraphrase of this part of the Lord's Prayer.

### Session Eleven  A Life of Prayer: *The Great Value of Prayer (Part 2)*

1. Charles Spurgeon, *Praying Successfully* (New Kensington, PA: Whitaker House Publishers, 1997), 62–63. (Edited for the modern reader; the sermon was originally titled: "Robinson Crusoe's Text: Psalm 50:15.")

2. John Piper, *When I Don't Desire God* (Wheaton: Crossway, 2004), 150–52.

### Session Twelve  Understanding God's Will: *The Guidance of God (Part 1)*

1. John Piper, "What Is the Will of God and How Do We Know It?," DesiringGod.org, August 22, 2004, www.desiringgod.org/ResourceLibrary/Sermons/ByDate/2004/179_What_Is_the_Will_of_God_and_How_Do_We_Know_It/. John Piper discusses how to make biblical sense of the will of God in the midst of the evil and sufferings of life. He writes, "For example, if you were badly abused as a child, and someone asks you, 'Do you think that was the will of God?' you now have a way to make some biblical sense out of this, and give an answer that doesn't contradict the Bible. You may say, 'No it was not God's will; because He commands that humans not be abusive, but love each other. The abuse broke his commandment and therefore moved His heart with anger and grief (Mark 3:5). But, in another sense, yes, it was God's will (his sovereign will), because there are a hundred ways He could have stopped it. But for reasons I don't yet fully understand, he didn't.' . . . And corresponding to these two wills are the two things you need in this situation: one is a God who is strong and sovereign enough to turn it for good; and the other is a God who is able to empathize with you. On the one hand, Christ is a sovereign High King, and nothing happens apart from His will (Matt. 28:18). On the other hand, Christ is a merciful High Priest and sympathizes with our weaknesses and pain (Heb. 4:15). The Holy Spirit conquers us and our sins when He wills (John 1:13; Rom. 9:15–16), and allows himself to be quenched and grieved and angered when He wills (Eph. 4:30; 1 Thess. 5:19). His sovereign will is invincible, and His will of command can be grievously broken. . . . We need both these truths—both these understandings of the will of God—not only to make sense out of the Bible, but to hold fast to God in suffering."

2. Bruce K. Waltke, *Finding the Will of God: A Pagan Notion?* (Grand Rapids: Eerdmans, 2002), 7, 59.

3. Charles Swindoll, *Stress Fractures* (Portland: Multnomah, 1990), 232–33.

4. Waltke, *Finding the Will of God*, 6–7.

5. The word "normally" is used here because, while God can choose to act or reveal himself in any way he chooses, he sets forth in his Word instructions for how he guides his children.

6. Waltke, *Finding the Will of God*, back cover. I am indebted to Waltke's research, insights, and practical applications into understanding how God guides his people.

7. Piper, "What Is the Will of God?" Piper writes: "God's will of command is the discerning application of the Scriptures to new situations in life by means of a renewed mind."

8. Waltke, *Finding the Will of God*, 59–187. Although these key factors are listed in Waltke's work, these factors (in some form) have been used and written about by Christian leaders through the centuries. Waltke has rendered a scholarly service by giving a good exegetical footing to these factors.

9. Steve Cornell, "Discerning God's Will: Four Primary Biblical Texts," Life on Purpose, July 14, 2007, http://thinkpoint.wordpress.com/2007/07/14/discerning-gods-will-4-primary-biblical-texts/. Cornell references Everett Harrison, "Romans," in *The Expositor's Bible Commentary* (Grand Rapids: Zondervan, 1976), 10:128.

10. Piper, "What Is the Will of God?"

11. Waltke, *Finding the Will of God*, 86–87, 92.

12. It is noteworthy that in Luke's Gospel Jesus also stated, "If you then, being evil, know how to give good gifts to your children, how much more will your heavenly Father give the Holy Spirit to those who ask Him" (Luke 11:13).

13. John Piper, "Be Filled with the Spirit," Desiring God Ministries, March 8, 1981, http://www.desiringgod.org/ResourceLibrary/Sermons/ByDate/1981/287_Be_Filled_with_the_Spirit/.

### Session Thirteen  Knowing God's Will: *The Guidance of God (Part 2)*

1. To develop a heart for God and to discover wisdom is an active pursuit. Prov. 2 speaks of acquiring wisdom in order to live life skillfully in the sight of God; you cannot be passive in seeking out God's wisdom. As you read through the verses notice the italicized words, which are *action words*! Prov. 2:1–9 [the personification of wisdom is speaking]: "My son, if you *receive* my words, / And *treasure* my commands within you, / So that you *incline* your ear to wisdom, / And *apply* your heart to understanding; / Yes, if you *cry out* for discernment, / And *lift up* your voice for understanding, / If you *seek* her as silver, / And *search* for

her as for hidden treasures; / Then you will understand the fear of the LORD, / And find the knowledge of God. / For the LORD gives wisdom; / From His mouth come knowledge and understanding; / He stores up sound wisdom for the upright; / He is a shield to those who walk uprightly; / He guards the paths of justice, / And preserves the way of His saints. / Then you will understand righteousness and justice, / Equity and every good path."

2. Bruce K. Waltke, *Finding the Will of God: A Pagan Notion?* (Grand Rapids: Eerdmans, 2002), 118, italics removed.

3. Westminster Confession of Faith (Committee for Christian Education and Publication, Presbyterian Church in America, 1990), chap. 5, sec. 1.

4. John Piper, "George Mueller's Strategy for Showing God," Desiring God Ministries, February 3, 2004, http://www.desiringgod.org/ResourceLibrary/Biographies/1531_George_Muellers_Strategy_for_Showing_God/.

5. Ibid.

6. George Mueller, *Answers to Prayer from George Mueller's Narratives* (Chicago: Moody, 2007), 11, 12.

## Session Fourteen The Mystery of the Trinity: *The Trinity (Part 1)*

1. Roy B. Zuck, *The Speaker's Quote Book* (Grand Rapids: Kregel, 1997), 221.

2. Very early in church history (around AD 168), the overseer (bishop) of Antioch, Syria, named Theophilus used the idea of God as a "Trinity" in his writing (*Theophilus to Autolycus* 2.15, in *Ante-Nicene Fathers*, 2:25). Theophilus used three days of creation as a "type" of the Trinity. He doesn't actually define the Trinity but does use this term for God, which infers that the concept of the Trinity was already in use at that time in history.

3. Wayne Grudem, *Systematic Theology* (Grand Rapids: Zondervan, 1994), 227.

4. Wayne Grudem, *Bible Doctrine: Essential Teachings of the Christian Faith* (Grand Rapids: Zondervan, 1999), 106.

5. "The Shield of the Trinity," Wikipedia, http://en.wikipedia.org/wiki/Shield_of_the_Trinity. The earliest attested version of the diagram is from a manuscript of the writings of Peter of Poitiers, ca. 1210.

6. C. S. Lewis, *Mere Christianity* (San Francisco: HarperCollins, 2001), 161–62.

7. James R. White, *The Forgotten Trinity* (Minneapolis: Bethany, 1998), 20.

8. Ron Nash, "The Law of Noncontradiction," Theopedia, http://www.theopedia.com/Law_of_noncontradiction, quoting R. C. Sproul.

9. R. C. Sproul, *Essential Truths of the Christian Faith* (Wheaton: Tyndale, 1992), 111–12.

10. William F. Arndt and F. Wilber Gingrich, *A Greek-English Lexicon of the New Testament and Other Early Christian Literature* (Chicago: University of Chicago Press, 1969), 623.

11. Samuel Storms, "Baptism of the Holy Spirit—Part 1," Enjoying God Ministries, November 6, 2006, http://www.enjoyinggodministries.com/article/baptism-of-the-holy-spirit-part-I. This article is recommended for an excellent historical and exegetical discussion on the difference between the baptism and filling of the Holy Spirit.

12. Grudem, *Bible Doctrine*, 223; emphasis in original.

13. John Piper, "Beyond Forgiveness: Blasphemy Against the Spirit," Desiring God Ministries, April 1, 1984, http://www.desiringgod.org/ResourceLibrary/Sermons/ByScripture/44/432_Beyond_Forgiveness_Blasphemy_Against_the_Spirit/.

14. Charles H. Spurgeon, "Unpardonable," Pre-Evangelism Ministries, 2005, http://www.spurgeon.us/mind_and_heart/quotes/s3.htm.

## Session Fifteen Eternally One God in Three Persons: *The Trinity (Part 2)*

1. James R. White, *The Forgotten Trinity* (Minneapolis: Bethany, 1998), 173; emphasis in original.

2. John Piper, *God's Passion for His Glory* (Wheaton: Crossway, 1998), 84.

3. White, *Forgotten Trinity*, 173.

4. John Piper, "Why Expositional Preaching Is Particularly Glorifying to God," Desiring God Ministries, April 27, 2006, http://www.desiringgod.org/resource-library/conference-messages/why-expositional-preaching-is-particularly-glorifying-to-god?lang=en.

5. John Piper, "God Created Us for His Glory," Desiring God Ministries, July 27, 1980, http://www.desiringgod.org/ResourceLibrary/Sermons/ByDate/1980/238_God_Created_Us_for_His_Glory/.

6. Piper, *God's Passion for His Glory*, 37.

7. "Shield of the Trinity," Wikipedia, 2012, http://en.wikipedia.org/wiki/Shield_of_the_Trinity.

8. Wayne Grudem, *Bible Doctrine: Essential Teachings of the Christian Faith* (Grand Rapids: Zondervan, 1999), 86.

9. Ibid., 104–5.

10. Ibid., 105.

11. White, *Forgotten Trinity*, 170–71; emphasis in original. Also keep in mind that each person of the Trinity is completely and fully God. This means that you cannot divide God into something similar to three slices of a pie—where the Father is a third, the Son is a third, and the Holy Spirit is a third. And you cannot say that all thirds added together make a whole. Each person possesses the whole being of God himself. Each person of the Trinity has all the attributes of God. No one member has any attributes that are not possessed by the others.

12. Wayne Grudem (*Bible Doctrine*, 114, 117) points out that there is a false teaching (that is, a heresy) known as subordinationism. Subordinationism says that the Son is not equal to (or that he is inferior to) the Father. Various forms of this heresy were debunked in the fourth century when the Arian controversy was settled. Subordinationism is not a biblical teaching and opposes the true teaching, which says that the Son is completely equal in essence and yet is eternally subordinate to the Father in role or function. Without a proper orthodox understanding of this truth, the doctrine of the Trinity begins to fall apart. Jesus is equal to the Father and yet subordinate in his role and function *only*. To tamper with this teaching is to ultimately muddy the waters of how the Father, the Son, and the Holy Spirit relate to each other within the Trinity as three eternally distinct persons and yet one God.

### Session Sixteen Jesus's Divinity: *The Uniqueness of Christ (Part 1)*

1. C. S. Lewis, *Mere Christianity* (San Francisco: Harper-Collins, 2001), 52.
2. John Piper, *What Jesus Demands from the World* (Wheaton: Crossway, 2006), 20–21.
3. William F. Arndt and F. Wilber Gingrich, *A Greek-English Lexicon of the New Testament and Other Early Christian Literature* (Chicago: University of Chicago Press, 1969), 895.
4. 1 Tim. 6:15 also uses the phrase, "King of kings and Lord of lords." It can be enlightening to compare 1 Tim. 6:15 with Rev. 19:16.
5. Dorothy Sayers, *Christian Letters to a Post-Christian World: A Selection of Essays* (Grand Rapids: Eerdmans, 1969), 14.

### Session Seventeen Jesus's Humanity: *The Uniqueness of Christ (Part 2)*

1. Phil Stringer, *The Foundations of Our World* (Cleveland: The Old Paths, 2011), 1:263.
2. F. F. Bruce, *The Person of Christ: Incarnation and Virgin Birth*, Basic Christian Doctrines, ed. Carl F. H. Henry (Grand Rapids: Baker, 1971), 125.
3. C. S. Lewis, *Miracles* (New York: HarperCollins, 1996), 174.
4. J. I. Packer, *Knowing God* (Downers Grove, IL: InterVarsity, 1973), 50.
5. William Hendriksen, *New Testament Commentary: Exposition of the Gospel According to Matthew* (Grand Rapids: Baker, 1973), 144.
6. R. C. Sproul, *Essential Truths of the Christian Faith* (Wheaton: Tyndale, 1992), 81; emphasis added.
7. The definition of "monophysitism" (from Walter A. Elwell, ed., *Evangelical Dictionary of Theology* [Grand Rapids: Baker, 1984], 730): "Derived from *monos*, 'single,' and *physis*, 'nature,' monophysitism is the doctrine which holds that the incarnate Christ had only a single, divine nature, clad in human flesh. It is sometimes called Eutychianism, after Eutyches (d. 454), one of its leading defenders. Since the Council of Chalcedon, which confirmed as orthodox the doctrine of two natures, divine and human, monophysitism has been considered heretical. Monophysites tended to divide into two main groups: Julianists, who held to the immortality and incorruptibility of Christ's incarnate body, and the more orthodox Severians, who rejected the Eutychian view that the human and divine were completely mingled in the incarnation. In the remnant of Syrian Jacobites and in the Coptic and Ethiopian churches (and to a limited extent in the Armenian) it survives to the present day." Some theologians illustrate the monophysite heresy by the analogy of dropping ink into a bottle of water. It is no longer purely ink nor is it purely water, but instead some kind of third substance. Thus, the heresy taught that with the mixture of the two natures of Christ the outcome was a whole different nature.
8. Sproul, *Essential Truths*, 81–82.
9. Matt Perman, "How Can Jesus Be God and Man?" Desiring God Ministries, October 5, 2006, http://www.desiring god.org/ResourceLibrary/Articles/ByDate/2006/1796_How _can_Jesus_be_God_and_man/. See also Wayne Grudem, *Systematic Theology: An Introduction to Biblical Doctrine* (Leicester, UK: Inter-Varsity Press and Grand Rapids: Zondervan, 1994), 561–62.

### Session Eighteen Kept by God: *Preservation, Perseverance, and Assurance (Part 1)*

1. Wayne Grudem, *Bible Doctrine: Essential Teachings of the Christian Faith* (Grand Rapids: Zondervan, 1999), 336–47.
2. William F. Arndt and F. Wilber Gingrich, *A Greek-English Lexicon of the New Testament and Other Early Christian Literature* (Chicago: University of Chicago Press, 1969), 109.
3. John Piper, "Eternal Security Is a Community Project," Desiring God Ministries, August 18, 1996, http://www .desiringgod.org/ResourceLibrary/Sermons/ByDate/1996 /964_Eternal_Security_is_a_Community_Project/; emphasis in original.
4. Louis Berkhof, *Systematic Theology* (Grand Rapids: Eerdmans, 1972), 548.
5. Grudem, *Bible Doctrine*, 336.

### Session Nineteen Living by God's Power: *Preservation, Perseverance, and Assurance (Part 2)*

1. John Piper, "Those Who Have Faith Are the Sons of Abraham," Desiring God Ministries, March 20, 1983, http://www.desiringgod.org/ResourceLibrary/Sermons/By Scripture/7/382_Those_Who_Have_Faith_Are_the_Sons_of _Abraham/. "Verse 7 says that 'those of faith are sons of Abraham.' And verse 9 says that 'those of faith are blessed with Abraham.' Surely, these are the same people: sons of Abraham, who will, therefore, enjoy the blessings promised to Abraham and his children. But it is clear from the connection between verses 8 and 9 that these people include Gentiles. Verse 8 quotes Genesis 12:3, 'In you shall all the nations (i.e., Gentiles) be blessed'—not just Jews. And from that Paul infers verse 9: 'So then, those of faith are blessed.' So the believers of verse 9 must include Gentiles, and since these are the same as the believers in verse 7 who are called sons of Abraham, the sons of Abraham must include Gentiles."
2. John Piper, "Sustained by Sovereign Grace—Forever," Desiring God Ministries, 1996, http://www.desiringgod.org /ResourceLibrary/Sermons/ByDate/1996/960_Sustained_By _Sovereign_Grace_Forever/. "His heart work is so powerful that he guarantees we will not turn from Him. This is what's new about the new covenant: God promises to fulfill by His power the conditions that we have to meet. We must fear Him and love Him and trust Him. And he says, I will see to that. I will 'put the fear of Me in their hearts'—not to see what they will do with it, but in such a way that 'they will not turn from me.'"
3. Louis Berkhof, *Systematic Theology* (Grand Rapids: Eerdmans, 1972), 548.
4. Millard J. Erickson, *Christian Theology* (Grand Rapids: Baker, 1985), 994. Erickson builds on G. C. Berkouwer's work, *Faith and Perseverance* (Grand Rapids: Eerdmans, 1958), 83–124.

## Session Twenty  God's Unique Character: *The Attributes of God (Part 1)*

1. John D. Hannah, *Our Legacy: History of Christian Doctrine* (Colorado Springs: NavPress, 2001), 11–12.

2. J. I. Packer, *Knowing God* (Downers Grove, IL: InterVarsity, 1973), 23–27.

3. Wayne Grudem, *Systematic Theology* (Grand Rapids: Zondervan, 1994), 160–61.

4. Fred H. Klooster, "The Attributes of God: The Incommunicable Attributes," in *Basic Christian Doctrines*, ed. Carl F. H. Henry (Grand Rapids: Baker, 1971), 23.

5. Grudem, *Systematic Theology*, 161–62; emphasis in original.

6. J. I. Packer, *Knowing Christianity* (Downers Grove, IL: InterVarsity, 1999), 55. Kevin DeYoung ("Tis Mystery All, the Immortal Dies," The Gospel Coalition, T4G 2010, 1, 9, 10) handles these questions by first defining that quality of God related to his immutability, called "impassibility," this way: "God cannot suffer and is incapable of being acted upon by an external force." In other words, people and angels cannot inflict suffering on God so that in some sense God becomes a victim of his creatures' sins. J. I. Packer (*Knowing Christianity*, 46–47) states: "No one can inflict suffering, pain, or any sort of distress on Him [God]. Insofar as God enters into an experience of suffering, it is through empathy for His creature and according to His own deliberate decision. He is never His creatures' victim." DeYoung also writes: "I can't stress this enough. To be impassible is not to be passionless. To be immutable is not to be motionless. God is always active, always dynamic, always relational." God is no stranger to joy and delight and he certainly empathizes with human pain and grief. DeYoung continues: "Clearly, in one sense it is patently obvious that God has an emotional life. Scripture tells us God is grieved; he is angry; he rejoices; he is moved to pity, full of mercy, overflowing in love. So if anger and joy and pity are emotions, then God has emotions. We should not be afraid to speak of God in the way Scripture does and the Bible is full of emotional language. If we try to push aside God's emotional life as nothing but a human way of talking about God (anthropopathism), the price will be too high. We'll be left with a God that seems hallow and distant. And yet, we can't simply say God has emotions just like we do. . . . So do not look to an angst-ridden, pain-stricken, eternally grieving God for comfort. Look to the cross."

7. Wayne Grudem, *Christian Beliefs: Twenty Basics Every Christian Should Know* (Grand Rapids: Zondervan, 2006), 23.

8. Grudem, *Systematic Theology*, 168.

9. R. C. Sproul, *Essential Truths of the Christian Faith* (Wheaton: Tyndale, 1992), 43.

10. Stephen Charnock, *The Existence and Attributes of God* (Grand Rapids: Baker, 1996), 1:389.

11. Ibid., 395–96.

12. Ibid., 43.

13. Anthony A. Hoekema, "The Attributes of God: The Communicable Attributes," in *Basic Christian Doctrines*, ed. Carl F. H. Henry (Grand Rapids: Baker, 1971), 28.

14. Walter A. Elwell, ed., *Evangelical Dictionary of Theology* (Grand Rapids: Baker, 1984), 452.

15. Louis Berkhof, *Systematic Theology* (Grand Rapids: Eerdmans, 1972), 62.

## Session Twenty-One  God's Shared Character: *The Attributes of God (Part 2)*

1. Jonathan Edwards, "The Christian Pilgrim," *The Works of Jonathan Edwards*, vol. 2 (Edinburgh: Banner of Truth Trust, 1974), 244.

2. John Piper, *Desiring God* (Portland: Multnomah, 2003), 18, 94, 288; emphasis in original.

3. When the Bible says, "The LORD's hand is not shortened, that it cannot save, or His ear dull, that it cannot hear," the mention of God's hand or ear, etc. are *anthropomorphisms*—God described in human terms so that we can understand.

4. Wayne Grudem, *Systematic Theology* (Grand Rapids: Zondervan, 1994), 188.

5. Stephen Charnock, *The Existence and Attributes of God* (Grand Rapids: Baker, 1996), 1:414.

6. J. I. Packer, *Knowing God* (Downers Grove, IL: InterVarsity, 1973), 37.

7. Louis Berkhof, *Systematic Theology* (Grand Rapids: Eerdmans, 1972), 66; emphasis removed.

8. Packer, *Knowing God*, 80.

9. Wayne Grudem, *Bible Doctrine: Essential Teachings of the Christian Faith* (Grand Rapids: Zondervan, 1999), 88–89.

10. Ibid., 89–90.

11. R. C. Sproul, *Essential Truths of the Christian Faith* (Wheaton: Tyndale, 1992), 39–40.

12. Grudem, *Bible Doctrine*, 91.

13. Charles Suprgeon, *The Treasury of David* (New York: Funk and Wagnalls, 1882), 5:73.

14. Grudem, *Bible Doctrine*, 90.

15. John Piper, *God's Passion for His Glory: Living the Vision of Jonathan Edwards* (Wheaton: Crossway, 1998), 36, 75.

## Session Twenty-Two  More of God's Shared Character: *The Attributes of God (Part 3)*

1. J. I. Packer, *Knowing God* (Downers Grove, IL: InterVarsity, 1973), 29; emphasis added.

2. Ibid., 153–54. Packer is quoting R. V. G. Tasker, *The General Epistle of James*.

3. Francis Brown, S. R. Driver, and Charles A. Briggs, *A Hebrew and English Lexicon of the Old Testament* (Oxford: Clarendon Press, 1974), 871–73.

4. Louis Berkhof, *Systematic Theology* (Grand Rapids: Eerdmans, 1972), 73.

5. R. C, Sproul, *Essential Truths of the Christian Faith* (Wheaton: Tyndale, 1992), 47.

6. Berkhof, *Systematic Theology*, 73–74.

7. Sam Storms, "Attributes of God: Justice and Wrath," Enjoying God Ministries, 2006, http://www.enjoyinggodministries.com/article/justice-and-wrath/; emphasis removed. Storms is using A. W. Pink's definition and description of the justice of God.

8. John Piper, *God's Passion for His Glory* (Wheaton: Crossway, 1998), 33, 141.

9. Wayne Grudem, *Bible Doctrine: Essential Teachings of the Christian Faith* (Grand Rapids: Zondervan, 1999), 93.

10. Packer, *Knowing God*, 134.

11. Grudem, *Bible Doctrine*, 99–100.

12. John Piper, *The Pleasures of God* (Portland: Multnomah, 1991), 23.

### Session Twenty-Three  The Sovereign God: *The Attributes of God (Part 4)*

1. John Piper, "Desiring God Conference," Challies.com, Informing the Reforming, October 7, 2005, http://www.challies.com/liveblogging/desiring-god-conference-session-one. Tim Challies is quoting John Piper.

2. Louis Berkhof, *Systematic Theology* (Grand Rapids: Eerdmans, 1972), 76.

3. "The Sovereignty of God," Theopedia.

4. R. C. Sproul, *The Invisible Hand: Do All Things Really Work for Good?* (Dallas: Word, 1996), 79.

5. R. C. Sproul, *Essential Truths of the Christian Faith* (Wheaton: Tyndale, 1992), 62.

6. Westminster Confession of Faith (Committee for Christian Education and Publication, Presbyterian Church in America, 1990), chap. 3, sec. 1.

7. Paul Smith, *Enjoying God Forever: The Westminster Confession* (Chicago: Moody, 1998), 66.

8. Sproul, *Invisible Hand*, 83.

9. John Piper, *Desiring God* (Portland: Multnomah, 1986), 29.

### Session Twenty-Four  The Mystery of Sovereignty: *The Attributes of God (Part 5)*

1. John Flavel, *The Mystery of Providence*, Reformed Literature, http://www.reformedliterature.com/flavel-the-mystery-of-providence.php, Introduction, 1.

2. John Piper, *For Your Joy* (Minneapolis: Desiring God Ministries, 2005), 24.

3. R. C. Sproul, *The Invisible Hand: Do All Things Really Work for Good?* (Dallas: Word, 1996), cover page. This concept is taken from the title of Sproul's book.

4. Westminster Confession of Faith (Committee for Christian Education and Publication, Presbyterian Church in America, 1990), chap. 5, sec. 1.

5. Further clarification: In Abraham's life, as recorded in Genesis 20, a king of the Philistines by the name of Abimelech took Abraham's wife, Sarah, to be a part of his harem. But God did not let Abimelech touch her. God told Abimelech in a dream: "I also *withheld you from sinning* against Me, therefore I did not let you touch her" (Gen. 20:6). God would not let Abimelech exercise his freedom to sin in this regard. Sproul rightly observes, "If I choose to sin this afternoon, God has the *power* to prevent me from sinning if He so chooses. He also has the *right* to prevent me from sinning since He is sovereign. If he 'permits' my sin, this does not mean He sanctions it or gives His permission in the sense that He deems it lawful. He may let it occur without intervening to stop it. . . . But what God permits to happen He still *chooses* to permit. That is, since He could stop it and decides not to stop it, He exercises His permission according to His good pleasure. In some sense He ordains that it happens or else it could not happen" (*Invisible Hand*, 82–83; emphasis in original).

6. Ibid., 83.

7. William F. Arndt and F. Wilber Gingrich, *A Greek-English Lexicon of the New Testament and Other Early Christian Literature* (Chicago: University of Chicago Press, 1969), 242.

8. R. C. Sproul, *Grace Unknown* (Grand Rapids: Baker, 1997), 143.

9. Ibid., 147.

10. Ibid., 150–51. The quote here and the preceding sentences are derived from Sproul's discussion of the nature of God's mercy and grace.

11. Ibid., 147.

12. John Piper, *The Pleasures of God* (Portland: Multnomah, 1991), 144–46. D. A. Carson arrives at the same conclusion in his classic work *The Difficult Doctrine of the Love of God* ([Wheaton: Crossway, 2000], 78): "When I have preached or lectured in Reformed circles, I have often been asked the question, 'Do you feel free to tell unbelievers that God loves them?' . . . It is obvious that I have no hesitation in answering this question from young Reformed preachers affirmatively: *Of course* I tell the unconverted that God loves them."

13. Charles Haddon Spurgeon, *The Treasury of the Bible*, "Jacob and Esau" (Grand Rapids: Baker, 1988), 7:93–94; emphasis omitted.

14. Charles Haddon Spurgeon, *Election and Holiness*, from the Spurgeon Archive, The New Park Street Pulpit, delivered on March 11, 1860, at Exeter Hall, Strand.